Praise for

The Special N
Planning Guide: How to Prepare
for Every Stage of Your Child's Life

"[This book] will become a classic for families who have special needs children....There is no other resource book like it for parents."
—Dee Lee, CFP®
Author, *Women & Money*

"A treasure chest of information...held together with family values that close gaps and lead to goals."
—Allen C. Crocker, M.D.
Associate Professor of Pediatrics
Harvard Medical School
Senior Associate in Medicine
Children's Hospital Boston

"A must-have reference...[that] will serve as a great tool to help families navigate through the many challenges, while giving them thoughtful and practical solutions."
—James T. Brett
Former member of the President's Committee for People with
Intellectual Disabilities

"An extremely valuable resource for both families and professionals who seek to provide for the current and future care and quality of life of an individual with special needs."
—Marvin Natowicz, M.D., Ph.D.
Vice Chairman
Genomic Medicine Institute
Cleveland Clinic

"Excellent...simply written and understandable, yet concise enough to serve as a road map that will assist families of persons with special needs to navigate the highway of life from childhood to adulthood."
—William A. Catelli, Jr.
Secretary
Board of Directors
The Arc of the United States

The

Special
Needs
Planning
Guide

The

Special
Needs
Planning

Guide

How to Prepare
for Every Stage of
Your Child's Life

by

John W. Nadworny, CFP®, ChFC

and

Cynthia R. Haddad, CFP®

Special Needs Financial Planning, LLC
Massachusetts

·P A U L·H·
BROOKES
PUBLISHING CO.®

Baltimore • London • Sydney

Paul H. Brookes Publishing Co.
Post Office Box 10624
Baltimore, Maryland 21285-0624

www.brookespublishing.com

Typeset by Spearhead Global, Inc., Bear, Delaware.
Manufactured in the United States of America by
Versa Press, Inc., East Peoria, Illinois.

The opinions voiced in this book are for general information only and are not intended to provide specific advice or recommendations for any individual. To determine which investments(s) may be appropriate for you, consult your financial advisor prior to investing. All financial performance referenced is historical and is no guarantee of future results.

The case studies appearing in this book are composites based on the authors' experiences; these case studies do not represent the lives or experiences of specific individuals, and no implications should be inferred.

Library of Congress Cataloging-in-Publication Data
Nadworny, John W.
   The special needs planning guide : how to prepare for every stage of your child's life / by John W. Nadworny and Cynthia R. Haddad.
      p.   cm.
   Includes bibliographical references and index.
   ISBN-13: 978-1-55766-802-8 (pbk)
   ISBN-10: 1-55766-802-7 (pbk)
      1. Parents of children with disabilities—United States—Finance, Personal—Handbooks, manuals, etc.   2. Children with disabilities—Care—United States—Planning—Handbooks, manuals, etc.   3. People with disabilities—Care—United States—Planning—Handbooks, manuals, etc.   4. People with disabilities—Legal status, laws, etc.—United States—Handbooks, manuals, etc.   5. Estate planning—United States.   I. Haddad, Cynthia R.   II. Title.

   HQ759.913.N33 2007
   332.0240087'0973—dc22   2007000716

British Library Cataloguing in Publication data are available from the British Library.

Contents

Contents of the Accompanying CD-ROM

The Special Needs Planning Guide: How to Prepare for Every Stage of Your Child's Life features a CD-ROM containing printable and modifiable versions of the following components, provided in PDF and DOC files:

About the Authors

About This CD-ROM

Personal Special Needs Timeline

Current Budget and Expenses Worksheet

Estimated Monthly Supplementary Expenses

Letter of Intent

About the Authors

Since the early 1990s, John and Cynthia have worked together as a parent and sibling team in special needs financial planning. They continue to share their passion and understanding in providing financial planning information to families with special needs as noted speakers on special needs planning for families throughout the country. They have combined their years of personal experience of special needs and professional experience in the field of financial planning to create a special Letter of Intent (see the appendix at the end of this book for a sample Letter of Intent).

John and Cynthia have also contributed to *Passport to Independence: Home, Work and Community—a Manual for Families* (Specialized Housing, Inc., 2002). They are also contributing authors to various publications and journals, including *Wall Street Journal, The New York Times, Kiplinger's Retirement Report, The Boston Globe, Business Week, Bloomberg Wealth Management, Worth Magazine, USA Today,* and other well-known periodicals.

John and Cynthia are registered representatives and offer securities through Linsco/Private Ledger, Member NASD/SIPC. Financial planning services are offered through Special Needs Financial Planning, LLC, in Massachusetts, a registered investment advisor.

John W. Nadworny, CFP®, ChFC, Special Needs Financial Planning, LLC, Massachusetts, http://www.specialneedsplanning.com

As a parent and professional, John has served on the Governor's Commission on Mental Retardation for three terms. He is currently the chair of the subcommittee on transitioning to adult services. He helped draft the Qualified Disabilities Savings Program proposal that has recently been submitted to President George W. Bush by the President's Committee for People with Intellectual Disabilities. In his second term on the Governor's Commission, John was the co-chair of the subcommittee on developing an overall plan for private–public housing partnerships between families and the Massachusetts Department of Mental Retardation. He also served on the Family-to-Family Advisory Board. John is a past member of the Board of Directors of The Arc of East Middlesex.

John and his wife, Susan, received Distinguished Citizen Awards from The Arc of Massachusetts in 1995 and 1999. They are an active family in Massachusetts Families Organizing for Change. John completed the Ironman USA Triathlon in 1999 to raise funds to help endow the Family-to-Family project, which was established to address Massachusetts's waiting list for residential services.

John has earned a master of business administration from Babson College, a master of science from Bentley College, and a bachelor of science from Bridgewater State College. He lives in Massachusetts with his wife and their children, Alexandria, Bennett, and James.

Cynthia R. Haddad, CFP®, Special Needs Financial Planning, LLC, Massachusetts, http://www.specialneedsplanning.com

As a result of her own experience with an adult brother with special needs, Cynthia has dedicated her financial planning practice to helping other families address their unique financial planning needs. She is currently a member of the Board of Directors for The Arc of Massachusetts and serves on the subcommittee for the upcoming capital campaign. She was honored to co-chair, along with her husband Mark, the 50th anniversary gala celebration for The Arc of Massachusetts in September 2005.

She is a contributing author to *A Special Needs Planning Guide for Families* (Jewish Family & Children's Service, n.d.), a collaborative publication between colleagues to aid families with special needs in the planning process.

Cynthia has served on the Central Middlesex Area Advisory Board for the Massachusetts Department of Mental Retardation and was a member of the committee for residential quality control. She is past chair of the Family-to-Family steering committee and has served as an advisor to the MARC Trust, Inc. (currently Planned Lifetime Assistance Network of Massachusetts, Inc.).

Cynthia has earned a bachelor of arts in finance and economics from Simmons College in Boston. Cynthia lives in Massachusetts with her husband and their children, Anthony and Lydia.

Foreword

Families who have a member with special needs have their own "special" needs. One of these needs is the hard fact that families must become skilled information gatherers and planners. This responsibility is one that is often resisted because of the pressures of daily life, the emotional challenge of recognizing one's own mortality, and the need for real care in how planning is done. As this book notes, "People do not plan to fail; they fail to plan." This timely book should help families take the necessary steps to construct solid plans and also to feel empowered by the work they have done.

As this information-packed book points out, many parents are overwhelmed at the prospect of planning for the various needs of their child with special needs. What this book does, however, is provide a clear roadmap and sets of guidelines to demystify the challenges of planning. And, it takes a different approach than many of the other books and materials available on planning.

First, the authors of this book acknowledge that planning is a lifelong activity. They repeatedly advise periodic reviews of existing plans to take into account life changes and emerging goals. The emphasis they give to this point is important because it suggests that planning is a way of monitoring the collective thinking about the child's future and, as such, provides opportunities for clarifying goals and the roles of people who have committed themselves to those goals.

Second, the authors take a holistic and broad view of what the planning activities are all about. The emphasis in this book is on the whole family's needs—not just the needs of the individual with special needs. Good planning takes into account the current and future needs of the parents, the other children, involved friends, and extended family, as well as the child with special needs. Taking the "family perspective" is critical to designing workable and supportable plans that affect multiple generations.

Third, the authors provide a clear and compelling framework within which planning should occur. It is noted that there are specific "pressure points"—transitions in the service delivery system and age-related changes—that serve as useful markers for planning activities. And, they discuss five specific factors that need to be considered at each of these pressure points—family issues, emotional needs, financial issues, legal considerations, and government benefits. This framework acknowledges the complexity of the process but gives the process useful structures so that a comprehensive and sustainable plan can be achieved.

Fourth, the authors emphasize identifying personal priorities, values, goals, and dreams in order to articulate a vision for the future. This emphasis is critical so that the plan reflects what the family wants to see happen. The authors challenge the reader to resist accepting what others recommend or say is possible if such advice is not respectful of the family's vision. To reinforce this perspective, the book contains wonderful vignettes written by family members about their own experiences in planning. These vignettes energize the text, adding real life experiences that illustrate how much can be achieved through careful planning. In addition, case studies are offered that bring together all of the elements of the planning framework.

A core theme in the book is the importance of preserving government benefits, and to this end, the authors provide important information on what these benefits are over the life cycle of the individual with special needs. Because government benefits may vary by state and over time, the authors make the case for securing professional assistance in the planning process. The task of choosing the right professionals is made easier because of the authors' useful set of guidelines and even suggested questions to use in interviewing prospective professionals.

The fact that both of the authors have a family member with special needs is evident throughout the book. This is a book written to help readers every step of the way and over time in achieving a vision. It's not a cookbook—it's a value infused discussion about what one needs to think about, when one needs to think about it, and how one can move ahead with purpose and confidence. By carefully explaining why planning really does matter, and then by providing the tools for planning in highly accessible terms, this book educates, encourages, and empowers families of children with special needs to take some control over the future.

Marty Wyngaarden Krauss, Ph.D.
Provost and Senior Vice President of Academic Affairs
Brandeis University

Preface

Our Story

We share a common bond with you—having a family member who has special needs. We are both well aware of the caregiving concerns that have been required of us. As it happens, we have both arrived at the same point in our careers from different directions.

Cynthia's Story

I was born into a family in which an older brother has special needs. I grew up watching my parents love and care for my brother while juggling the needs of the whole family, and I am prepared to be a lifetime support for him.

John's Story

I was well into developing a career and family when a third child was born with special needs, a life event that immediately (and for some years dramatically) changed the course of family living and priorities. Yet I recognized that my family had begun a journey for which few to no road maps existed to guide our way.

It may be fate that the two of us ended up in the same profession and in the same firm, but it is not by chance that we have dedicated our work to helping people, like ourselves, who are responsible for the lifetime care of a family member with special needs. Our past experiences, personal knowledge, and professional expertise on these issues have enabled us to make a difference in the financial security of many families like yours.

Special needs planning is unlike the traditional *Mainstream financial planning*-style financial planning, where you buy a home, raise your children, plan for college education, and make provisions for retirement. Special needs planning is planning for *two* generations. Many adult children with a disability must be supported to some extent their entire lives, even long after their parents have died. Our approach reaches beyond the limited boundaries of wills and trusts to provide you with a comprehensive plan to address your family's particular needs. We do not believe that there is one single solution or financial product that fits the needs of every family. Instead, the planning process drives the needs for implementation of individual products and services. We do believe that proper financial planning is the cornerstone enabling you to coordinate your financial and legal affairs so that you can implement the vision that you have for your child.

From the dramatic increase in the number of inquiries and requests that we receive daily from our web site and other referrals, we realize that there is a lack of information readily available and easily accessible for families throughout the country. We hope that this book will allow us to reach beyond our direct capacity and provide information to as many families as possible, to help them in the planning process. With this book, we have shared our thoughts and expertise on the key issues with which many families are confronted and have provided reasonable strategies to help families accomplish their goals. We thank all of the families that we have worked with over the years for allowing us to play an active part in helping them enrich the lives of their family member.

Acknowledgments

In our journeys, we have come across so many dedicated and caring individuals who, like ourselves, have committed their expertise to helping families plan for a meaningful, secure, and independent future for their family member. We would like to acknowledge the significant contributions made by the following four individuals, who have collaborated with us in this endeavor.

Leo V. Sarkissian, Executive Director, The Arc of Massachusetts, for his insights and contributions on understanding government benefits. His leadership in advocacy has made a tremendous difference for our family members as well as the thousands of others throughout the Commonwealth of Massachusetts and the country.

Theresa M. Varnet, an attorney with Fletcher, Tilton, and Whipple, LLC, for her knowledge and contributions on understanding special needs trusts, guardianships, and less restrictive alternatives to guardianships. She has tirelessly educated and counseled thousands of individuals throughout the country on the importance of such legal matters.

Barbara D. Jackins, an attorney with Mason and Goldberg, LLC, for her guidance and contributions in helping to make such a technical area of understanding complex trustee standards and practices user friendly.

Dafna Krouk-Gordon, Executive Director, TILL, Inc., for contributing her expertise in planning and understanding the complexities of a family transitioning into the adult service world. She has pioneered the movement for community living and employment opportunities for individuals with disabilities since 1980.

There are many others who have helped us to shape the essence of this book and have cheered us on along the way. We would especially like to acknowledge the following individuals and express our appreciation for their faith in us and in our abilities.

Marty Wyngaarden Krauss, Provost, Brandeis University, for supporting our dream to write a book and for introducing us to Paul H. Brookes Publishing Co.

Nancy Mark Honig, of Internet Gorilla Marketing Group, the creator and webmaster of http://www.specialneedsplanning.com. After managing hundreds of inquiries to our web site from families throughout the world, she made it clear to us that a book on special needs planning was needed.

We would also like to thank all of our friends at Bay Financial Associates, LLC, especially John Kerr, Lisa Logan, Tom Loonie, Misty Claveloux, and Erin Granger, as well as show our appreciation to the folks in the Linsco/Private Ledger Advertising Compliance Department, especially analyst Cyrille Mahfoud for reading the text and expressing his interests and suggestions. We would like to thank the many employees of the Massachusetts Department of Mental Retardation and the not-for-profit agencies that provide the direct support and services to our own families. Their dedication to supporting the lives and rights of individuals with disabilities is unwavering. In particular we would like to thank Judy Curry for demonstrating the value and strength of meaningful family support. We would like to thank the team at Paul H. Brookes Publishing Co., especially Rebecca Lazo, Steve Peterson, Emily Moore, Jen Lillis, and the many others who guided us along the way.

Last, but certainly not least, we would like to thank our spouses, Susan Nadworny and Mark Haddad, for their encouragement, patience, and steadfast support. Susan especially has shared her thoughts and been our conscience while writing this book. She is an extraordinary example of the wonderful things parents can do for their children.

Introduction

When we first began planning for families with disabilities in the early 1990s, it was frustrating to us as planning professionals; the only information available involved planning for the death of a parent or primary caregiver. Obviously, planning for the death of a parent of a child with a disability is paramount because that parent is often the lifeline for the child's security. There was some information available about using wills and trusts, which are simply legal devices that provide for the orderly administration of assets upon death, but neither device guarantees nor provides for your family member's security. There was, however, no information readily available to address all the unique and complex planning considerations for the lifetime of both the parents and the child. Without implementing a plan that would maximize both public and personal resources under all circumstances, there may be no money available when it is most needed.

Although we personally lived and felt the financial importance for planning for the care of a child with special needs beyond the lifetime of the parents, we never truly realized that there were so many factors involved in working with families under these circumstances. We underestimated the significance of each individual family's values and how so many emotional factors could affect the planning process. We never realized how difficult it was to simplify and communicate the complexity of government benefits—and how important advocacy is in keeping the benefits funded. We did not anticipate finding that families would have such a false sense of security after completing their wills and trusts. We did not have as great an appreciation of how our personal emotions and planning affected our own lives or those of the families we have assisted. We did, however, understand how important it was to plan.

With this in mind, we have identified the most critical components in special needs planning as the Five Factors that must be addressed to develop a comprehensive plan:

- Family and support factors

- Emotional factors

- Financial factors

- Legal factors

- Government benefit factors

These Five Factors are used throughout the book to help you take into account the many facets that affect decision making in special needs planning. In our work with families, we aim to increase their awareness of the Five Factors and how to use them to pull all of the pieces together.

Unfortunately, there continues to be a void of information on comprehensive planning to provide an individual with disabilities the resources needed to have an enriched life. The goal of this book is to walk a family through the various stages of life and provide guidance and knowledge of the unique planning techniques and strategies for special needs planning. We have developed the special needs planning timeline that is based upon the age of your child to guide your family along the planning process. The timeline is used to identify the various key special needs planning pressure points such as early intervention, transition planning to school and adult services, guardianship issues, Supplemental Security Income and Medicaid eligibility, and residential needs. Developing and following your own personal special needs planning timeline will enable you to be proactive in your planning for your family's financial security.

In planning for the needs of a family, the process does not usually begin by planning for the end of one's life. The primary goal is to achieve financial independence and security during a lifetime. The most common concerns to plan for are 1) living longer than expected (thus outliving the extent of assets), 2) dying earlier than expected, or 3) becoming disabled along the way. To name a few common goals, most parents want to provide for their children's education, be financially independent at their retirement, minimize income and estate taxes, and provide protection in the event of a disability or premature death. For families with a member with a disability, to consider that needs only occur when a parent or caregiver dies provides an incomplete plan and misses the point of achieving financial security during that member's lifetime.

In the context of traditional financial planning, each financial goal typically has a standard solution to help achieve that goal. Where there is a question regarding an investment or a tax issue or an insurance product, the answer can easily be found. There is an unlimited supply of resources and information available at our fingertips to address traditional financial planning strategies. Financial models using software can define the amount of savings required to achieve a specific goal. This approach is considered to be the traditional financial planning process.

In special needs planning, however, there are no simple solutions, no easy answers, and no general guidelines or statistics to help quantify the amount of money needed to provide for an individual with disabilities. We took it upon ourselves to find answers for families. The traditional financial planning pyramid is the foundation of the financial planning process. We have created the special needs planning pyramid, which identifies the unique elements in special needs planning, so that special needs planning has its own cornerstone tool. This book addresses all of the elements of both planning pyramids to provide the most comprehensive approach to building a firm foundation for the entire family.

One of the missions of this book is to identify all of the factors involved in special needs planning. By combining our own personal experiences and professional expertise, we have come to develop solutions, define answers, and provide general guidelines to help identify and quantify the needs of families and individuals with special needs.

The special needs planning process includes guiding a family through the stresses of trying to manage a world of uncertainties. Because every family is different and unique, there is not one clear path that measures success. Having enough money may not be the only concern. We would like to believe that we can make even a small difference for each family and that we can help them to make a difference for their family member with disabilities. Over the years, we have met with hundreds of families that have been struggling, not only with the financial planning needs of their child but with all of the Five Factors. We have worked with families that face insurmountable challenges each day. These include families with children who are profoundly disabled and require 24-hour intensive care. These include older families that care for their adult child at home. These include families whose lives have changed in one moment. We continue to be amazed by these families—their strength and their vision.

Our main goal in writing this book was to share the knowledge that we have gained over the years in working with families who face similar planning challenges and share similar goals. In the sections throughout this book labeled Special Needs Planning Stories, we share many family stories we have encountered throughout our career, and in the sections labeled Special Needs Planning Pointers, we share the helpful planning strategies we have identified and developed. The extended case examples throughout this book are intended to showcase specific needs that a family might want to prepare for and illustrate the planning process a family may use to make their preparations. It is with great pleasure that we present this book to you, the reader, with the intent to pass on what we have learned.

This book is written as a tribute to the many families that have pioneered before us. We are thankful to them for allowing us to become a part of their lives. From them we have learned so much. They have showed us the true meaning of success.

What we do every day is very personal and affects our entire purpose, both of being who we are and doing what we do. We have been blessed with family members who have taught us the true meaning of love and of independence. Cynthia's brother, Ron Haddad, and John's son, James Nadworny, have shown us the purpose of life in its fullest. We dedicate this book to them—our true champions!

To my wife, Susan, I continue to be in awe of your patience and persistence in all that you do with James. The strength of your love has been the cornerstone of our entire family.

To my children Alexandria and Bennett, the life lessons I never imagined I could teach you, James has taught you. The love you all share for one another makes me so proud to be your dad.
—John W. Nadworny

To my parents, Al and Marjie, and my brothers, Bruce, Ron, and Steve. You have helped to shape my heart and soul, and for this I am forever grateful.

To my husband, Mark, you graciously stepped into my world of special needs 13 years ago and have gently encouraged me to follow my passions.

To my children Anthony and Lydia, you continue to teach me every day about how special life truly is.
—Cynthia R. Haddad

1

The Special Needs Planning Timeline

This book will serve as a guide to help your family plan for the future. Reading through it may relieve your anxieties about planning, or may raise your awareness about the need to plan. Because every family's specific situation is unique, it is not possible to find one single solution, one financial product, one legal document, or one residential model that fits the needs of every family. There are, however, some basic guidelines and rules that can be applied to form a basis for a planning strategy.

COMPARING TRADITIONAL FINANCIAL PLANNING WITH SPECIAL NEEDS PLANNING

When we first began speaking to groups of families, we learned that we had to clarify the distinction between planning for the needs of families that had a member with special needs and the needs of the typical family. The basic needs of both special needs families and traditional families overlap at various stages. The baseline needs of purchasing a home, saving for college, retirement, and estate distribution are similar in both special needs planning and traditional planning. In addition to these needs, families with special needs face additional challenges. Clearly, it is not recommended for families with special needs to adhere to the motto of "I'm spending my kids' inheritance." Having a child with special needs requires that families plan for two generations, because the child with disabilities may need parents' financial assistance and support into and throughout adult life. This is a common thread throughout this book.

There are any number of resources in the media, books, magazines, and newsletters available to raise awareness and education for the financial and legal planning needs of traditional families. Traditional families can find an answer to a basic planning question by calling in to a talk radio host, writing a letter to the financial editor in the local paper, or attending public seminars and educational workshops. Information for families with special needs is not as easily accessible—nor are the answers families seek as generally applicable.

In order to illustrate the differences between traditional planning and special needs planning, we have developed a special needs planning timeline (see Figure 1). This timeline outlines the various planning stages, or *planning pressure points*, that families with children with disabilities need to consider. It demonstrates the differences between the traditional planning timeline and the special needs planning timeline. Keep in mind that families with special needs will want to consider all the aspects of the traditional family planning timeline; however, in addition they will need to incorporate all the points on the special needs planning timeline. These planning pressure points are stages that align with natural life transitions in families with children with disabilities. For a child with special needs, the planning pressure points indicate a change in services and/or benefits available. In addition, these are often the points in time when parents feel the pressure to begin planning. We identify these points as an indicator that action is needed, and these points highlight the unique planning differences in special needs planning. Each planning pressure point indicates some very specific planning considerations, which will be discussed in detail in later chapters. In later chapters, we provide strategies for the various stages of planning (pressure points) and discuss the Five Factors to consider for each stage, including family and support factors, emotional factors, legal factors, financial factors, and government benefit factors. We will then illustrate the issues and applicable planning stategies using actual case examples from families that we have worked with over the years. We recommend that families build their own personal planning timeline as they begin the planning process.

THE KEY STAGES OF SPECIAL NEEDS PLANNING

We have developed a simplified approach to help families understand the complexities of special needs planning based upon our timeline of planning pressure points determined by the age of the child. Families have very little time to spare already but do indeed need the facts and figures to help them map a course of action to achieve financial security for themselves and their family. By reading the section that pertains to your child's age, you will get a quick overview of the basic points to consider and actions to be taken for that particular planning stage. By reading the entire book, however, you will get the detail necessary to develop an overall strategy for the future.

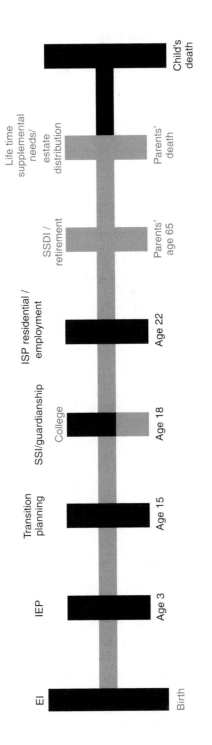

Figure 1. The special needs planning timeline illustrates all of the pressure points that individuals plan for. The distinction with special needs planning is that you must plan for the traditional family goals while incorporating the unique requirements of raising a child with special needs. (*Key:* EI = early intervention; IEP = individualized education program; SSI = Supplemental Security Income; ISP = individual service or support plan; SSDI = Social Security Disability Insurance.)

Stage I (Birth to Child's Age 3)

If your child's disability is diagnosed between birth and age 3, the primary focus at that point is on understanding the diagnosis and obtaining early intervention (EI) services from professionals in the areas of physical therapy, occupational therapy, speech therapy, and medicine. EI services focus on the child as an integral member of the family. EI programs are mostly home- and community-based. Services can include diagnostic testing through hospital or school screenings and referral services to diagnostic or direct intervention programs.

EI and other services are provided in accordance with an individualized family service plan (IFSP), developed in consultation between families of infants and toddlers with disabilities and the EI support team. The team can consist of occupational therapists, physical therapists, speech therapists, social workers, and other medical professionals. The IFSP is provided for by Individuals with Disabilities Education Improvement Act (IDEA) of 2004 (see boxed explanation). Providing intervention services early on builds opportunities to help strengthen families. A typically developing child would not require such services.

Please keep in mind that not every disability is identified at birth. Many symptoms can be difficult to recognize at first, and a diagnosis may come later. Getting a later diagnosis

Enacted in 1975 as PL 94-142, the Education for All Handicapped Children Act, now called the Individuals with Disabilities Education Improvement Act (IDEA) of 2004 (PL 108-446) is the federal law for special education services. This law requires state and local education officials to provide appropriate special education services for eligible students in the least restrictive environment. See the web site for the Committee on Education and the Workforce at http://edworkforce. house.gov/nclb.htm for more information. Also see the U.S. Department of Education web site at http://www.ed.gov and the National Dissemination Center for Children with Disabilities web site at http://www.nichcy.org.

or having a disability emerge at a later age may require a family to make adjustments in this portion of the timeline.

Stage II (Child's Age 3–15)

When your child reaches age 3, the family's first experience with transition will occur. You will be introduced to the educational system, and your child will need to be determined eligible to receive services through an individualized education program (IEP). The IEP is also provided for by IDEA'04. This will begin with an assessment of your child's abilities and needs. Occasionally the school district will accept an EI resource plan and suggestions. In most cases, however, the public school system prefers to do its own assessments. It will then provide recommendations for school-based services. Integrated public preschools and some privately funded preschools will support your child's IEP by allowing time for specialists to be a part of your child's school day. The parents' role is critical in working to coordinate with educators and service providers to set measurable goals and objectives for their child. IEP teams can include a number of professionals and are required by law to do so. Thus begins your journey of educational advocacy and understanding your roles and rights in the process, as well as the various programs, services, and supports schools may offer your child.

Stage III (Child's Age 16–21)

When your child turns age 16, if you have not already done so, you should begin the transition planning to high school. At this point it is important to maximize the entitlements of education to provide opportunities for vocational exploration, daily living skills, and independence. Your child's abilities are primarily identified, and his or her needs for future care both residentially and vocationally should be identified between the ages of 16 and 18. It is important to locate and establish contact with the government agency in your state that will provide adult services to your child when they are no longer receiving educational services—which will most likely be at age 21 or 22, depending upon your state of residence.

At age 17½, guardianship and/or alternatives to guardianship need to be addressed (see Chapter 4). It is also important to begin the exploration of residential and vocational options in your area by identifying the various service provider agencies. Attend workshops and family support groups on such topics as future planning, transition planning, and financial or estate planning. Learn as much information as possible about the variety of adult services and supports in your state and how to access them.

Most local family support agency groups will offer educational workshops and training for families. Inquire with your local chapter of The Arc, Autism Spectrum Disorders Support Center, Down Syndrome Congress, school special education parent advisory council, or other support agencies. Get on their mailing lists or visit their web sites (see the Bibliography section titled Web Sites to Investigate). Speak with other parents and share ideas—we all share the common thread of wanting what is best for our children.

Between the ages of 18 and 21 or 22, you will need to plan to insure that your child has a smooth transition into adult services. There are still many opportunities for higher education at age 18 to consider. Typically developing young adults graduate from high school and move to higher education or employment. Young adults with disabilities may also be faced with decisions concerning additional education (college, adult education, or vocational training); however, in addition to these considerations, parents will also want to focus on their independence. In fact, for some families *independence* is the primary focus. At this stage, understanding your child's rights and ensuring everything is in proper order is paramount to his or her success in any postsecondary opportunities. It is also important to be aware of various legal and financial issues that will affect your child's financial security and eligibility for government benefits and services.

At age 18, your child is no longer a minor in the eyes of the law. Although in some situations parents may continue to make all financial, medical and legal decisions on behalf of their child with disabilities, the child has the legal right to make his or her own decisions. Physicians, educators, and service providers have no legally binding obligation to act upon your instructions on behalf of your child. This is where the issues of guardianship—or less restrictive alternatives to guardianship—need to be considered. (This issue is discussed further in Chapter 4.)

Also at age 18, your child may be eligible for Supplemental Security Income (SSI) based upon his or her own asset level. Although this is an entitlement program, your child needs to be eligible to receive these benefits. Basically, the individuals with disabilities cannot own assets in excess of $2,000 to qualify for SSI benefits. They can, however, own a home, a nominal life insurance policy, a vehicle, and a prepaid burial account as assets that would not count against their eligibility. The section in Chapter 4 on government benefits will provide greater details. In addition, you can visit the Social Security Administration web site at http://www.ssa.gov for further information.

Stage IV (Child's Age 22 and Beyond)

Turning age 22 (or in some states, turning age 21) is another major milestone, and the entitlements of public education stop. Therefore, the individual with disabilities is no longer entitled to receive services from the special education system. There are no federal or state laws guaranteeing entitlement to services after the age of 22. Access to residential, vocational, and transportation services become a major challenge for many families. If you have not already done so, this is a critical time to better understand the state agency from which you may receive services. See the section on government benefits in Chapter 4 to learn more about locating the most appropriate state agency from which your child may receive services. Obtain as much information as possible about residential models and availability of services, and keep in mind that options do exist out there!

This is where the culmination of the efforts in your own personal planning, which you have hopefully initiated previously, will come together. Being creative with personal and public financial resources, as well as having a clear vision for your child, can make a tremendous difference in his or her life.

2

An Overview of Special Needs Planning

WHY IT IS IMPORTANT TO PLAN

The lives and options for individuals with disabilities have changed dramatically over the last 30 years. A generation ago, options were limited. There were two choices: a person could stay at home with his or her family or be placed in an institutional setting. The theory was that an institutional setting could provide the best lifetime care for the individual. There were limited supports and few options available if the family chose to care for their child with disabilities at home. Years of advocacy and hard work at least provided for every child to have a legal right to a public education. The persistence and dedication of parents of prior generations has resulted in free appropriate public education (FAPE) becoming an entitlement for all children.

Although obtaining an appropriate and meaningful education for a child with disabilities continues to be a challenge, the fact that there is a legal entitlement provides a basis to pursue the best education for your child. Unfortunately, there is no legal entitlement that guarantees an individual with disabilities an appropriate residential placement or supports for his or her quality of life when he or she leaves the school system.

The fact that most entitlements end when an individual leaves the school system is frequently a shock for many families. In addition to the lack of legal requirements to provide residential supports and services to individuals with disabilities, there are many issues that contribute to the need to plan ahead for the long-term security and financial needs of individuals with disabilities. The five most compelling issues are

1. Increasing population of people with disabilities

2. Increasing demands for services

3. Lengthening life span of people with disabilities

4. Increasing costs of long-term care

5. Shrinking government resources

Families should never assume that their other children will take on the role of caring for their sibling with disabilities in the event of the disability or death of the parent. Lives are much too complex. Families are geographically distant. There is no easy access to government benefits. Advocacy for the child can often be a full-time job for a sibling to assume. Compromises on the part of the siblings with their own families to care for are often unrealistic for parents to expect. Parents themselves may also require long-term care, and families need to be mindful of planning for such a contingency.

Dealing with the uncertainties of the future can be stressful and difficult. It is important to acknowledge that there are financial challenges and compromises to be made. You must realize that both personal and public resources are limited. Regardless of how successful an individual is, he or she may not be able to generate all the wealth necessary to care for his or her own child for that child's entire lifetime. On the other hand, the government may not be willing to pay the amount necessary for an individual to achieve his or her full potential.

The current trend in futures planning is to develop a person-centered planning model.

Overall, we have found the person-centered planning process to be very successful in helping parents to create the ultimate vision for their child's future. Unfortunately, there has been little to no information available on guiding a family through the steps of how to financially support the outcome of the person-centered planning process. We hope to remedy this lack of information by helping you develop a plan that takes into consideration the strengths and weaknesses, as wells as hopes and desires, of your child or family member. Because many families may not have the opportunity to participate in a person-centered planning process, using the Five Factors of special needs planning outlined in this book will

> Person-centered planning is a process-oriented approach to empowering people with disability labels. It focuses on the people and their needs by putting them in charge of defining the direction for their lives, not on the systems that may or may not be available to serve them. This ultimately leads to greater inclusion as valued members of-both community and society.

ensure that the completed plan reflects the preferences of the family. To do so takes careful planning and consideration of a number of variables that, if coordinated properly, can best maximize the financial resources available to achieve your overall vision.

. . .   **Special Needs Planning Story**   . . .

We were invited to participate in a person-centered planning process to help us determine a vision of the environment that is most appropriate for James to thrive in. One of the most valuable aspects of this process was that we were better able to see James as a person from other people's perspectives. For example, I often find myself helping James with many simple tasks each day. After listening to others in the group, I realized that he had the ability to be more independent than I allowed him to be. We learned so much about James from the many people involved in his life outside of our family. Ultimately, the value of this process helped us envision what James's life might be like in the future. Although the process helped us to create James's vision with him, it was also somewhat frustrating because we did not have any specific answers about where the money would come from.

. . .   —James's parents   . . .

As government resources continue to shrink, and the population of individuals with disabilities continues to increase, it is becoming clear that families also have to have personal financial resources (either from savings and/or income) to provide for their family member. In some cases, however, it may be financially impossible for an individual to have enough money to provide for all that is needed. The process of special needs planning not only involves saving your own money but identifying and maximizing any and all government resources available.

In many cases, it may cost too much money for parents to be able to personally pay for all of the requirements needed. Because of this, families have begun to explore more creative options to provide for the security and independence of their child. For example, many families have pooled their resources together as a group to purchase homes and fund the expenses of ongoing supports and staffing. If this is something that you may be interested in further researching, you may wish to consult *Passport to Independence* (Specialized Housing, Inc., 2002). The only way that a family may have the option to participate in a privately funded residential program is to plan ahead. Even if you have adequate resources, you still have to plan ahead to find the most appropriate program. Planning today allows a family to provide options for residential and lifestyle supports needed in the future.

Maximizing both public resources and private resources increases the possibility of being able to financially support the person-centered plan. Service providers continue to struggle with limited budget constraints and high staff turnover. Families tired of receiving minimal supports and services often combine their resources to supplement those needed. Although every individual has his or her own personality and needs, many dreams have been realized by creatively pooling resources between groups of families.

Advocacy groups such as The Arc of the United States (http://www.thearc.org), the Autism Society of America (http://www.autism-society.org), and the National Alliance for the Mentally Ill (http://www.nami.org) continue to provide a voice for people with disabilities and their families. We encourage you to remember that it is in working together that we can provide opportunities for ourselves and others. Neither families nor providers can always independently provide the resources to help an individual with disabilities achieve his or her fullest abilities. The most effective means to providing an individual the opportunity to achieve a full life is to maximize both public and private resources.

Special Needs Planning Pointer

Comprehensive financial planning is the cornerstone enabling you to coordinate your financial and legal affairs so that you can implement the vision that you have for your child. We must be creative and utilize all resources and opportunities to help our family members with disabilities achieve full lives in the community.

A LOOK AT SPECIAL NEEDS PLANNING

Financial planning for families caring for a person with special needs differs from financial planning for the traditional family, where goals are rather simple—to build a cash cushion for emergencies; to provide protection in the event of an illness or death of a parent; to buy a home in a nice neighborhood; to raise children, to plan for college and perhaps graduate school expenses; to plan for retirement years; and to leave whatever is left to children, grandchildren, and charities after death. What makes planning particularly challenging

> The birth of a child with disabilities will probably change the course, but the destination is the same—creating opportunities for our children, and providing long-term security for our families.
> —Susan, James's mother

for our families with special needs is the necessity to provide for *two* generations, considering the parents' and entire family's financial security *as well as* the continued lifetime needs of the family member with a disability. We call this *special needs planning*.

Special Needs Planning Pointer

In traditional planning for families, the financial responsibility of planning for a child ends when he or she completes college or reaches the age of majority at 21. In special needs planning, the financial challenges of planning are greatest when your child's entitlements end or when he or she leaves the school system at age 21 or 22, depending upon the state of residence. By beginning to plan early on, you will identify or possibly even create more options and alternatives for your child when he or she leaves the school system.

Comprehensive special needs planning allows families to maximize their own personal resources while protecting the child's eligibility for receiving government benefits. There are frequently competing financial goals that a parent or caregiver of an individual with special needs encounters. The task of allocating personal resources in a way that enables you and your family to achieve your financial objectives requires an integrated plan. Identifying the goals of all family members and pulling together all of the pieces become the key to a successful plan.

THE SPECIAL NEEDS PLANNING PYRAMID

The special needs planning process includes traditional planning, but also addresses the unique requirements of raising a child with special needs. The key is in building a firm foundation.

The traditional financial planning pyramid, which forms the cornerstone of financial planning, illustrates the building blocks for financial success. With any pyramid structure, we need to first establish a firm foundation on which to build. The stronger the foundation, the greater the likelihood of achieving financial security becomes. The special needs planning pyramid integrates the planning requirements for traditional families with the unique planning requirements of a family with special needs. Figure 2 displays two pyramids, with one revealing the typical financial planning considerations that all families encounter and the other revealing the additional considerations that families with special needs must examine and address.

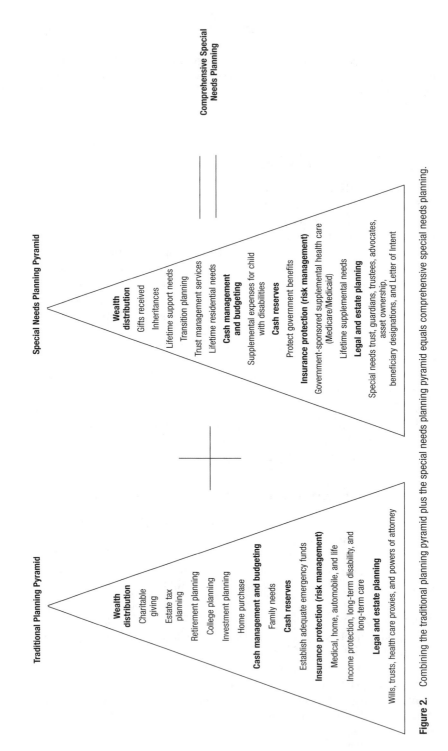

Figure 2. Combining the traditional planning pyramid plus the special needs planning pyramid equals comprehensive special needs planning.

The Pyramid Foundation: Legal and Estate Planning

Legal and estate planning is not just for the elderly or the wealthy. The first building block in special needs planning is to draft proper wills and trusts. One of the unique features in this process for families with a special needs member is to maintain the child's eligibility for government benefits. Not too long ago, a common estate planning practice was to disinherit a child to protect his or her eligibility. Now, the proper use of a special needs trust can allow a family to leave an inheritance for the benefit of the child while maintaining his or her eligibility for government benefits. In the event that you do not have a will in place at the time of your death, called dying **intestate,** the state of your residence will dictate the distribution of your estate. The state will also appoint a guardian or a successor guardian for your child if you have not named one in your will. Guardians, trustees, and advocates should all be named in your estate planning documents. These individuals should be familiar with your child and share your vision for his or her future when you are no longer able to fulfill these roles in the event of your death and/or disability.

Another part of estate planning is the ownership of assets and beneficiary designations of insurances, annuities, and retirement plans. In typical family planning, it is common to name the second beneficiaries on insurance policies and retirement plans as *children equally.* In special needs planning, naming the children equally as second beneficiaries may result in an unintentional loss of the child's eligibility for government benefits. It is critical to have the ownership and beneficiary designations carefully coordinated with your overall estate plan.

Although not a legal estate planning document, a **Letter of Intent** (see the appendix at the end of this book for a sample) is one of the most important documents that you can complete for your child's future caregivers. This is not a stand-alone document; it should be incorporated into your estate planning process. Not only does it provide the pertinent information about your child's needs and the individuals involved in his or her life, it also provides an opportunity for you to communicate your desires and visions of what you would like your child's life to be like when you are no longer alive.

A Firm Establishment:
Insurance Protection (Risk Management)

Risk management—or insurance protection—is perhaps the second most important building block to financial security. In an instant, an unforeseen catastrophe or illness could change your financial picture for life. Not only is it important to protect the family's lifestyle and income needs in the event of a premature death or disability of a parent, but also it is critical to plan for the supplemental lifetime needs of the child with special needs.

Special Considerations for Life Insurance in Special Needs Planning   The use of life insurance in special needs planning is somewhat different than in traditional financial planning. It is critical to plan for the financial problem of one of the most catastrophic events in life—a parent's death.

In planning for a traditional family, often the largest amount of life insurance protection is purchased for the wage-earning parent. Following this same strategy is one of the most common errors a family with special needs tends to make. One cannot assume there is no financial value lost in the event of death of the primary caregiving parent. Although it is difficult to place a financial value on a parent who does not work outside of the home or provide the majority of the income to the family, it is critical to account for this value. This often means that you have to look at each parent to determine his or her human life value. This human life value is ultimately converted to a dollar value to determine the life insurance protection needed.

Income Replacement   In the traditional planning model, the amount of life insurance needed is often simplified to be a function of the annual income. For example, to determine the life insurance need of a wage earner, a simple technique is to multiply your annual earnings by 5 to 10 times—or the number of years you want to ensure that income for your family is continued. This means that if you earn $100,000 per year, you should have from $500,000 (5 times) to $1,000,000 (10 times) of life insurance protection. A more detailed approach would be to complete a capital needs analysis. This is the analysis that most life insurance professionals and financial planners use. This calculation involves determining the present value of money needed to pay for the short-, mid-, and long-term goals a family identifies. For families with special needs, insurance coverage requirements often extend well beyond the traditional family's timeline of having enough money to support children through their school years. Special needs planning requires planning for two generations, anticipating a possible need to support the child with disabilities beyond the school years and throughout his or her life.

In special needs planning, the first step in determining life insurance needs is to determine the loss of income to the household with the death of a parent. Next, it is important to identify the expenses that will continue upon the death of that parent, particularly money needed to address future family goals. Looking at income alone can be misleading, because variations in saving and spending affect planning. In the event that a family spends a larger percentage of their monthly income and saves less, they have two options: 1) to insure for this larger amount to maintain the family lifestyle or 2) to anticipate lifestyle changes required by the family due to a decrease in income after the death of a parent. For families who are diligent at saving for their future (for retirement, education, supplemental needs, etc.), a loss of income may prevent the ability to maintain this saving pattern. Families must address issues of both current spending to maintain their lifestyle and their savings and investments for the future.

The other common error in purchasing life insurance is buying only term life insurance. Term insurance is life insurance that is designed to last for a predetermined number of years, such as 5, 10, 20, or possibly 30 years if applied for at an early age. Term insurance is appropriate if the need for protection is only for a temporary period of time. In special needs planning, the need is not temporary—it is permanent. As we have discussed, the need to address that second generation of financial issues comes into play once again. There may be a need for permanent life insurance protection, rather than term life insurance that only lasts until the children have grown in 20 years. A recommended strategy is to aquire a combination of both term insurance as well as permanent insurance (see Chapter 9 for a review of types of life insurance).

Important Supports: Cash Management and Budgeting

Basic **cash management** looks at your income versus your expenses. Having an understanding of your cash in and cash out is critical to success in future planning. This helps you differentiate between your needs and your wants, limit spending on luxury expenses that are not affordable, minimize debt, keep good financial records for budgeting and tax preparation purposes, get a handle on your net worth summary, and build your cash reserves. In addition to the current cash flow and budgeting needs of your family, it is important to provide for the supplemental expenses for the child with special needs.

Building Upward: Cash Reserves

Adequate **cash reserves** for emergencies and/or opportunities should be part of every family's financial planning. Generally, 3 to 6 months of living expenses should be available in reserves. This amount, however, depends on an individual's health, age, and employability. In special needs planning, a key component of long-term financial security is maintaining eligibility for government income benefits from Social Security and/or SSI—especially after the child is age 18 (see Chapter 4 for a discussion on government benefits). Reserves for families with special needs may also include additional money for potential medical emergencies, short-term disability of a parent, change in caregiving requirements, loss of support, or other financial needs specific to the family.

Structure for Life: Homeownership and/or Lifetime Residential Needs

Owning a home is often one of the first long-term financial goals for a family to achieve. In special needs planning, there is often an added goal of purchasing a home or condominium for a family member with disabilities. In addition, families would need to have resources available not only to maintain this second home but also to provide for the lifetime supports of the family member with a disability.

More Building Blocks

A number of the typical issues that families associate with traditional financial planning move more toward the top of the pyramid for special needs planning, including investment planning, college planning, retirement planning, estate tax planning, and charitable giving. Add the special considerations of trust management, transitional/vocational planning, lifetime support needs, and inheritances to the list, and you have a complete picture of the considerations that need to be addressed by families with special needs.

Investment Planning In families with special needs, **investment planning** addresses not only rates of return but also trust administration and investment management services. Finding a professional familiar with the unique requirements of distributions from special needs trusts is critical in protecting the beneficiary's eligibility for government benefits (see Chapter 9 for a list of trustee standards).

College Planning In traditional financial planning, determining the savings required to fund a 4-year college education is not too difficult to calculate because there is a defined beginning and ending point. The special needs planning process, however, may consist of additional considerations. Although some individuals with disabilities will attend college or other postsecondary education, and parents may want to plan for the related expenses, parents may also require additional services during that phase of their lives. Paying for educational advocacy services, supporting the transition to adult services, providing for residential costs, and allowing for lifetime supports create a much greater financial need than simply funding 4 years of college tuition expenses.

Retirement Planning For typical families, **retirement planning** involves establishing a regular savings plan to make certain that there is sufficient money available to maintain a lifestyle to which you and your spouse have grown accustomed. In special needs planning, parents may have to delay their retirement date or make adjustments in their lifestyle, including the ability to travel or relocate, due to the needs of their child. Combining the supplemental income need of the child with a disability with the parents' income needs can be a complex process. Saving enough money to achieve retirement planning goals may be more challenging for families with special needs because one parent may need to remain at home with the child and forego access to employer-sponsored retirement plans and benefits.

To the Point: Wealth Distribution

Wealth distribution for a typical family often ends upon the death of the second parent. There may be no pressing need to provide for the financial needs of a typical child after they have become an adult. A basic concept is to distribute one's remaining estate to the children equally. There may also be considerations for estate tax minimization and planning strategies, which could include the luxury of charitable giving intentions. In special needs planning, it is paramount to be certain that there are adequate assets readily or easily accessible to provide for the lifetime needs of the dependent with special needs. In addition, distributing the remaining estate to the children equally may not be fair. It is, however, also important to point out that equal distribution and fair distribution may address two different concerns, particularly in families that have a member with special needs. For example, traditional planning at the death of the second parent usually involves dividing all assets equally among the children. In special needs planning, however, frequently the estate is divided so that a larger portion is left to fund the lifetime needs of the child with a disability. The ultimate distribution of an estate involves many considerations, some of which are the age of the children, the levels of support the children need, and the availability and quality of government benefits. The needs of each child are unique and can vary significantly. Well-intentioned family members who offer gifts and inheritances need to be mindful of eligibility for government benefits for the child with disabilities. As with so many of the other aspects of special needs planning, wealth distribution must take into account two generations.

APPLYING THE CORE PLANNING POINTS IN THE FIVE FACTORS OF SPECIAL NEEDS PLANNING

Traditional comprehensive planning involves cash management, investment planning, tax planning, education planning, retirement planning, insurance planning, and estate planning. In addition to the traditional planning areas discussed earlier, comprehensive special needs planning emphasizes these core planning points in the Five Factors:

1. Family and support factors

2. Emotional factors

3. Financial factors

4. Legal factors

5. Government benefit factors

The key is in pulling the pieces together to address all Five Factors in each phase of planning (see Chapter 4 for a detailed discussion of the Five Factors). To simplify this process, we have identified the core planning points of special needs planning to consider for each of the Five Factors. The core planning points work with every stage of the planning timeline outlined in Chapter 1, and should be reexamined from time to time to be certain that the recommendations stay current with your family's needs.

These core planning points are by no means an exhaustive list of planning points, but they do provide a baseline of what should be considered in special needs planning. The case examples later in the book incorporate these planning points within the specific stages of planning and address more unique requirements based on the age of the child.

Family and Support Factors (Core Planning Points)

1. Ask the people whom you want involved with your family member's life whether they want to be involved. Although someone may say that they want to be involved, it is still not enough to assume that they are able to carry out those responsibilities. For this reason, it is important to begin to teach an appropriate and willing successor the ropes. Plan to speak to those individuals you would like to see as guardian, trustee, trust advisor, caregiver, or advocate.

2. Help prepare future guardians and successors for their roles. Bring them with you to meetings with your advisors, to family support workshops, and to meetings with providers. Find other opportunities to introduce them to your child's world, such as school or family activities, and social or recreational programs. Encourage other people to actively participate in the meetings and activities surrounding your child's care. This will help you to feel more supported in your efforts for your child. It will also prevent you from missing any details that can be important in the long term. Sometimes meetings and activities can become emotional. Having another support person with you who may not be as emotionally involved as you are can help to keep balance in a meeting.

3. Complete a Letter of Intent (see the appendix at the end of this book for a sample and the CD-ROM included with this book for a blank version). Update it at major transitions in care or services, or at least annually on your child's birthday. The Letter of Intent is your primary means of communicating exactly what you envision for your child to future caregivers.

4. In the event that other family members, such as grandparents, want to include your child in their gift or estate plans, encourage them to speak with advisors who specialize in disability planning. The key emphasis should be on protecting your child's eligibility for government benefits, not excluding them from gifts or inheritance.

5. When other family members or friends want to help, explain to them how they can help. Perhaps you could use household help, child care for your other child (or children), emotional support, or financial support. It is important to express what your needs are so that others can help you where or when you need it the most. Attend educational workshops on the many topics offered by local agencies to help keep you informed and give you practical ideas on how you can engage your family and friends.

6. In the event that you do not have strong family ties within your community, frequently state agencies will set you as a priority in allocating resources for support. Contact the agencies in your area that support your child's disability to obtain relevant information. Consider exploring this option if you do not have local family and support.

7. Let your personal circumstances be known to providers in the event that a special situation occurs, such as divorce, death of a family member, personal health problems, or financial hardship. There are often ways that they can help in those circumstances.

Emotional Factors
(Core Planning Points)

1. Talk to other parents and caregivers who have similar circumstances.

2. Encourage your other children to meet and talk with children, similar in age, who also have a sibling with disabilities.

3. Keep in mind that things will change over time. It is important to plan for the vision you have for the future.

4. Seek professional help when needed, and do not expect that you will have all the answers at once.

5. Take care of your own personal and financial needs first. Your child depends upon both your good health and your personal financial security.

6. Be patient with your spouse, and remember that he or she is most likely on your side when it comes to making decisions about what is best for your family. Sometimes the stress of managing a family with special needs can cause us to forget to support the person we need the most.

Financial Factors
(Core Planning Points)

1. Carefully review your financial plan. If you have not yet made a plan, you should try to make it a priority. You may contact a CERTIFIED FINANCIAL PLANNER™ (CFP®) or an other advisor who specializes in disability planning issues. You should work with a planner who holds the professional designation of CFP® practitioner. In addition to this designation, you should also ask about their expertise in special needs planning and how they are compensated. To further confirm their knowledge in special needs planning, you could ask them to explain to you what SSI and Social Security Disability Insurance (SSDI) are, and ask how each program applies to your personal situation (see Chapter 9 for more information).

2. Obtain adequate life insurance, long-term disability insurance, and long-term care insurance coverage for primary caregivers.

3. Identify all employer-sponsored benefit plans for which you are eligible. These may include retirement benefit plans; long-term disability; life insurance (yourself, your spouse, and your dependents); flexible spending accounts; and reimbursements for legal, financial planning, or tax preparation fees.

4. Do not establish savings or investment accounts in your child's name, to prevent disqualifying him or her for government benefits upon turning age 18.

5. Unless you have a high level of certainty that your child will attend college and not require government entitlement benefits, it is not advised that you use a 529 College Savings Plan to save for your child.

6. Maintain a current inventory of your assets and liabilities with account numbers, ownership, and beneficiary information. Make certain that your spouse, trustees, and executor have this list.

Legal Factors
(Core Planning Points)

1. Carefully review your estate plan. If you have not yet made a plan, you should make it a priority. Estate planning minimum requirements would include: will(s), durable power of attorney, health care proxy, and a supplemental needs trust (or special needs trust).

2. Contact a qualified attorney who is knowledgeable in disability law in your state of residence. Because one of the legal strategies of special needs planning often involves protection of government benefits, primarily Medicaid benefits, elder law attorneys may be most familiar with disability law. An attorney who practices disability law should also be a member of the professional organization of The National Association of Elder Law Attorneys (NAELA). In addition to asking an attorney for his or her credentials and experience in this area, you should also ask if he or she is an active member of NAELA. As with determining whether a financial planner is qualified to advise you on disability issues, you should ask an attorney to explain what SSI and SSDI are and how each program applies to your personal situation.

3. Name a guardian for your child or children in the event of your premature death or disability. Obtain consent from this individual before naming him or her in writing.

4. Identify your beneficiary designations on all group life insurance and retirement plans. Make certain to update and coordinate the primary and contingent beneficiary designations with your overall estate plan.

5. Identify your beneficiary designations on all personally owned life insurance, annuities, and retirement plan accounts. Make certain to update and coordinate the primary and contingent beneficiary designations with your overall estate plan.

6. Other family members may wish to provide financial assistance to your child, either by making gifts during their lifetime or by leaving inheritances upon their death. You should communicate with them that no gifts should be made directly to your child or established in your child's name; instead, offer to help them find the best way to leave a gift that benefits the child. Suggest that they consult with your advisors or have their advisors consult with yours before making any gifts or estate plans. Depending upon the amount of the gift and whether there will be annual gifts made, you may consider funding a special needs trust (see Chapter 9 for more information on funding).

Government Benefit Factors (Core Planning Points)

1. You are your child's best advocate. Stay connected with your state and local advocacy agencies that provide service and support for your child's disability.

2. Learn the difference between government benefits to which your child is entitled and those for which they are eligible (see Chapters 4 and 9 for more information on government benefits).

3. Know and pursue your child's legal rights and entitlements. Learn the system and how it works in your state.

4. Do not be afraid to question how things work, such as how services are obtained and how funds are allocated.

5. If you need help understanding or navigating the system of services, hire a professional advocate.

6. Maintain eligibility for your child's government benefits at all times, even if he or she is not currently receiving them, by carefully monitoring any current or potential assets in your child's name.

7. In the event a spouse dies, the surviving spouse should apply for social security survivor's benefits promptly. In some cases, benefits will be paid from the time you apply and not from the time the spouse died. For more information on social security survivor benefits, visit http://www.ssa.gov.

3

Practical Steps in the Planning Process

The planning process is really a matter of asking yourself some tough questions—about your vision, your values, and your ability to see this vision come to life by taking action. In special needs planning, we need to incorporate these questions at three levels: the parents' needs, the children's needs, and the integrated needs of the family. This process makes special needs planning comprehensive.

Planning for the death of a parent is paramount in the planning process, because parents are the lifeline for their child's security. Families are frequently led to believe that they have completed the planning process after they sign their wills and trusts. Although these legal documents provide for the orderly administration of assets upon death, neither guarantees your family member's security. Completing the legal documents without integrating the financial aspects is a piecemeal approach to planning.

Even when families take another step after signing their estate planning documents and purchase life insurance to fund a special needs trust, this should not be the final step. Parents may have safeguarded their child's financial security upon their death, but they have not provided any guidance in developing the vision they have for their child's lifetime. Providing only for your child upon your death is a nonintegrated approach—or rather, a piecemeal approach—which is not effective.

Even when planning for a traditional family, the primary goal is not to plan only for when the parent dies. The goal is to achieve financial independence and security for both you and your family members during your lifetime as well as at your death. In addition, when planning the needs for a traditional family, the process does not usually begin by planning for the end of one's life, yet we have found that families that have a child with disabilities often do the legal work but do not address where the money will come from to meet their personal needs and the needs of their child. The most common concerns of traditional planning are to plan for the event that an individual lives longer than expected (and outlives their assets), dies prematurely (sooner than expected), or becomes disabled along the way. It is well documented that typical families want to provide for their children's education, achieve financial independence at their retirement, minimize income and estate taxes, and provide protection in the event of a disability or a premature death, to name a few common goals. To consider that family needs only occur when a parent or caregiver dies provides an incomplete plan and misses the point of achieving financial security during the parents' lifetime.

Families often ask what they should do first—financial or legal planning. Regardless whether you elect to begin the process by meeting with a financial planner or attorney, the following two steps are required prior to the meeting: 1) Identify and prioritize your goals, and 2) list your resources available. Based on this information, you can begin to determine with your financial and/or legal advisors the most appropriate legal documents that you should have.

Special Needs Planning Pointer

By doing the first two initial steps in the financial planning process (i.e., identify goals and list assets and resources) prior to the legal planning process, you will at least have a good understanding of your financial situation to help determine the extent of the legal documents required. These steps will determine whether the value of your assets are large enough to warrant specific estate tax planning techniques in addition to the basic estate planning needs. Without developing a clear and current picture of your financial matters first, you can end up with inappropriate legal documents being created. This can then lead to the use of inappropriate financial products, and can ultimately lead to unnecessary legal and financial fees.

UNDERSTANDING THE PLANNING PROCESS—STRIKING A BALANCE

The comprehensive special needs planning process involves a sequence of events to be followed in planning for your personal security and the financial security of your child. This sequence of events will often vary with each family, based upon their own goals and values, ages, health status, and financial resources.

One of the major obstacles that families encounter in the beginning of the planning process is that they are overwhelmed with information and emotions. There are so many different choices that are now available to individuals with disabilities, from education, to employment, to social activities, to residential opportunities. Everything is important, but it is necessary to determine the priorities first.

In order to simplify this planning process, we recommend breaking it down into three primary components. The first component is to plan for the parents' financial security and future goals. The second component is to plan for the children's financial security and future goals. The third component is to integrate the first and second components with any and all government benefits and supports available.

First Component—Planning for the Parents' Needs

The first component in the special needs planning process is to identify a comprehensive baseline of financial security required for the parents and/ or primary caregivers. It is not possible to provide financially for your child if you do not have personal financial security for yourself. This baseline addresses the requirements needed to maintain the family's current lifestyle for the short term, intermediate, and long term. Depending upon the age and financial well-being of the parents, this stage usually addresses the basic needs of the family—food, clothing, and shelter—as well as the long-term retirement needs of the family. These goals are tangible, easy to measure, and usually do not change significantly.

The most important step in this component is to gain control of your current spending and saving habits. You need to analyze your current cash flow of income and the expenses needed to maintain your family's current lifestyle. Ask yourself, what does it cost for you to maintain your present lifestyle? If your expenses are greater than or equal to your income, the potential for achieving future goals is not likely. As elementary as this appears, often the more a family earns, the more they spend rather than save. If this is the case, you need to take a good look at your income and spending habits. You may have to modify your spending habits or explore ways in which you can increase your income if you wish to implement a plan of action to achieve other long-term goals.

Second Component—Planning for the Child's Needs

The second component is to identify the baseline of security required for your children's financial security. For the typical child, the most common concern is providing the child with the financial opportunity to attend college. This requires calculating the cost for 4 to 6 years of college—often a definable goal. Because the planning needs of a typical child usually have established beginning and end points, they are easy to quantify with some level of accuracy.

For the child with special needs, the most pressing concern may be providing for his or her supplemental lifetime planning needs; this may be in addition to planning for the more quantifiable goal of some type of vocational or postsecondary education for that child as well. This requires the following

1. Identifying the short-term, intermediate, and long-term costs of services, annual support costs, and supplemental expenses (current and future)

2. Identifying residential costs for purchase and/or rental of residential property

3. Identifying and maximizing eligibility for government benefits

Identifying and quantifying the costs associated with these items may be difficult, depending on the age of your child. You can use basic models based upon your child's current abilities until your child's abilities change or are further defined.

Third Component—Integrating Parents' and Child's Needs

The third component is to integrate the entire family's needs and goals, in order to strike a balance. In the event that there are inadequate resources available to achieve your own personal goals, as well as those for your children, compromises have to be made. In many cases, the compromise will be for the parent to work past the traditional retirement age of 65 to provide for the child's financial security. In some cases, parents will compromise their own goals to provide the best opportunities for their children. An additional planning component in special needs planning is to explore options and alternatives available within the guidelines that the state provides for services and supports. This is done not only to maximize personal resources, but to also maximize government benefits when appropriate and integrate these into the plan.

As you go through the planning process, it is important to keep in mind that there are many elements in planning for your child that you do not have control over. In addition, you must realize that it may not be possible for you to save all of the money that your child will need. Because you do have greater control over your own security, which includes minimizing personal expenses and establishing a regular savings plan, it is important to provide for your own security first. It is not possible for you to care for your child if you do not plan for yourself. The key in the comprehensive special needs planning process is to strike a balance between

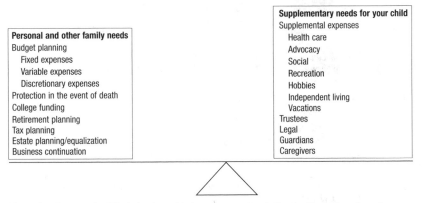

Personal and other family needs	Supplementary needs for your child
Budget planning	Supplemental expenses
Fixed expenses	Health care
Variable expenses	Advocacy
Discretionary expenses	Social
Protection in the event of death	Recreation
College funding	Hobbies
Retirement planning	Independent living
Tax planning	Vacations
Estate planning/equalization	Trustees
Business continuation	Legal
	Guardians
	Caregivers

Figure 3.   An example of the balancing act between personal and other family needs and supplementary needs for your child.

the personal and other family needs and the supplemental needs for the child (see Figure 3).

BASIC PLANNING STEPS

Most people find it helpful to have a concrete list of steps to follow when beginning the financial planning process. It does not have to be overwhelming if you break it down into manageable pieces. The basic steps of financial planning often are to

1. Identify and prioritize your goals

2. List your resources and expenses, including personal net worth, income sources and earnings, and expenses

3. Identify gaps between both personal and governmental benefit resources and desired goals

4. Identify strategies to fill the gaps

5. Implement a coordinated plan of action based on priorities

6. Periodically review and monitor your plan

These steps are a starting point, and are the steps often used in traditional financial planning. Consider this framework as you get ready for the more detailed special needs planning steps (see Table 1).

SPECIAL NEEDS PLANNING STEPS

The special needs planning timeline is the framework for special needs planning as we have outlined in Chapter 1 and illustrate in case examples for each stage in Chapters 5–8. You should begin to build your own spe-

Table 1. Guide to comprehensive special needs planning steps

1) Address preliminary issues   Done_____

Determine what you want for the future of your family member with a disability for both during your lifetime and upon your death or for when you are no longer the caregiver. Focus on areas such as living environment, employment, social life, religious affiliation, medical care, and final arrangements.

2) Estimate probable costs   Done_____

This is difficult to estimate because of future uncertainties, but do the best you can. Determine the amount that you currently supplement and any future expenses that you might anticipate as your child's needs change. Closely examine any effect if government funding is reduced or reallocated.

3) Identify financial resources   Done_____

Review government benefits, family assistance, inheritances, investment earnings, legal settlements, and insurance. If a deficit exists, select appropriate funding vehicles and determine how you can make adjustments to achieve your goals.

4) Choose trustee(s)   Done_____

They will manage the trust funds today and in the future when you are no longer able because of health or death. Select someone you trust to tend to the provisions of your documents.

5) Choose advocate(s)/guardian(s)/caregiver(s)/trust advisor(s)   Done_____

These are the key persons who will make sure your wishes are carried out. Ask them to be involved in your child's life and what you envision their role to be.

6) Execute will(s)   Done_____

Make certain that your child with special needs does not receive a direct inheritance from your estate. Leave your child's share to a special needs trust.

7) Establish a special needs trust   Done_____

The trust will manage the resources, protect government benefits, provide supplemental funds as needed, and specify distribution of remaining assets to successor beneficiaries.

8) Have a coordinated plan   Done_____

Asset ownership should be arranged to ensure the legal documents function as designed. Jointly held property, individual assets, beneficiaries on retirement plans, life insurance policies and annuities, and property ownership should be arranged in accordance with your financial and estate plan.

9) Letter of Intent   Done_____

This is not a legal document but provides the format to communicate your desires and concerns to future caregivers, advocates, guardians, trustees, and trust advisors. Update it periodically with any changes or corrections, but do so at least annually on your child's birthday.

10) Update your plan   Done_____

Update your plan periodically. This includes a review of legal documents, trust agreements, financial instruments, asset ownership and beneficiary designations. Also periodically reconsider the appropriateness and abilities of those selected to serve as successors for guardian, caregiver, advocate, trustee, and/or trust advisor.

cial needs planning timeline based upon your current age, your child's age, your goals, and the planning pressure points to consider. Your timeline should list your personal goals as the parent (first component) and the goals for of all your children (second component). Identify each of the planning pressure points based upon the age of your child with special needs. When you complete the timeline, you will then be able to see how these goals are integrated (third component). By creating your own personal special needs planning timeline, you will have identified the framework of your goals and the time period for which to plan.

Step 1: Identify and Prioritize Your Goals

Begin by determining the vision you want to have for your family today and after you are gone. This is where we begin. Just as when you plan a trip, you start with the destination first and explore ways to get there. Make it simple by prioritizing your financial concerns. Some common concerns that families identify include how to

- Maintain their current lifestyle in the event of a premature death of a parent or primary caregiver

- Provide the opportunity for all their children to achieve their maximum potential, including funding for college and postsecondary education programs

- Maximize eligibility for any and all government benefits for their child with disabilities—both during their lifetime and upon their death

- Explore options and alternatives for the most independent residential lifestyle possible for their child with disabilities

- Have adequate savings for financial independence for their own retirement

- Protect their income and assets in the event of the disability of a parent or primary caregiver

- Minimize income and estate taxes within prescribed IRS legal limitations

- Determine how to apportion their estate among their children in the most equitable manner

Often, it is difficult to even define a goal. Sometimes simply by listening to others and discussing your concerns, it becomes easier to identify your goals. We then recommend prioritizing the goals as short term, intermediate, or long term. This will help to build your own special needs planning timeline.

It is important to point out that having a child with disabilities can require a family to redefine the classical financial planning terms of short-term, intermediate, and long-term goals. Financial planning textbooks will refer to a short-term planning goal as something that would be needed immediately and/or within the next 5 years, an intermediate planning goal as one to be achieved in a 5- to 10-year period, and a long-term planning goal as one to be achieved in a period greater than 10 years. In planning care for a child with disabilities, however, we often must look at things differently. We recommend considering these traditional planning periods as a general guideline to help determine the time periods for which to plan. For example, saving for your child's physical residence, which may be 20 years away, is more of an intermediate goal for families. This is an identifiable goal with a definable time period. To use another example, planning for your child's lifetime supplemental needs has a long-term time period. In fact, this goal could conceivably be an infinite planning goal that often exceeds your own life expectancy. By following the special needs planning timeline, families with disabilities can plan flexibly and for two generations.

Defining Traditional Goals   The relevance in defining a goal as either a short-term, intermediate, or long-term goal is that it helps you to

1.   Prioritize the order of each goal

2.   Determine a plan of action

3.   Establish benchmarks to measure whether you are achieving your goals

4.   Determine the most appropriate financial and legal tools to be used to achieve each goal

Each goal, whether short term, intermediate, or long term, requires a careful analysis of the needs and the savings available to achieve this goal based upon the time remaining until the invested funds are needed. The investment objective will change depending on the timeframe for needing the money; an investment objective is the financial focus of the investment, such as the level of risk you are able to assume and the rate of return you require on your investments. For example, if there is a goal to be achieved in more than 10 years, the investment objective may be more growth oriented—a growth-oriented investment has greater potential of long-term gain, but the value may fluctuate more in the short term, and could potentially lose value at some points during the planning timeframe. Alternately, if there is a short-term goal to be achieved in less than 5 years, maintaining the safety of the principal investment, and having less fluctuation in value, becomes more important.

For short-term needs, planning is focused on having adequate liquid savings for emergencies and unexpected expenses. A simple rule of thumb is to have 3–6 months of living expenses available in the bank and/or money market accounts. Although liquid savings tend to have lower rates of return, they may provide **safety of principal**. The key is to receive a return *of* the money, not necessarily to have a return *on* the money. An investment in money market funds is not insured or guaranteed by the Federal Deposit Insurance Corporation or any other government agency. Although the fund seeks to preserve the value of your investment at $1.00 per share, it is possible to lose money by investing in the fund.

For intermediate needs, planning is focused on accumulating savings in nonretirement accounts that can be accessed without having to pay a penalty. The investment objective may primarily be focused toward growth, with a secondary objective of safety of principal.

For long-term needs that are earmarked to be available during your retirement years, planning is generally focused on accumulating savings in retirement plan accounts. The investment objective is primarily focused toward growth of principal.

Defining Special Needs Planning Goals For a typical family, an intermediate savings goal might be paying for college tuitions, which are often a 4-year commitment. For special needs planning, an additional intermediate savings goal might be purchasing a home for your child with disabilities. Defining the specific dollar amount required to purchase a home can vary dramatically from state to state, from family to family, and from child to child. It is important, however, to at least establish a baseline for which to plan. To define the amount of savings needed to achieve this goal, many financial planners use the example of purchasing a condominium unit. The purchase of any physical structure would be basically the same, with some variations in structure and layout (or accessibility) based on the child's abilities. The primary distinction would be to anticipate any requirements for significant modifications to the home to meet the needs of the individual. Nonetheless, these are definable intermediate goals.

Continuing to provide for the lifetime supports required to enable your child with disabilities to live away from you in a separate residence are considered long-term savings goals. Regardless of the number of years until the child moves into the residence, the support needs may continue for his or her lifetime. In developing the long-term planning strategy, the long-term support needs of your child should be integrated with your personal long-term cash requirements. In planning ahead, this involves recognizing an increase in your cash-flow needs during your retirement years by the estimated amount of money required to support your child in his or her residence. For example, in traditional retirement planning it is frequently recommended to establish your retirement income goal to be 75% of your preretirement expenses. In supporting the lifetime needs of your child, his or her additional estimated expenses should be added to your own retirement income goal.

Special Needs Planning Story

Our son, Derek, had become friendly with his classmate, Peter. They attended a high school program together for years. Derek, who has a cognative disability, and Peter, who has a visual impairment, just seemed to hit it off. We also became friendly with Peter's parents. Our goal was always to see Derek living independently. Through Peter's parents, we heard about a program where we could purchase a condominium unit in a seven-room house for $95,000 and personally pay $1,000 per month for services. Initially we were nervous about being able to afford that for the rest of our lives. But after we factored in my state pension, income from Jim's retirement savings, and Derek's government benefits, we felt we could make some changes in our expenses and be able to afford Derek's supplemental costs. He and Peter have been living on their own for 18 years now. Since then, the program expenses have gone up, but things have worked out perfectly!

· · · —Jim and Laura · · ·

Step 2: List Your Resources and Expenses

Determine Your Personal Net Worth To determine your net worth, simply list everything that you own (your assets) and subtract all that you owe (your **debt obligations** or **liabilities**). The easiest way to do this is to gather the most recent statements of each investment and savings account. Then categorize the assets that you own as **liquid, retirement, nonliquid,** or **other assets.**

- Liquid assets are those assets that can be converted into cash within 5 business days. These may include savings and checking accounts, certificates of deposit (nonindividual retirement account [IRA]), money market accounts, treasury bills or savings bonds. Some liquid assets, such as stocks, bonds, and mutual funds, may fluctuate due to market conditions. Therefore when redeemed, they may be worth more or less than your original cost.

- Retirement assets are those investments held in retirement plan accounts, where a penalty occurs if distributions are taken prior to age 59½. These include IRA accounts (e.g., traditional IRAs, Roth IRAs, rollover IRAs), employer-sponsored retirement plans (e.g., 401[k]s, 403[b]s, and tax-sheltered annuity accounts), and tax-deferred annuities.

- Nonliquid assets are those investments that cannot easily be turned into cash within 5 business days. These include business interests, boats, investment property, recreational vehicles, artwork, collectables, and personal property.

- Other assets do not typically convert to cash for investment purposes. These include personal residences and vehicles.

After you list your assets, the next step is to list all of your debt obligations—these are called your **liabilities.** Again, the easiest way to do this is to gather the most recent statements of each account. There are two types of debt, **secured** and **unsecured.** *Secured debt* requires use of collateral to secure the loan. *Unsecured debt* does not require the use of collateral to secure the loan. After you have gathered all of your statements, categorize them as follows:

- Short-term debt obligations are those that would be paid off within 5 years. These include credit cards (unsecured debt), personal loans (unsecured debt), passbook savings loans (secured debt), and auto and boat loans (secured debt).

- Intermediate term debt obligations are those that would be paid off within 5–10 years. These include home equity line of credit (secured debt), loans against retirement plan accounts (secured debt), loans against the cash value of life insurance policies (secured debt), student loans (unsecured debt), and business loans (often secured debt, but can be unsecured).

- Long-term debt obligations are those that would be paid off in a period greater than 10 years. These include mortgages (secured debt).

In order to calculate your total net worth, you need to add up all of your assets, then subtract all of your liabilities.

Determine Your Income Sources and Earnings   Income can be categorized in two basic ways—**earned** and **unearned.** Earned income is received while you are working, either from wages or self-employed earnings. Unearned income is income generated from your investments in stocks, bonds, mutual funds, and real estate (rental income). Additional income sources at retirement may be from Social Security, pensions, and retirement plan distributions.

Parents' Income Sources   During your earning years, unearned income is usually reinvested. During retirement years, income and dividends from investments are often used to pay for expenses. Additional sources of income may be received from gifts and/or inheritances.

Adjustments to Income   It is important to keep in mind that your current level of income may be reduced due to the demands on your time required to provide for your child's unique needs. Even a self-employed parent may have a loss of earnings due to the requirements of attending medical appointments and the accompanied loss of billable hours. Many typical couples are dual-income households. Having two working parents means not only more current income but also a better ability to maximize retirement savings and receive benefits from employers. The loss of earnings from one parent needing to be the primary caregiver will have an impact not only on the current income but also on saving for future goals.

As your child's needs become more definitive, and as services become more available when your child enters school, the primary caregiver may have an opportunity to work outside of the home, if only on a part-time basis. During this period of double income earnings, it is important to maximize contributions to retirement plan savings for yourself and college savings for your other children.

As your child leaves the safety net of the school system and its entitlements, circumstances will change significantly. You will be facing another pressure point: the transition to the adult service world. Upon your child's graduation from school, for the most part you will be transitioning from a world of entitlements to the world of service eligibility. This is where benefits, either in the form of services or supports, are subject to the funding available in your state's budgeted services for residential and day programs. Keep in mind that the time required for your new level of advocacy efforts may limit your time for employment opportunities.

Child's Income Sources   At some point your child with disabilities may receive his or her own employment income. He or she may be gainfully employed from an independent employer, corporation, or supported work program subsidized by the state. Clearly, the level of income depends on his or her abilities as well as opportunities in your area.

Income sources for your child may also be received in the form of SSI. SSI is perhaps one of the most important income benefits. It provides a monthly income allowance and usually makes the person eligible for Medicaid health benefits. SSI is administered through the Social Security Administration and is available, based on financial need, to low-income people who are elderly or have a physical or intellectual disability. Prior to age 18, a child's eligibility is determined based upon a parent's income and assets. If the parent's assets exceed $2,000, the child is ineligible for SSI until age 18. Upon the child's 18th birthday, the child's own income and assets determine eligibility.

The key is to make certain that an individual with a disability does not have more than $2,000 in available assets and that he or she is under an annual income limit. The assets include cash, savings accounts, certain property, inheritances, custodial accounts, or other assets. Those assets that do not count include the individual's home, an automobile, a burial plot, a prepaid funeral plan, life insurance (under $1,500 cash value), and clothing.

Another source of income for your child may be SSDI. A person can receive SSDI benefits either from his or her own work record, or, if he or she qualifies as a disabled adult child (DAC), he or she can receive SSDI benefits from a retired or deceased parent's work record. Primary eligibility for SSDI benefits occurs when the person and/or parent has paid into the Social Security system.

Identify Public Resources Available   In special needs planning, one of the primary goals is to maximize the child's eligibility for government benefits. Prior to becoming age 18, a child's government benefits are limited. Private health insurance benefits, education entitlements, and some respite or family support are the main sources of benefits prior to age 18.

Upon turning age 18, the child may be eligible for a number of benefits. Table 2 lists some of the major government programs that have been established for people with qualifying disabilities. Although the list is lengthy, one must keep in mind that government benefits are considered to be either **entitlements** or **public benefits programs** (refer to the section in Chapter 4 and Chapter 9 on government benefits for details). In special needs planning, it is important to distinguish between entitlement programs and public benefits programs.

Special Needs Planning Pointer

Using a combination of your own income and resources as well as one or more government benefits may provide the additional resources needed to make a residential program possible. It is also very important to protect your child's eligibility for these programs even if they are not currently receiving benefits, as they may have a future need. Obtaining the entitlement benefits is the first step to developing a base from which you can begin to seek the most appropriate public benefits programs for your son or daughter. It is important to explore each option and be creative in the way you use each program. Since every person is different, it is up to you to shape the program around your child's needs, rather than trying to shape your child's needs around the program.

Table 2. A list of government benefit programs available for people with disabilities

Entitlement programs	Eligibility programs
Medicare	Housing subsidy (under housing finance agencies)
Medicaid	Rental subsidy (under Section 8 housing)
Group adult foster care funding (under Medicaid)	Flexible family supports
Social Security Disability Insurance (SSDI)	Residential supports
Supplemental Security Income (SSI)	Transportation
Federal and military benefits	Adult day service programs
Veterans benefits	Supported employment
Railroad retirement benefits	
Civil service retirement benefits	

Determine Your Expenses Some families maintain detailed summaries of their monthly expenses, using cash-flow software or expense logs. If you do not record the details of your expenses, you may be able to determine an estimate of your monthly expenses by subtracting your checking account's ending monthly balance from the beginning balance, and then adding back any deposits. After several months calculations, you could determine an average of your monthly expenses using this method. In an ideal world, we would recommend keeping a detailed budget that specifically lists all income and expenses. But in the real world, many people do not have the time or the interest to maintain such detailed records.

Expenses can be **fixed, variable,** or **discretionary** and are defined in more detail next. Figure 4 shows an example of budgeted expenses.

Fixed expenses are those expenses that do not change frequently and that must be met on a regular basis. They include housing expenses (mortgage, property taxes/rent), car loans, and other loans.

Variable expenses are those that we have some control over but are generally classified as necessities, such as housing repairs and maintenance, utilities, and food.

Discretionary expenses are those that we have control of and are not required. They include vacations, dining out, and entertainment.

Family Needs The value of classifying your personal expenses is that you can determine what expenses you can control. The greater control you assert over your expenses, the greater capacity you will have to achieve your goals. Basic cash-flow and budgeting principles state that if, at the end of each month, your expenses exceed your income, you need to reevaluate your spending and explore ways to reduce your expenses. Once you have an idea of what it costs to maintain your family's current lifestyle, you can then determine whether your goals are reasonable and/or achievable given your cash-flow needs. Having competing

Current Budget and Expense Worksheet

	Monthly	Annual
Mortgage or rent	$1,400.00	$16,800.00
Telephone	$90.00	$1,080.00
Utilities	$150.00	$1,800.00
Taxes	$300.00	$3,600.00
Water	$75.00	$900.00
Maintenance	$100.00	$1,200.00
Homeowner's or renter's insurance	$50.00	$600.00
Other		
Total housing costs	$2,165.00	$25,980.00

	Monthly	Annual
Child and adult day services		
Caregiver	$50.00	$600.00
Pet care		
Other		
Total care costs	$50.00	$600.00

	Monthly	Annual
Automobile payments	$225.00	$2,700.00
Gas	$90.00	$1,080.00
Maintenance	$200.00	$2,400.00
Automobile insurance	$100.00	$1,200.00
Parking fees		
Other		
Total transportation costs	$615.00	$7,380.00

	Monthly	Annual
Groceries	$800.00	$9,600.00
Child lunches		
Adult lunches	$25.00	$300.00
Miscellaneous foods		
Other		
Total food and beverage costs	$825.00	$9,900.00

	Monthly	Annual
Personal premiums	$225.00	$2,700.00
Spouse premiums	$175.00	$2,100.00
Total life insurance costs	$400.00	$4,800.00

	Monthly	Annual
Personal new expenses	$50.00	$600.00
Spouse new expenses	$100.00	$1,200.00
Child new expenses	$50.00	$600.00
Tailoring		
Dry cleaning	$20.00	$240.00
Laundromat		
Other		
Total clothing costs	$220.00	$2,640.00

	Monthly	Annual
New purchases	$35.00	$420.00
Maintenance		
Other		
Total furnishing costs	$35.00	$420.00

	Monthly	Annual
Personal taxes		
Spouse taxes		
Total federal tax costs		

	Monthly	Annual
Personal taxes	$1,750.00	$21,000.00
Spouse taxes		
Total state and local tax costs	$1,750.00	$21,000.00

	Monthly	Annual
Personal taxes		
Spouse taxes	$375.00	$4,500.00
Total self-employment tax costs	$375.00	$4,500.00

	Monthly	Annual
Personal	$600.00	$7,200.00
Spouse		
Total Medicare costs	$600.00	$7,200.00

	Monthly	Annual
Spending money	$300.00	$3,600.00
Personal care	$50.00	$600.00
Personal products		
Total personal costs	$350.00	$4,200.00

	Monthly	Annual
Medication	$30.00	$360.00
Health insurance	$50.00	$600.00
Dental insurance	$50.00	$600.00
Disability insurance		
Office visits	$20.00	$240.00
Other		
Total health expenses	$150.00	$1,800.00

	Monthly	Annual
Tuition fees		
Books and materials		
Exam fees		
Therapy fees		
Exercise club fees		
Other		
Total education and self-improvement costs		

Figure 4.   A current budget and expense worksheet completed for the Barry family.

(continued)

Figure 4. *(continued)*

Current Budget and Expense Worksheet

	Monthly	Annual
Credit card payments	$1,750.00	$21,000.00
Home equity payments		
Personal loan payments		
School loan payments		
Subscriptions	$10.00	$120.00
Cable service	$45.00	$540.00
Internet service	$15.00	$180.00
Other		
Total debt and installment payments	$1,820.00	$21,840.00

	Monthly	Annual
Dining	$100.00	$1,200.00
Movie or theater tickets		
Sports		
Hobbies		
Other		
Total entertainment costs	$100.00	$1,200.00

	Monthly	Annual
Winter		
Spring		
Summer	$200.00	$2,400.00
Fall		
Total vacation and holiday costs	$200.00	$2,400.00

	Monthly	Annual
Church	$75.00	$900.00
Charities	$50.00	$600.00
Alma mater	$8.00	$96.00
Other		
Total charitable contributions	$133.00	$1,596.00

	Monthly	Annual
Birthdays	$30.00	$360.00
Weddings and anniversaries	$25.00	$300.00
Work related		
Baby and wedding showers	$35.00	$420.00
Religious events		
Holidays		
Other		
Total gift costs	$90.00	$1,080.00

	Monthly	Annual
Savings		
401k contribution	$900.00	$10,800.00
529 Plan for Patrick	$100.00	$1,200.00
Joint investment account	$500.00	$6,000.00
Other		
Total savings	$1,500.00	$18,000.00

goals for the same dollars will cause frustration and inaction in planning for your goals.

Special Needs Planning Pointer

If increased expenses are a result of your child's supplemental needs, you should also explore ways in which to find reimbursements and/or entitlements. See the section on government benefits in Chapter 4 for ideas.

Supplemental Cash-Flow Needs of the Child with Disabilities
The estimated supplementary expenses worksheet (see Figure 5) helps to determine what it will cost to create your vision of your child's lifestyle, including taking into consideration current needs, future needs, and lifetime needs. Identifying those expenses that a parent and/or caregiver currently provides, or will eventually provide, enables you to calculate an estimated future need. The amount that you determine as your child's needs should be included as part of a parent's expenses in determining retirement and estate planning needs. This worksheet should be used as a

Estimated Monthly Supplementary Expenses

Child's Name Alan Barry   Date January 2007

Housing	Current	Future
Rent/mortgage	$200.00	$200.00
Utilities	$25.00	$90.00
Maintenance		$25.00
Cleaning		$20.00
Other		
Total	$225.00	$335.00
Care assistance		
Live-in care		
Respite care	$90.00	$300.00
Custodial care		
Guardian		$50.00
Other		
Total	$90.00	$350.00
Food		
Home	$50.00	$150.00
Eating out		
Special foods		
Other		
Total	$50.00	$150.00
Personal needs		
Health and beauty		$35.00
Clothing	$10.00	$10.00
Telephone		$25.00
Other		
Total	$10.00	$70.00

Health needs	Current	Future
General		
Therapy		
Nursing		
Medications		$15.00
Insurance		
Other		
Total		$15.00
Recreation		
Sports		$15.00
Vacations		$80.00
Entertainment		
Camp		
Computer		
Cable		$25.00
Total		$120.00
Transportation		$50.00
Education (tutor)		
Employment		
Special equipment		

Total estimated monthly supplementary expenses $375.00 $1,090.00

Figure 5. An estimated monthly supplementary expenses worksheet completed for Alan Barry. The estimated current expenses show what the Barrys will need to plan for while Alan is living at home with them, while the estimated future expenses show what will need to be planned for when Alan is living independently.

guideline in your planning process. It is important to recognize the fact that the needs of your child will change constantly over time, as will his or her abilities. As your child ages, his or her physical and cognitive abilities may change, and in some cases the ultimate outcome may be a greater need for increased long-term supports.

Supplemental Needs for Younger Children with Disabilities (Child's Birth to Age 15)   The estimated supplementary expenses worksheet includes the more common expenses that families incur for their child with special needs. For younger families, in many cases there will not be a significant increase in the tangible costs involved in raising a child with special needs over that of raising a typically developing child. For example, the increased expenses may not be for traditional extracurricular activities but may still include expenses that would naturally be absorbed by a parent, such as

- Specialized child care
- Legal and educational advocacy

- Private tutoring

- Special foods

- Therapies

- Counseling

- Adaptive equipment

- Other medical needs not covered by insurance

During the years when a child is young, the cost of child care may, in many cases, be approximately the same as that for a typically developing child. If there are significant medical or behavior issues, however, the cost of the additional help may not be the only factor. You just might not be able to find anyone reliable that you can count on. If this is the case, it is suggested to make every attempt to connect with a local not-for-profit agency to seek some form of respite supports. Everyone needs a break!

· · ·　　　**Special Needs Planning Story**　　　· · ·

When I first attended a meeting of aging parents who were on a waiting list for residential services and heard other parents share their thoughts and frustration about their inability to secure an appropriate residential placement for their child still living at home with them, it suddenly brought my life fast-forwarded to the future. Although I never thought that I would have a child with disabilities, it really didn't seem all that different because he was still so innocent and lovable. I only imagined his innocence would last forever. My life changed immediately when an elderly parent looked at me and said with great emotion, "People will not always look at your child and call him cute."

· · ·　　　　　　　　—John, James's father　　　　　　　　· · ·

As your child approaches adolescence, it may become more difficult to find someone who is comfortable caring for your child. Although society has changed significantly and children with disabilities are more likely to be accepted in the community, the thought of having someone watch your adolescent child while you enjoy an evening out—or even a break in your day—may not always be accepted by others. The neighbor next door who used to babysit your young child may not feel as comfortable watching an adolescent. In fact, even as we write this book we are struggling to find the right words to use—is it "babysitting," "child watching," "adolescent caring," or something else? It costs more money and is more difficult to find care so parents can simply have an evening out. If there are family members nearby, often a grandparent and/or aunt or uncle of the child may be willing to help out. If it is at all possible, engage the child's future guardian, caregiver, or trustee to spend time with the child as often as possible. When that person takes an active part in your child's life, he or she gets to know your family and your child well from those experiences. Your child will also have the opportunity to build a relationship with this individual sooner rather than later. It also may be necessary to hire extra help for family vacations or to carve out time alone with, and for, your other children. It is difficult to find trusting, qualified individuals to provide such care. It is also an added expense to the customary costs of child care, and can extend beyond the typical years that child care is needed.

• • •   **Special Needs Planning Story**   • • •

We felt very strongly after a year of hospital stays and surgeries with our son, Billy, that we wanted to spend time alone with our daughter, Julie, on her 16th birthday to celebrate with her and her friends. She needed to just be sweet 16 and know that life could be fun and simple at times. Because there were no public funds available for us to pay for respite hours or caretakers, we had to hire one of his aides to spend the weekend with Billy while we spent the weekend alone with Julie. This was an expense well worth spending.

• • •   —Billy's mother   • • •

As your child approaches the teenage years, it is important to become integrated into his or her community. This can be challenging and often can result in spending extra money to provide such supports. There is a growing recognition of the importance for increased social and recreational activities beyond the family unit. Older siblings are involved in their own activities and social life and may not have the time to spend with their brother or sister as they once did. In order for your child to participate in typical teenage activities, you may need to pay for someone to accompany him or her. There are specialized programs for social, recreational, and travel opportunities beyond the classroom. Often these programs can be accessed for a fee, and they should be included in your budget.

Special Needs Planning Story

When we found out that our daughter may only receive residential services when we either become very ill or die, we decided to take the matter in our own hands. Fortunately her needs were not significant, and we were able to purchase a condominium with other families where she would have the supports necessary to have an enriched life.

· · · —Bethany's father · · ·

Supplemental Needs for Transitioning Families (Child's Age 15 to End of School)

During this stage, the estimated supplementary expenses worksheet (Figure 5) should focus on more lifestyle expenses that you would like to continue providing for your child after his or her graduation. It is difficult to plan for such expenses, due to the uncertainty of available funding for residential placement, transportation, and vocational programs. You may, however, have an idea of the desired lifestyle that you could envision your child living, including such details as location, hobbies, activities, interests, special foods, therapies, and so forth. You may not have an idea yet of the vocational abilities of your child. Therefore, you may not have any idea of additional expenses required for such items as transportation and job coaching, but additional costs should be anticipated.

· · · **Special Needs Planning Story** · · ·

When our son Brian was 16 years old, we were invited to an open house of a home for individuals with disabilities. We initially did not think that we would benefit by attending because Brian was only 16, and we quite frankly never envisioned Brian living outside of our home. We were amazed to see that residents with even more challenges than Brian were able to live on their own. It was a great experience to see how happy the residents were. Our views on Brian's abilities definitely changed.

· · · —Brian's father · · ·

The key of this transition stage is to begin exploring options and alternatives for your child's residential and vocational needs upon graduation. Residential and vocational services may or may not be fully provided by your state's programs. Therefore, it is important to focus on the cash-flow that will be needed to provide for the supplemental needs not covered by public resources or services such as transportation. These supplemental needs could include special health and hygiene requirements, recreation, advocacy, or special foods and therapies. In many cases, residential placement and transportation is limited. Today, primarily due to lack of public funding and a desire for greater control, parents are seeking alternatives to the fully funded model and services, whereby the government provides full residential supports that are often limited in quality and care. By utilizing both public resources and personal income and savings, many families are developing creative residential models.

A proactive approach for developing a desirable residential and day or vocational program is to interview several provider agencies in your area. The most appropriate government agency for your child will usually provide an assessment to determine the requirements of your child as he or she makes the transition to adulthood. In some cases, this assessment is thorough and you will feel good about it. In other cases, you may question the accuracy, or perhaps the thoroughness or the competency, of the assessor, or possibly the general disposition of your child at the time of the assessment. If you do question the assessment or the placement, it is strongly recommended that you hire an independent third party who can perform an evaluation and provide alternative options. It is very common for parents to obtain an independent evaluation of their child for educational programs and services. It is less common, however, for parents to consider paying for an independent evaluation of their child's residential and/or vocational needs and options. Many residential service providers will provide an independent evaluation of your child's life skills abilities to help determine the residential needs for the child. Consulting with residential service providers will also give you some insight into the various options that are available.

Special Needs Planning Pointer

It is quite interesting to find that parents will hire advocates, and at times attorneys, to help them secure the best education for their child, but do not consider doing so for residential and vocational placements. Although a residential placement or a day program may not be an entitlement benefit, it is important for you to make sure that you are receiving the most appropriate supports and services for your child. Having an independent consultant who is aware of the various programs and options available will enable you to design the best program for your child's needs. The more knowledge you have about how the system works and the various agencies and models available, the more power you will have in making these decisions when the time comes.

Supplemental Needs for Older Families (Adult Child/Post School) As your child's needs become more defined in adulthood, completing the estimated supplementary expenses worksheet (Figure 5) should help quantify his or her lifetime needs. This information is then used to determine the level of supports your child requires. Once the support requirements are identified, you can determine the amount of money necessary to maintain his or her lifestyle, including, for example, costs of social and recreational programs, hobbies or extracurricular activities, additional staff needs for daily activities, budgeting, or even medical assistance. Identifying the earlier expenses and needs should also help you to plan for the ultimate distribution of your estate upon your death. Additional expenses to consider are primarily those to help maintain the independence of your child with a disability; these may include additional supports for guardians, advocates, trustees, and professional advisors. Additional travel expenses during holidays and birthdays, so that your child can be with siblings and other family members in other locations, need to be included. Consider your family traditions for holidays and special occasions and ways to continue these traditions. Do you have a special tradition for birthdays or a favorite meal or event that you would like to continue? Does your child have his or her own Christmas tree to decorate or always have a new and special outfit for holidays? Are there any special family traditions for Hanukkah or other religious holidays?

· · ·   **Special Needs Planning Story**   · · ·

My son is now 27; when he was 22, I was not ready for him to move out of our house. Since he had his brothers and sisters at home, he was "part of the crowd" when all of their friends were at our house. Now, the other children have been moved out of the house for 10 years and we need help. We're tired and could use a break. When we were planning for our retirement years, we never planned to have to pay for his quality of life as well as our own. I wish that we had planned better.

· · ·   —Steven's mother   · · ·

It is also important to be mindful that expenses for health care and medications that are not covered by insurances will increase, either due to inflation factors or due to increased needs. Because of these issues, the level of support required to maintain the present living situation is likely to increase. These potential increases should be factored into the budget for future planning.

• • • **Special Needs Planning Story** • • •

When my parents died three years ago, my sister needed limited supports and was happy living in a residence with two roommates. For years things were going very smoothly, and her supplemental expenses were very low. In fact, the only additional expenses she had were from her hobby of collecting hats—which she loved to do. When one roommate suddenly became ill and passed away, she went into a period of depression. Because her communication skills were limited, it was very difficult to detect how great the emotional distress was for her. She then had multiple hospitalizations for depression. But due to insurance regulations, she could not stay in the hospital for any length of stay. This resulted in our having to change her living situation, because she now needed 24-hour supervision. Although our state provided for her residential placement, it became a challenge to be able to maintain her original living situation. We had to hire an advocate to help us obtain the additional services she needed. Fortunately, the money my parents left in her special needs trusts was available for us to hire the advocate. We developed a plan that involved our paying for an intern to be with my sister, to give her the supplemental supports that we felt she needed. Although the state was willing to provide for her basic needs, we felt that we should do better than that for her.

• • • —Brooke's sister • • •

Step 3: Identify Planning Gaps

After you identify your goals and available resources, the next step is to identify any shortfalls that will prevent you from achieving your goals. Common planning gaps are often found in the event of a premature death and/or disability of a parent, or not having adequate savings to meet your lifetime goals. Naturally, each family will identify their own unique issues and planning deficiencies based on their personal financial situation, family values, and overall priorities.

In special needs planning, it is important to identify where the gaps are in each of the factors. It is not only about the money. It is about coordinating all of the factors, to minimize the impact of gaps in any one area. The following are examples of common gaps in the Five Factors:

• **Family and support factors**

  No family members living locally

  Family members are unable or unwilling to help

No individuals available to be a successor caregiver

No connection with a family support organization

Inability to identify appropriate personal care attendants

High employee turnover in residential and day programs

- **Emotional factors**

Frustration of not knowing a diagnosis

Uncertainty of the child's future abilities and how to plan

Fear of making incorrect planning decisions

Feeling overwhelmed with day-to-day challenges

Anxiety of coordinating and meeting the health care needs of the child

Personal health concerns of a parent

- **Financial factors**

Not saving enough for parents' own retirement needs

No protection in the event of a death and/or disability of a parent or caregiver

Inability to meet current cash-flow needs

Lack of discipline in saving

Loss of employment and income due to tending to the needs of the child

No liquid emergency reserve

Poor investment decisions

Excessive debt

- **Legal factors**

No current wills or trusts in place

Legal documents that do not protect the child's eligibility for government benefits

Assets owned improperly

Improper beneficiary designations

Inability to identify appropriate guardians and/or trustees

Lack of proper estate tax planning

- **Government benefit factors**

Not maximizing eligible or being disqualified for government benefits

Inadequately funded state government eligibility programs

Waiting lists for services

Understaffed government agencies

Limited and/or ineffective advocacy efforts for key issues in your state of residence

According to the special needs planning timeline (Figure 1), planning pressure points are determined by the age of the child. Planning gaps are identified by analyzing your current resources and determining whether they are adequate to meet your goals over the short term, intermediate, and long term. Planning strategies vary, based upon the age of the parent, the age of the child, the government funding available, and family savings and income. The shortfalls or gaps are then solved by utilizing the most appropriate planning tools.

In special needs planning, it takes one parent—if not both—to be the advocate for their child. The more involved and aware parents are about the options and entitlements for their child, the greater potential they possess to make their future vision a reality. Although the primary intention of this book is to discuss the financial implications of raising a child with disabilities, your child's success is also determined by your advocacy.

If there is a gap or loss in any one area, it affects the whole plan. For example, if a parent has to return to work upon the death of a spouse because of improper planning, he or she may lose valuable relationships that he or she had begun to establish for the benefit of the child. Not only does the loss of income affect planning, but the loss of momentum and resources creates a setback to the future opportunities of the child.

It is difficult to simply write a formula that quantifies the value of the relationships you develop and the knowledge that you gain through EI and the school system as your child develops. One of the most important planning tools available to document all of this information for the surviving spouse, family members, or guardian is the Letter of Intent (see the appendix for a sample and the accompanying CD-ROM for a blank version).

Special Needs Planning Story

In the event that my wife and I both died together, we knew that our friend Audrey would be the best caregiver for our son. Audrey is single and a professional and has a very promising career that requires her to travel and work long hours. She adores Bobby, and he adores her too. Despite her career goals, she has told us that she would quit her job to take care of Bobby as her own. Although we felt this was commendable, we were also realistic that this would be a great financial setback in planning for her own financial independence. In our planning, we had enough life insurance to take care of Bobby's needs, but we wanted to make sure we could plan for Audrey's needs as well. We just didn't think it would be fair for Audrey to give up her career and her personal financial security. Because of this we purchased additional life insurance that would provide enough money to fund an IRA for Audrey and pay her health insurance premiums and any incidentals that she might have.

· · · —Bobby's father · · ·

· · · **Special Needs Planning Story** · · ·

We thought that we were financially secure in knowing that I had lots of life insurance on my life and a small policy on my wife. This was because I had a successful career and my wife had a part-time job, while the rest of her time was spent overseeing our daughter's care. She spent her days arranging her therapies and developing relationships with various agencies to maintain our support network. When she died suddenly, I had no idea where to turn. Because of her being so proactive, there were many people willing to offer their help and guidance. However, because this was in many respects a whole new life for me, I had trouble adjusting to this other side of care[giving]. It has been over a year, and I am just now able to return to a somewhat reasonable work life. The loss of income was significant. But the loss of these relationships and the continuity in my daughter's life has had a far greater impact than the loss of the second paycheck. Although I was able to survive through everything, I wish I had done a little more planning to help provide for us through the initial adjustment period.

· · · —A grieving father · · ·

Step 4: Identify Strategies to Fill the Gaps

Most often, a parent's primary concern is to provide financial security for their child in the event of their death. This is perhaps because death is one of the certainties of life. When a planning gap exists in this area, it can cause a number of problems in special needs planning. Each of the Five Factors (family and support, emotional, financial, legal, and government benefits) is immediately and equally important upon the death of a parent or primary caregiver—there is a major impact on all of the Five Factors. There are also a variety of strategies available to fill this gap, as well as other planning gaps. The key is to identify the most appropriate strategy to meet your planning goals.

For example, the use of estate planning tools (especially wills and special needs trusts) coordinated with some form of life insurance (**second-to-die insurance** or individual life insurance) can provide a simple solution to fill the financial and legal gaps that will arise upon the death of one or both parents. This is a very common planning strategy that is fairly easy to implement.

This strategy, however, may not be the most appropriate solution for every family. It may indeed address the financial and legal factors, protect eligibility for government benefits, and provide the money needed to care for the child with special needs. At the same time, it may create more gaps in the family and support factors by giving the impression that the parents did not treat all children fairly or equally. It may also create emotional factors for the child who did not receive a direct inheritance as did his or her siblings. Coordinating all of the factors must be considered for each planning strategy.

・ ・ ・   **Special Needs Planning Story**   ・ ・ ・

Who said that money can cure all problems? When my parents died, my sister Misty was so irate that she did not receive a direct inheritance from their estate like the rest of us that she almost created a schism in our family. When she learned that my parents intentionally did not leave her anything directly but left her inheritance to a special needs trust, with me as the trustee, she went into a total outrage. We couldn't even get her to realize that the life insurance proceeds that went to the trust left her with more money than the rest of us. It was awful. Misty had worked so hard to achieve her independence and manage her illness that this created a setback in her progress. She interpreted Mom and Dad's actions to be condescending of her abilities to manage her own money and to be independent. She did not understand that it was to protect her eligibility for her SSI and housing benefits, and provide extra money for her when she needed it. And the fact that she now needed to ask me for money from her trust added another element of frustration. It took several months and several thousands of dollars in legal, financial, and family therapy fees to work through this with her. Clearly, we should have gotten her involved before my parents died.

・ ・ ・   —Misty's sister   ・ ・ ・

All of the Five Factors must be considered to develop the most appropriate planning strategies. Because every family is unique, there is no standard solution that can be applied for all families. Throughout this book we have used Special Needs Planning Stories and Special Needs Planning Pointers to give the reader an appreciation of the various planning factors that must be considered. In some of the later chapters (Chapters 5–8), case examples are used to further illustrate various ways to apply different planning strategies and appreciate their impact on all Five Factors.

Step 5: Implement a Coordinated Plan of Action

When a plan is completed, the most important step is to take action and to implement the recommendations made. If you have gone through the entire planning process, from identifying your goals and gathering information through developing recommendations, and you do not implement the recommended course of action(s), you have not made any further progress towards achieving your goals. You might as well have done nothing.

Special Needs Planning Pointer

Planning for your future is necessary. Acting on your plan is essential.

Just as the beginning stages of the planning process can be overwhelming, the actual implementation can also be overwhelming and time consuming. It may not be possible to immediately accomplish and implement all of the recommendations required to fully complete your plan. If that is the case, at least begin with the step that you feel is most critical, timely, and achievable for your family. Take the step that you feel you have the most control over. Because a comprehensive plan may involve other professional advisors, agencies, and family members, it may take time to coordinate all of the steps.

In many cases, people procrastinate because they are not sure if they have identified the best options available. Do not let this prevent you from moving ahead. Your plan should be flexible enough to allow for you to easily make changes. If you overanalyze the details, you can end up wasting critical time in moving forward with your plan. In some cases, you may feel that the recommendations do not fully meet the needs of your family, or you may not trust the advice that you have received. Hopefully, by this point in the planning process, you have already developed a great deal of confidence in the advisors whom you are working with. If you have these kinds of concerns, however, they may prevent you from implementing your plan and cause you to waste valuable time. Because these decisions will have a significant impact on the future of you and your family, you should consider obtaining a second opinion from a trusted advisor who has established an expertise in planning for individuals and families with disabilities. It is important to do whatever is necessary for you to begin implementing your plan.

If nothing else can be accomplished, at least get your legal documents in order and pursue any and all government benefits for which your child is eligible. An improperly planned estate can have the most detrimental impact upon your child's future. Planning before a crisis occurs allows you to explore options and alternatives, rather than implementing at the last minute what may not ultimately be the most favorable course of action. Of course, completing the Letter of Intent (see the appendix at the end of this book for a sample and the accompanying CD-ROM for a blank version) is also another great starting point, which requires only your investment of time.

Special Needs Planning Pointer

The steps to a successful implementation process are as follows. 1) Prioritize the recommendations based on your goals and your family's special needs planning timeline. This may be determined by the complexity of the recommendation, there may be additional costs involved that you are not yet able to afford, or there may be some actions that are timely and must be completed by a certain date (i.e., your child turning age 18 or 22, year-end tax planning deadlines). 2) Schedule a completion date for each recommendation. 3) Schedule follow-up meetings with your financial planner, attorney, accountant, service coordinator, and other advisors to keep you focused and on target.

Implementation of recommendations will most likely follow a step-by-step process. These steps can be shared by a number of individuals. If you are a husband-and-wife team, you may find it helpful to split responsibilities between the two of you. If adult children are involved, they may be able to take responsibilities for researching services and/or benefits eligibility. If the individual with a disability has participated in developing the plan, he or she may also be able to share in the implementation of the plan by interviewing trustees and/or agencies. If you have a service coordinator, you may be able to ask him or her to assist in finding additional services and/or benefits available. Ask for help wherever appropriate. The key is to take action.

Step 6: Periodically Review and Monitor Your Plan

Special needs planning is an ongoing process. The needs of the individual will change, the financial situation of your family will change, and the availability and eligibility of benefits and services will change. All of these changes require that you periodically review and monitor your plan. You should make certain that the plan is still serving its intended purpose and is up to date with current laws. If changes occur, appropriate revisions should be made.

You should also be mindful of the state rules and statutes regarding services and eligibility. It may be difficult to remain current with constant changes taking place. Your advisors can help you to be aware of any significant changes that would apply to your plan. Periodic reviews will help you to stay on top of any changes necessary.

Reviews should be made prior to your child's reaching a planning pressure point (prior to age 3, age 15, age 18, or age 21 or 22). In addition, reviews should be made if there has been or will be a change in his or her health, level of supports needed or provided, employment status, or financial status, to name a few. Reviews should be made if there are changes in a parent and/or caregiver's employment, financial situation, health, or marital status (death or divorce), changes due to the birth of another child, and so forth. Even changes in grandparents' health should prompt a review with their advisors as well as your own.

By getting your name on mailing lists, or e-mail lists, with various agencies serving your child's needs, you will be kept informed of important topics and changes in the system. Attend workshops and educational forums whenever possible to keep yourself abreast of any changes in information.

4

The Five Factors to Consider in Special Needs Planning

One of the major obstacles that can prevent families from planning is that they are frequently consumed by daily crises. The thought of planning ahead can simply be overwhelming.

Realizing that each family situation is unique, we have identified the Five Factors that must be considered in conjunction with special needs planning:

- Family and support factors

- Emotional factors

- Financial factors

- Legal factors

- Government benefit factors

These Five Factors, and the way they affect planning, must be considered as you progress through each pressure point on the special needs planning timeline (see Chapter 1). It is important to develop an understanding of each of these factors because they do have a significant impact on how a family proceeds in their planning strategies. Both controllable and uncontrollable factors exist that will influence success in the planning process. Families need to define the influencing factors and determine which they have the ability to change—and those that they do not.

Since the birth of (or the realization of) raising a child with special needs is usually unexpected, the emotional impact can immobilize us and prevent us from making any financial decisions. Depending upon the extent of the disabilities, we may find that we are responsible for the life-time needs of a person who may be dependent upon us forever. Instead of the requirement to plan for the tangible goals that are often anticipated, we are now faced with the challenge to plan for the unknown. Because of the unique needs of families who have a member with special needs, we have to consider all of the Five Factors (family and support, emotional, financial, legal, and government benefits) to develop a coordinated plan that provides for the lifetime needs of our family members.

The cost of raising a child with special needs can vary dramatically, from child to child, family to family, and even state to state. Published information about the cost of raising a child with special needs is simply not available. Families cannot readily locate information to help ease their fears and uncertainties about financial decision making. Most of the time, we have no previous life experiences to reference in order to help us pre-pare for what it will take to raise a child with disabilities.

This book will give you examples and guidelines from which to build. It is important for you to keep in mind that your son or daughter is an individual with unique abilities and needs. Because each family is also unique, it is not possible to precisely predict all of the costs that will be needed to provide for the lifetime needs of an individual with disabilities. You can, however, begin to develop some rough estimates of the potential costs of your child's support needs just by determining whether they will require assistance for any or all activities of daily living. Discussions with your child's physicians, teachers, therapists, and other supportive peo-ple will help you to determine your child's future abilities for independ-ence. The key to determining the ultimate costs of providing for your child's lifetime needs is to identify his or her abilities and determine how they translate to the level of supports that will be needed. For example, some individuals with disabilities will always need to have the presence of a caregiver, while others may be able to stay home alone for some periods of time, and still others may be able to live independently.

By considering all of the factors that this book discusses, you will be better able to begin the process of identifying the most optimum alterna-tives available for your family. You will also be better prepared to explore the options available to achieve the best alternative for your family.

PULLING THE PIECES TOGETHER

The numerous financial planning books in print that address the needs of typical families indicate that the general public is struggling to address basic financial planning needs. Typical families have been educated to take action to plan for their financial security—to begin saving early for college expenses and maximizing savings for retirement—but they do not always feel confident about how to begin.

Unfortunately, no one ever tells us, as families with special needs, that we should start to save for our child's future. In fact, earlier advice was simply to make sure that you never put any money in your child's name because it might interfere with his or her eligibility for government benefits. This thought process frequently leaves parents with the assumption that the government will provide for their child. We have learned that the government does not provide a guaranteed source of income and security to adequately meet the needs of every individual with disabilities. Because of this deficit in services, it is important to begin the planning process by managing the Five Factors of special needs planning. We hope that we can help educate others by combining our personal experiences with our professional expertise.

It is difficult to find a balance between adjusting from daily events and crises and being able to establish and implement a long-term planning strategy. Families are frequently faced with the challenges of managing day-to-day events, and their daily lives can make them feel as if they are constantly in a crisis management mode. Planning requires taking a step back to analyze where we are and developing a vision of where we want to be. Although it may be difficult to balance between a crisis mode and a planning mode, it is very important to set aside the emotions and begin the planning process. Pulling all of the factors together may be a challenge, and it may take some time, but it is achievable and important to success. The sooner we realize that it may never be possible to precisely identify the specific amount of money needed to care for every contingency, the sooner we are able to begin the planning process. We soon realize that we cannot do everything, but we can do something. Because there are many uncertainties in our lives, early and effective financial planning assures us that we are doing all that we can to protect all that we can. The key is in pulling the pieces of the Five Factors together, as is illustrated in Figure 6.

Family and Support Factors

Every family situation is unique. Understanding the personal characteristics of your family and support network will make a difference in how you approach the planning process. Every family has different goals, which evolve around the following

- Family and lifestyle values
- Extended family involvement (e.g., brothers, sisters, aunts, uncles, grandparents, friends, neighbors)

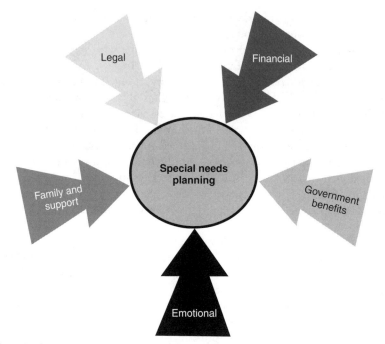

Figure 6. Planning for the future by pulling together all the pieces of the Five Factors of special needs planning.

- Sibling considerations (e.g., ages, involvement, abilities, interests)
- Careers (e.g., one income versus two incomes)

   Family and Lifestyle Values   Each family's values of money and desired lifestyle differ. The goals and dreams that you have for your child with special needs may differ from the goals and dreams of other parents in many ways. For example, you may feel that you want your child to live with you throughout your lifetime, or you may want him or her to be as independent as possible. Determining whether your child will continue living at home with you or ultimately moving to an independent living situation has significant impact on your long-term financial planning needs.

   Some families' financial situations require them to rely solely on government benefits. If this is the plan, the primary planning focus should be on protecting the child's eligibility for government benefits (e.g., SSI, SSDI) throughout his or her lifetime. The secondary planning focus should be to save whatever is possible to provide at least a minimal supplement. Because people are vulnerable to an ever-changing political environment, it is important to establish a safety net that goes beyond the baseline of support that is provided by the government. Your ongoing advocacy and involvement in the life of your child with disabilities is essential.

Even if a family feels that the government is responsible for their child's care, it does not mean that the government will do all that it is socially responsible to do. In fact, it may be that the government will stop paying for services or benefits that your child is currently receiving, such as dental care, prescription drugs, podiatry care, and other services. As an example, the government recently discontinued issuing new funding subsidies for low-income rental housing programs throughout the country via Section 8 vouchers. These rental subsidies were a popular tool in funding creative living options for individuals with disabilities. Budgets are voted on every year, and benefits are constantly changing. This makes legislative advocacy essential to maintain government services and supports and to maximize the benefits your child receives.

Special Needs Planning Pointer

At the very least, parents should plan to leave enough money at their death so that someone can be hired to provide oversight as a guardian or an advocate. Do not underestimate the time, advocacy, and real dollars that you, as a parent, provide. Asking another to assume your role or a portion of it must be accompanied by the financial assistance required to make it possible. It is a lot to ask another adult child or friend to assume the role of the parent without any financial assistance or guidance. In fact, unless you leave enough money to make it possible for them to help, they may not be able to do so.

There are, however, some families that feel that they do not want government assistance or interference. They may have the financial resources to provide for the lifestyle that they envision for their child without the dependence of government funding. There are a variety of private-pay residential models available throughout the country, as well as in-home assistance available to families who wish to have the child to continue to live at home.

Family customs, traditions, and values will also guide you in the planning process. If you have family members close by and everyone takes care of one another, or you live in a multifamily house or community with others to share the caregiving, you may not have a vision of your child living separately and might not wish to plan for that outcome. How your family celebrates holidays and birthdays may be another very important issue to consider. Continuing with family traditions, such as birthday cakes, Christmas or Hanukkah presents, special foods, and other customs may be important to you. Attending religious services and arranging for someone to take your child to them may be a consideration. Some families want to make certain that travel arrangements can be made and afforded for siblings or relatives to be together on holidays. With families often living in different cities, it may be necessary to hire a staff person to travel with your son or daughter to visit other family members for the holidays. Alternately, a sibling may not be able to afford the expenses of traveling to come home for the holidays. Providing for these supplemental expenses may make a significant difference in allowing your family to participate in special occasions together. Your family values and traditions will be able to continue in the best way possible if you provide for them in your planning.

· · ·   **Special Needs Planning Story**   · · ·

In our family tradition, you do not leave home until you are married. My sister Diane has Down syndrome. She has no plans of getting married, so she still lives at home. She is able to help our elderly mother with the household chores and is the primary reason why my mother can still be at home. They help each other. At this point, we haven't even talked about any plans for when my mother passes on and where Diane will live.

· · ·   —Diane's sister   · · ·

The Extended Family   In the event that there are no immediate family members available, a network of close friends can help provide support. Having a close network of friends and neighbors can be a valuable resource in the event of an emergency, and can also be helpful with issues of day-to-day living. In the event that there is limited family, this not only affects the emotional needs but also the financial needs of having to pay for supports.

· · ·   **Special Needs Planning Story**   · · ·

We do not have any family in this country. If it were not for the kindness of a few special teachers and friends who have become a part of our son's life, our daughter would be totally alone in caring for her brother. These special people are with us for holidays and birthdays and have become such an important part of our family. Now, we even consider their children as part of our own extended family.

· · ·   —Sam's mother   · · ·

If you have no close friends or family involved in the day-to-day activities of your life, it is very important to document your wants, needs, likes, and dislikes, as well as your vision for your child. Without something in writing, a potential future caregiver is burdened with learning the system that you took so long to learn. In addition, it can put your child at a great disadvantage and potentially can set him or her back in terms of development. This is why the Letter of Intent (see the appendix at the end of the book for a sample and the accompanying CD-ROM for a blank version) is such an important tool to use.

Special Needs Planning Pointer

Parents should make a point to complete the Letter of Intent (see the appendix and the accompanying CD-ROM for a blank version) to document the important aspects of their child's life. Share it with the future caregivers today and make it a living document. Do not just leave it up to others to figure everything out after you are gone.

Siblings It may be difficult to talk about the time when parents will not be around to care for their child. Some children may not want to be involved with the future caregiving responsibilities of their brother or sister with disabilities. Others are more than willing to do so in one capacity or another. Sometimes the roles of guardian, trustee, or social worker are defined by the nature of the relationships between family members. But sometimes a brother or sister wants to just be a brother or sister rather than a lifetime caregiver. It is critical that parents communicate their vision and their expectations to all of their children before they die or before the siblings are required to assume this role.

If there are adult children who have expressed an interest in helping, it is important to get them involved in the planning process early on. Try to include them in service planning meetings, house meetings, meetings with your financial planner and attorney, social activities, and any other aspects of the life of your child with disabilities. It is perfectly acceptable to have an adult child attend meetings with the financial advisor and attorney. In fact, it is quite advantageous. The more involved everyone is, the more comfortable they become, and service providers will appreciate knowing who to contact in the absence of the parents.

If siblings are not able or willing to be the future caregivers, it is very important to allow them to express their feelings and intentions about their future role. Sometimes parents hope that all of the children in the family will work together for the best interests of one another, and put the needs and interests of the child with disabilities first. The reality is not always so. Parents should not just assume that the other children will meet their expectations. They may need to reach out to professionals who have the expertise, time, and abilities to provide for their child's future care.

There are a number of organizations that have services established to provide assistance to caregivers for these support needs. See PLAN, Inc. (Planned Lifetime Assistance Network, http://www.nationalplanalliance. org), PALS, Inc. (Personal Advocacy and Lifetime Support, http://www. palsinc.org), and other local support networks. There are also sibling support groups for both younger and adult siblings. See information and workshops for sibling support groups at The Arc's Sibling Support Project and Sibshops at http://www.thearc.org.

· · · **Special Needs Planning Story** · · ·

My 44-year-old brother was living at home with my aging parents. Their plan was that he would continue to live in the family house or live with me when my parents died. Until I attended an adult sibling support group, I never knew that there were options available to us. I became involved as his advocate and served on our local Citizen Advisory Board for the Department of Mental Retardation and local chapter of The Arc. With the information that I learned, I was able to help my parents and my brother move forward in planning for his future today, while my parents are still alive. He is now living in a supported apartment in town, enjoying his independence, while my parents are proudly seeing his abilities soar. We are all in a much better position to support his future needs.

· · · —Cynthia, Ron's sister · · ·

Careers In addition to viewing the family as the potential source of supports, there may also be financial responsibilities associated with other family members. Initially, planning needs for more than one child may require financial compromises. One of the issues facing families is that, in many cases, households have only one spouse in the workforce while the second spouse stays at home to care for the family member with a disability. Careers may have to be put on hold. Loss of earnings, a reduction in disposable income, and loss of retirement savings can also occur. In many families, the option exists to choose between one or both parents being wage earners. In cases where families have a child with disabilities, there may be no choice. One parent may need to stay at home either full or part time.

Special Needs Planning Story

When our son was 1 year old, he developed a significant seizure disorder. Ordinary activities of daily living, even as basic as mealtimes, became a major challenge for our whole family. We tried to get help from various government agencies for personal care attendants. But after the appeal process to Medicaid, the arbitrator's determination was "the parent was the best suited caregiver." Because of this decision and the inability to secure the additional supports that were needed for our family, my wife was forced to sell her business that she built to enable her to stay home with our son as his primary caregiver. We had no choice.

• • •   —Jason's father   • • •

Emotional Factors

Emotional Obstacles to Planning   People do not plan to fail; they fail to plan. The fact that most people are unfamiliar with many of the financial and legal terms involved in the planning process is not why they fail to plan. Reluctance to plan is sometimes the result of not being able to set aside emotions. Often a parent may feel intimidated to plan for the future because they are overwhelmed not only by the day-to-day details but also by having to envision the future beyond today. It is very normal to feel intimidated by not knowing what to expect in the future. Even in a typical family, it is common to avoid planning for the future. It is not uncommon for a parent or caregiver of any age to be reluctant to plan for the ultimate day that they will no longer be able to care for their child. By not setting aside our emotions and failing to plan, however, we miss opportunities to see our children achieve full lives and find connections with their community.

Special Needs Planning Story

I never could have imagined my life without my 40-year-old son, Adam, living at home with me. It wasn't until I became ill [that I] realized it would be best for him to be settled in his own home before I died so that he wouldn't have the total loss of his mother and his home all at once. Letting him go was the hardest thing to do. But now that I see how happy and well adjusted he is, I am so proud of him. Just think, I would have missed this opportunity.

• • •   —Adam's mother   • • •

Times of Family Crisis We do have a choice; we can either be proactive and plan, or we can be reactive in a time of crisis. In many cases, families begin the planning process in the time of crisis—most often upon the illness or death of a parent or other family member. The problem with this approach is that planning in time of crisis is often based on emotions and can result in less desirable outcomes. Even if a well-thought plan already exists, it can be tempting to change it in a time of crisis, although many are advised not to do so at that time.

. . .   **Special Needs Planning Story**   . . .

When Dad was first diagnosed with cancer, our entire family was overwhelmed. My brother's first reaction was to want to move from his staffed-apartment back home with my mother. It took a great deal of counseling and support from his staff to help him and us to deal with the emotions and the reality that our parents will not be around forever. It would have been awful if he were to move back home at this point and lose all that he has achieved.

. . .   —Jimmy's sister   . . .

In a perfect world, a family will develop a plan and follow the overall strategy. The fact is, even in cases where there is a carefully considered plan, crises do occur. In the event of a crisis, it is extremely important to seek advice from professionals, because it is very easy to become overwhelmed with emotions and make poor decisions. Your financial planner, attorney, and/or accountant should be contacted in the time of a crisis in order to help facilitate any changes that may need to happen. Professional guidance in a time of crisis can often help in the decision-making process, since a professional will not be emotionally involved. Most likely such a person will be abreast of current trends in disability law and planning and can advise you on appropriate options, strategies, or any changes that you should make at this point.

It is important *not* to plan immediately after you experience a personal crisis. In fact, if you already have a plan in place, it is recommended *not* to make any immediate changes. Unless there is a true emergency that requires immediate attention, or unless there are some specific legal and/or financial strategies that have to be executed in a timely manner, it is recommended to wait between 9 months and 1 year before making any major lifestyle changes or financial decisions. The reason professionals encourage people to wait is because it is possible to make a decision based upon a passing emotional state. Such a decision can ultimately have life-time ramifications. Allowing yourself time to adjust to a new situation will help to remove emotions from the decision-making process.

Emotions as a Catalyst   Emotions are important in helping you create a vision for your family member. Emotions can drive us to passionate feelings, both positive and negative. Passionate parents have for many years been the ones to make a difference in the quality of life for their children. It is this passion—and the reluctance to accept the status quo of the current system—that has made it possible for our family members with disabilities to become more independent in the community. You cannot, however, make long-term planning decisions based solely on emotions and passion. You need to first create the vision. Keep in mind that your vision may need to be modified based on the reality of your child's abilities and the resources available to him or her. Then plan creatively to maximize the resources available to you to achieve your vision.

Your passion can be used to execute a plan of action in the event that the current service delivery system does not support your vision. As long as your vision is substantiated by a carefully considered plan, you can change the system. This can take years, or even a lifetime. But if you plan ahead, you can achieve your goals. Parents of generations before us have brought the disability movement to where it is today. Your emotions and passion will provide the motivation and perseverance to make a difference. Emotions can lead us to move mountains for our children. This is perhaps one of a parent's greatest assets in advocating for their child.

Throughout the planning process, you may find that the current system and its accessibility (or rather inaccessibility) to supports are roadblocks to achieving the vision for your child. You will find yourself becoming your child's best advocate in order to help him or her achieve his or her greatest potential. You will be surprised at how much you can accomplish when you are passionate about it.

Special Needs Planning Pointer

We have been fortunate enough to work with families, who, over 20 years ago, decided that they wanted their children with cognitive disabilities to live independently in the community with adequate supports. This was at the time when institutions were the common "home" for individuals with cognitive disabilities. Since they were the first to take on a venture like this

(continued)

(continued)

in our area, they were very nervous. It was the passion and dream of these parents who came together to create their own residential home and supports by utilizing their own private resources to pay for the cost of the program. Today this program continues to thrive as their children continue to grow. (For further information, see http://www. specializedhousing.org)

Raising a child with special needs changes our perception of the world and also changes how the world views us. Our perceptions concerning just about everything can change—especially concerning money. Our emotional state often affects the decisions we make in our lives and in our planning. In the beginning (after learning that a child has a disability), parents may struggle with negative emotions. Anger concerning the situation, guilt and questioning what went "wrong," and sadness for yourself and the loss of your typical life are all common emotions that surface. Over time, we found in our experience that we were able to grow to a more positive perception, as our emotions changed, as we gained understanding and as moments of joy and pride with each milestone helped sustain us. Our views also extended to other family members and their perception of our situation, as they experienced different challenges and emotions. We eventually acquired a different perspective of the world and those around us— sometimes more positive, sometimes not.

Denial Can Delay Diagnosis and Planning   Denial surrounding the child's diagnosis and its resulting circumstances can prevent families from planning. This is very common in families that have a child with mental illness, often because the child has been undiagnosed for many years. Asperger syndrome is a relatively new diagnosis; it is not unusual to find that such a child that has a very high IQ score is not only gifted, but has social issues that may require supports for his or her entire lifetime. Before beginning the planning process, parents and the child (often as an adult) should try to get a better understanding of the diagnosis. It is important to not get overwhelmed by a diagnosis and to plan for the child to have financial safety nets in place as part of your overall planning strategy. Every child is different and has unique needs. It is best to plan defensively and be flexible, as circumstances will change.

Planning defensively involves implementing the special needs planning strategies that will protect your child's eligibility for government benefits in the future. Regardless of your child's abilities and needs today, defending his or her eligibility for future benefits should be a key aspect in your overall planning strategy. It is also important to maintain flexibility in the event that your child does not require government benefits. Planning defensively today should allow for flexibility in the future.

· · ·   **Special Needs Planning Story**   · · ·

I received a phone call from a daughter asking me to please call her mother to make an appointment for financial planning. Her brother had developmental delays and received government benefits. He also had a substance abuse problem, which the family was in denial of. Ten years ago, the mother heard me speak about financial and estate planning issues. She kept my card. She was concerned that when she dies, her son would inherit a significant amount of money that he would simply spend to support his habit. She didn't want to leave this burden to her daughter to take care of, but her husband would not accept that the son had a problem. Because they could not come to an agreement on how to plan for the son's future inheritance, they have not been able to do any planning. Unless they plan properly, the son will receive his share of their estate, lose his government benefits, and have money available to support his addiction. Hopefully, they will soon be able to set aside their emotions, and be proactive in their planning.

· · ·   —Cynthia   · · ·

Challenges Couples Can Face   Sometimes it is difficult for couples to plan together with a shared vision of their child's abilities and needs. One parent may be more accepting of the child's diagnosis, while the other parent may be in denial. The results of this emotional disconnect between parents is often improper planning, or no planning at all, since they cannot come to an agreement on what is best. In order to reconnect emotionally, couples may need to seek professional counseling.

There are numerous emotions that parents and siblings feel at various stages and planning pressure points. It is important to accept and to anticipate that at times you will feel tension, fear, and frustration, but we hope you will also experience feelings of accomplishment and pride at every planning pressure point. Avoid feeling guilty, since it is quite natural to feel greater emotional stress at the various pressure points. Try to locate parent and sibling support groups in your area to reinforce the idea that you are not alone in what you are going through.

Special Needs Planning Pointer

Sometimes it is incredibly difficult to overcome some of the emotional pressures of raising a child with disabilities. It may be necessary to seek professional medical assistance. Do not hesitate to talk to your doctor about your feelings or seek support from other parents. There are numerous support groups available. Finding one that works for you can ease feelings of isolation and provide opportunities to learn from others. A simple online search should help to locate one of these groups in your area.

Financial Factors

Starting at a very young age, we learn about the value of money. Throughout our lives we associate the value of money with our life experiences, such as paying for our own college education, purchasing a car, buying a house, and saving for our children's college and our ultimate retirement—all in addition to the daily expenses of our desired lifestyle.

Your Family's Financial Values or Standards It is important to talk about the value of money and what it means to you, because you can pass these values on to future caregivers and other family members. How you feel about money can also have an impact on what you can achieve for your child's future. It does not do any good if you do not share your values of money with others. If parents do not articulate their vision, their financial capacity to achieve their goals, and their financial intentions, their vision for their child may not happen. Not only is it important to express your values to your financial advisors, trustees, guardians, and legal advisors, but also to your other family members. These individuals most likely will be the ones to follow through on implementing the plan that you have for your child.

Special Needs Planning Pointer

Take a moment to ask yourself, "What does money mean to me?" Then take time to share those values with your family—this can be expressed in your Letter of Intent (see the appendix at the end of this book and the accompanying CD-ROM for an example) as well.

Bringing Family Members into Your Discussions There are many ways to discuss your vision and your finances. It is often easiest to begin this process in a gradual manner and in an informal environment. Although it is important to have all family members in agreement, scheduling initial discussions in a formal meeting or a large family setting is not always the best. We recommend that you speak to one child at a time, to get their feelings about their willingness to help. This will offer them an opportunity to share ideas with you, rather than you telling them what you are hoping will happen. Remember, caring for a family member with disabilities is a lifetime commitment that you do not want to force on anyone, yet it is important for them to understand your intentions.

After everyone has had an opportunity to discuss their feelings and ideas in an informal way, you may wish to plan a discussion with everyone at once. Since every family's dynamics are unique, you will find the best way to communicate with your family. The following steps should help to move the communication process along smoothly:

- Share your vision.

- Talk about the amount of money you plan to have available to support your vision. You do not have to reveal all of your financial information. You can choose to mention only the financial aspects that pertain to the needs of the family member with a disability.

- Determine the best person to take on each role. For example, who is the best with finances? That person may be a good trustee or trust advisor of a special needs trust (see the section in Chapter 9 on special needs trusts). Who is most involved in the day-to-day life of the child? That person may be a good guardian.

- Ask family members if they feel able to perform their roles independently. If not, design your plan to give them resources to work with. For example, let them know that they could hire an investment advisor to help with the trust management or a social worker to help oversee supports.

In our combined 30-plus years of planning, one of the biggest obstacles that we have encountered is that people do not feel comfortable talking about how much money they have. Even professionals in the field of providing services to families, including government agency employees that serve families, do not feel comfortable talking about money or the specific costs of providing services to individuals with disabilities.

· · · **Special Needs Planning Story** · · ·

Although Charles is receiving all the benefits that he is eligible for and living independently, we feel that it is not enough for him to simply have what the government provides. We supplement his expenses by approximately $1,000 a month. This gives him the sense of self-worth and control to be able to do what he likes rather than do what someone else wants him to do. He has schizophrenia, and his sense of self-worth is most important to his ability to function in life. In working with our financial planner and our attorney, we made arrangements for our other son to provide this supplement to support Charles' needs without jeopardizing his government benefits when we are no longer able to.

. . .   —Charles' father   . . .

Sometimes parents feel that they must treat all of their children equally. They feel that their children expect it. In many cases, however, children without disabilities are more than willing to forego any type of inheritance in order to guarantee security for their brother or sister with a disability. They understand the financial realities and would rather make sure that their brother or sister is taken care of and would not expect that everything is shared equally.

One of the first steps necessary for you to be able to achieve financial security for your child is to overcome the reluctance to discuss the issues of money. We all know that it takes money to pay for services, staff, housing expenses, employment supports, transportation, education, health care services, and the like. We also know that the government does not have an endless supply of money to fund these types of services.

Maximize Eligibility for Government Benefits   With this in mind, families should plan to maximize eligibility for government benefits while also maximizing their own personal resources. It is important to be realistic about what funds are available to your family member (both personally and publicly), how to secure them, and how to allocate them. For further information on public resources, see the section in this chapter on government factors.

Understand Where You Are and Where You Would Like to Be
In order to maximize your own personal resources, you must first understand where you are financially. Do you have the money to do the things you and your family like to do today? Are you happy with where you are financially? If not, what can you do to change things?

The next step is to know where you want to be. What lifestyle do you envision for you and your family, today and in the future? What do you consider retirement—is it when you stop working full time, when you stop working the hours that you currently work, or when you begin to work part time or pursue a hobby for income? What do you want to do for your vacations, travel time, fun time, and the like? How philanthropic do you want to be? Where do you envision living when you retire? In what type of environment do you envision your child living? Do you envision him or her living totally independent from you, or do you intend to always be involved in the daily activities of your child's life for as long as you are able to?

Create a Plan The next step is to prepare an action plan to get you where you want to be financially. This is where having qualified advisors to guide you through the planning process can be most beneficial.

The key issue to consider in financial factors is maximizing personal resources. This includes maximizing tax planning strategies, both income tax and estate tax planning. The proper use of financial products can also be an important contributor to financial success. You should also incorporate your group employee benefits in the planning process. These would include your group health, life, and disability insurance coverage; retirement plans; stock option plans; stock purchase plans; flexible spending accounts; and so forth. Determine those benefits that are currently available to you and your family as well as those available to your family upon your death and/or retirement. You should also determine which employee benefits are transferable and/or portable upon termination of your employment. Adequately protecting your income and assets in the event of a premature death and/or disability of a parent is critical.

Any type of planning process, from planning a vacation to building a house, has a defined beginning and ending point. The traditional financial planning process involves identifying resources and listing specific goals that can be quantified. Some common examples of quantifiable goals might include paying cash for your next automobile, saving for 4 years of college tuition payments, purchasing a second home for retirement, or generating a retirement income equal to 65%–75% of your preretirement income.

Planning for a family member with disabilities can be a much more challenging process. There may be no defined beginning or ending point. The needs and abilities of the individual can change rapidly and vary significantly over time. It is only natural for the family of a young child to want to have a concrete plan in place that provides adequate assets and resources for their child's lifetime needs. Families must realize, however, that it may not be possible to predict accurately the long-term costs involved in providing supports for an individual over his or her lifetime.

Assumptions can be made regarding future expenses. We can somewhat accurately determine the costs of a physical residence (a house or a condo) in a geographic area based on current market values. We can also estimate the costs of maintaining a physical residence. Often, however, we cannot always accurately determine the costs of supports until the needs are identified. Once the needs are somewhat identified, we can develop a range of the probable expenses necessary to provide these supports today and in the future. Before implementing a residential plan, it is highly recommended that you work with an independent consultant to determine the level of supports required. You then need to develop a model that meets both your personal preferences and your financial abilities to maintain the model, both during your lifetime and upon your death.

So how do we determine how much money is needed? And how much is too much? Just as the educational needs of every child are unique, so are the long-term planning needs of every individual with special needs. Even two individuals with a similar medical and/or cognitive diagnosis can have significantly different support requirements. With these varying requirements, costs will also vary. There is no clear answer; the best we can do is to maximize all resources and coordinate all of the Five Factors. That is why it is so important to have a comprehensive plan and to reevaluate it periodically.

Legal Factors

The legal rights and public awareness of individuals with disabilities have increased over the years. Because of the advocacy efforts of individuals and families, laws have been enacted to protect these rights. It is important to know your rights as well as the rights of your family member with disabilities. Understanding and using the law will enable the individual with disabilities to achieve their maximum potential. Knowing how and when to use these laws is an essential part of the planning process. Keep abreast of information and changes in the law through your local advocacy agency.

For more information on rights to public education, see information on the IDEA at http://wrightslaw.com/idea.htm. For more information on employment rights, see the Americans with Disabilities Act (ADA) of 1990 (PL 101-336) at http://www.ada.gov. For more information on the Social Security Act Amendments of 1994 (PL 103-432) and benefits, see http://www.ssa.gov.

Estate Planning The accumulation of wealth often takes many years. Estate planning simply helps to direct how you want your wealth distributed upon your death. As difficult as it may be to discuss, the reality is that we will not live forever. Properly executed documents enable you to choose how your family is cared for and how your wealth is distributed. Without these documents, at your death the governing laws in your state of residence will determine how your assets are distributed and who will be the ultimate caregiver of your minor children.

All of your legal estate planning documents, which include wills, trusts, health care proxies, powers of attorney, and guardianship provisions, should be reviewed with your attorney at least every five years. In addition, you should review the ownership of your assets, including any U.S. government savings bonds (which are frequently overlooked). The beneficiary designations of your retirement plans, annuities, and life insurance policies should also be reviewed periodically and coordinated with your overall financial and estate plan.

Some parents leave equal shares of their estate to all of their children out of a desire to be fair to each. Parents should consider, however, that what is fair is not always equal, and what is equal is not always fair. The completion of the financial and estate planning process will help to determine an appropriate distribution of your estate.

Some parents do not leave any inheritance to their children with special needs. They leave all of the inheritance to the other children, with the hope that they will use a portion of the funds to take care of the individual with special needs. This would be considered a "morally obligated" gift to the child receiving the inheritance. Although this may protect eligibility for government benefits for the child with special needs, it can create additional problems for the one who inherits the assets. For example, income earned on those assets would be taxed to the recipient, not to the family member with special needs. Or, if that person later became divorced, those funds would be included as his or her own assets, and most likely have to be divided with the other spouse. This is where the use of proper estate planning tools and techniques, such as a special needs trust, would be a more appropriate strategy, enabling parents to leave an inheritance to a child with special needs without disqualifying eligibility for government benefits (see the section on special needs trusts in Chapter 9).

· · ·   **Special Needs Planning Story**   · · ·

I had always planned on being guardian of my brother Robert when my parents died. They disinherited Robert in their will and left their entire estate to me rather than split between the two of us. They trusted me to do the right thing with it. I knew it was a big responsibility for my entire family. What I did not realize was that it would cause so many financial problems for us. When we applied for financial aid for my oldest son, the college considered this money as my resource, even though I set it up in a separate account and only used it for Robert. As a result, we received less financial aid for my son and are now struggling with how to pay for his tuition. My wife thinks we should use some of Robert's money to help pay because he is why we did not receive more in financial aid, and we'll get it when Robert dies anyway. I just can't do that to Robert or to my parents' memory. This is something that I definitely did not expect, and I don't think my parents would have had any idea either. They certainly did not get the right advice.

• • •   —Robert's brother   • • •

The distinction in estate planning for individuals with special needs and those without is that, in special needs planning, the planning extends for two generations. Beyond that, there must also be planning strategies to protect and maximize any and all government benefits for the individual with special needs. Nevertheless, we must still incorporate the planning techniques to minimize potential estate taxes.

For families who have a child with a disability, much is written about planning for "what will happen after the parent dies." It is very important to talk about planning during your lifetime rather than just upon your death. Although it sometimes causes upset and anxiety to think about and plan for your ultimate death and what will happen to your child, financially and legally those issues are clearly defined and can be addressed through purchasing insurance and implementing basic legal work. Your basic estate planning documents include wills, trusts, powers of attorneys, and health care proxies. Again, it is critical to address this early on in your life (and your child's), while you are still able to make good decisions.

Special Needs Planning Pointer

To help prevent you from acting emotionally in time of crisis, it is important to review your financial and legal plans periodically, at least every five years, with your advisors. Make certain that ownership and beneficiary designations of assets are current and coordinated with your estate planning documents and current eligibility requirements. It will be less likely that you will have to make any significant changes if things are relatively up to date before a crisis arises.

As mentioned earlier, many people develop a false sense of security after signing their wills and trusts. Yet wills and trusts are only legal devices that provide for the orderly administration of assets. Neither guarantees your child's financial security. Without implementing a plan, beyond executing wills and/or trusts, that will provide adequate funds under all circumstances, there may be no money available when it is most needed, such as during a parent's retirement, disability, and/or death. The use of proper legal documents, and the coordination of your overall estate plan with your financial plan, is critical in developing an integrated plan that meets your needs as well as the needs of your child with a disability.

. . .   **Special Needs Planning Story**   . . .

Upon my mother's death, I initially felt comforted knowing that my mother had recently met with a disability law attorney to plan her affairs. Since I do not live near my sister with special needs, I had my personal attorney review the legal documents when my mother died. Everything appeared to be in order until I contacted the life insurance company, [which] informed me that my sister and I were equal beneficiaries on my mother's policy. This meant that the money my mother originally intended to help provide for my sister's needs actually disqualified her for benefits. If my mother had only coordinated designating the beneficiary of her life insurance policy with her estate plan, this would never have happened. I wish I had known.

. . .   —Marian's sister   . . .

Other legal considerations in special needs planning would include issues of

- Guardianship and less restrictive alternatives to guardianship

- Special needs trusts

- Trust administration

- Legal settlements

Guardianship and Less Restrictive Alternatives Guardianship is a legal means of protecting children and "incompetent adults" (in legal terms, adults who cannot take care of themselves, make decisions that are in their own best interest, or handle their assets due to a physical or mental disability). When the court determines that a person is incapable of handling either their personal or financial affairs and appoints a guardian, the person with a disability is referred to as the guardian's "ward."

The subject of guardianship for an adult child with disabilities is of concern to most parents. Parents of children with severe disabilities often assume that they can continue to be their adult child's legal guardian during the child's entire life. Although it may be obvious to a parent that a child does not have the capacity to make informed decisions, legally an adult is presumed competent unless otherwise determined to be incompetent after a competency proceeding. Once an individual reaches the age of 18, the parent is no longer the individual's legal guardian. The act of giving reasoned and well-informed consent when making a decision may be beyond the adult child's ability. Parents need to explore legal options available to protect their child from unscrupulous individuals who may exploit their child's inability to make informed choices.

Making the decision to seek the appointment of a guardian is a complicated issue. A petition for guardianship should not be filed automatically simply because a child has reached the age of 18. Parents, or other potential guardians, must carefully consider the person's individual circumstances, including strengths and weaknesses, needs, and best interests, before deciding to seek guardianship. If an individual with a disability is capable of making some but not all decisions, one or more of the alternatives to guardianship discussed following should be considered. These alternatives to guardianship proceed from least restrictive to most restrictive:

1. A **joint bank account** can be created to prevent rash expenditures. Arrangements can be made with most banks for benefits checks, such as Social Security or SSI payments, to be sent directly to the bank for deposit. In addition, arrangements can be made authorizing the bank to send certain sums of money on a regular basis to a specified party, such as the landlord, or the person with a disability for spending money. This helps provide structure to allow for budgeting and money management. (Remember to keep this account balance below $2,000.)

2. A **representative payee** can be named to manage the funds of a person with a disability who receives benefits checks from Social Security, Railroad Retirement, or the Veterans Benefits Administration. Benefits checks are sent to the representative payee, who manages the funds and spends them for the benefit of the individual with the disability. The representative payee has authority only over income from the particular check (or checks) for which he or she is the designated payee.

3. A **durable power of attorney (POA) for property** is a legal document that grants one person the legal authority to handle the financial affairs of another. This is useful for persons who are mildly or moderately incapacitated and capable of choosing another person to handle their money. There are both drawbacks and as advantages to the use of a POA. With a POA, the individual with special needs still has the legal authority to make decisions. For example, he

or she can commit to a contract that is not in his or her best interest and can be held to that contract. Also, the person with disabilities can withdraw the POA at any time and can remove the agent verbally or by the physical act of destroying the POA. Generally, the use of a POA should be used when the individual with disabilities has the capacity to make basic meaningful decisions and does not require full guardianship but may not be able to make complex financial decisions without support.

4. A **durable POA for health care**, also known as a **health care proxy,** should be considered for individuals who are presently capable of making decisions about their health care and wish to anticipate possible future incompetence. This is a legal document that enables a competent individual (the **principal**) to designate a health care agent to make health care decisions should the individual become incompetent to make them.

5. An **appointment of advocate and authorization** allows a person with a disability to designate an agent to advocate on his or her behalf with administrative agencies such as the state department of cognitive disability, the department of mental health services, or the department of medical assistance. The agent can be granted specific powers, such as access to rehabilitation and school records, as well as the authority to release records, to approve placement or services, to attend meetings, and to advocate generally on behalf of the individual with a disability. The document must be in writing, witnessed, and, depending on state law, notarized.

6. **Trusts** may be an appropriate alternative to appointment of a guardian in some circumstances. A trust is a legal plan for placing funds and other assets in the control of a trustee for the benefit of an individual with a disability. Creating a trust will be less expensive than a guardianship, in that no bond is required; it will keep the courts, and their associated costs, out of one's life (in most cases permission of a court is not needed to make disbursements from the trust or to make investments); and it protects the beneficiary's assets without requiring that he or she be declared incompetent by a court. A special needs trust (see later in this section and in Chapter 9) may also make it possible for the beneficiary to receive the benefit of extra income without losing valuable state and federal benefits. A trust set up without regard to the eligibility laws may disqualify a person with disabilities from SSI, Medicaid, and other important benefits.

7. As mentioned previously, **guardianship** is an option for persons who, because of mental illness, developmental disability, or physical disabil-

ity, lack sufficient understanding or capacity to make or communicate responsible decisions concerning their care and financial affairs. Guardians are approved and appointed by the court. Guardianships are also supervised by the court annually, by the guardian providing a report on the status of the ward. The following list of alternatives to guardianship is not exhaustive. Additional ones may be available, depending on where the person with disabilities lives and the presence of his or her natural supports. If you would like more information concerning guardianship or alternatives to guardianship, you may call your local or state chapter of The Arc, NAMI, ASA, or other advocacy organizations in your state. Some of the types of guardianship include

a. A **guardian of the person** is responsible for monitoring the care of the person with disabilities, also called the ward. The guardian need not use his or her own money for the ward's expenses, provide daily supervision of the ward, or even live with the ward. The guardian must attempt to ensure, however, that the ward is receiving proper care and supervision, and the guardian is responsible for decisions regarding most medical care, education, and vocational issues.

b. A **guardian of the estate or conservatorship** should be considered for persons with disabilities who are unable to manage their finances and have income from sources other than benefits checks, or have other assets and/or property. The guardian or conservator is responsible for handling the ward's financial resources, but is not personally financially responsible for the ward from his or her own resources. In most jurisdictions, the guardian or conservator must file an annual accounting of the ward's funds with the court.

c. A **guardianship** may be limited to certain areas of decision making, such as decisions about medical treatment, in order to allow the ward to continue making his or her own decisions in all other areas. The benefit of a limited guardianship is that the guardian's responsibilities can be tailored to fit the ward's special needs in the least restrictive manner. Further, under a limited guardianship, the ward has not been declared incompetent.

d. A **temporary guardian or conservator** may be appointed in an emergency situation when certain decisions must be made immediately. Generally, a permanent guardianship or conservatorship must be requested along with the temporary appointment. The duration of a temporary appointment is dictated by state law.

The Special Needs Trust Trusts provide for the orderly administration and distribution of your assets. The use of a special needs trust is a key element in special needs planning. The special needs trust allows you to leave an inheritance to your child without disqualifying him or her for government benefits. It is important that you do not leave an inheritance outright to the name of a child who is receiving government benefits—or who may potentially require government benefits. It is also important to note that you do not have to disinherit your child, nor do you have to leave his or her share to another person with the intent of that individual providing oversight and care. You can direct the portion of your estate to the special needs trust to provide supplemental financial support for the child with disabilities and still protect eligibility for government benefits. You can direct any share of your estate to be distributed to the special needs trust, including your house, savings and investment accounts, life insurance proceeds, and/or retirement plans. Because there is specific language required in a special needs trust, you need to work with a knowledgeable disability law attorney that has experience drafting special needs trusts. Additional information about different types of trusts can be found in Chapter 9.

Trusts are legal documents that provide a means to hold money or property for the benefit of another person. The individual who sets up the trust is called the **grantor.** The individual(s) who benefit from the income and/or principal of the trust are called the **beneficiaries.** The trustee is the person or financial institution whom you elect to manage the trust. It is the trustee's responsibility to follow the guidelines established by the trust (see the section on trust administration later in this chapter for further details).

Trusts can be funded in various ways, either during your lifetime or upon your death. It is like a bucket that must be filled, and you provide direction to the trustee or trustees as to how the money in this bucket is to be distributed. Keep in mind that without making provisions for assets to be directed into the trust, you would provide only an empty bucket.

Special Needs Planning Pointer

If funded properly, at your death the special needs trust will provide the basis for your child's future financial security. It will protect eligibility for government benefits and will make additional money available to supplement the beneficiary's needs. The most important point, however, is to make certain that the special needs trust is properly funded. One of the most common errors in planning is that parents assume that their child's

(continued)

(continued)

security is guaranteed after they complete the trust document. By completing the legal paperwork alone, you have only completed one of the Five Factors of special needs planning. Tending to all of the Five Factors and making sure that there is enough money in the trust to pay for your child's needs will enable your vision for your child to be realized.

Legal Settlements Individuals can become disabled due to some form of accident or negligence. In the event that an individual or a family presides in a legal settlement and receives a monetary award, it is important to implement some special needs planning strategies. One of the primary goals is to protect the individual's eligibility for government benefits. In addition, the individual may not have the capacity to handle such a large sum of money and may require the safety net of a special needs trust. Prior to taking receipt of any financial judgment, it is recommended that families speak with an attorney and financial planner who specialize in planning for individuals with special needs. The effect on the beneficiary's eligibility for government benefits must be carefully considered before electing to receive any monetary settlement. If the individual has become disabled after the age of 22, any Social Security benefits received will be based upon the individual's Social Security record. This is different from an individual whose disability was documented to occur before age 22, who will receive Social Security benefits based upon his or her parents' work history.

· · ·   **Special Needs Planning Story**   · · ·

When I was 30 years old, I was in a car accident that left me unable to work. I receive monthly income from Social Security based upon my work history. My previous employer continues to provide my health insurance and I am receiving a monthly income from their group long-term disability policy. Since my injury, I have been living at home with my parents.

Seven years later, I was presented with options from the settlement. I could have elected to receive either a lump-sum payment amount or a life time income. I wanted to buy my own home and live more independently. Based upon an analysis of my goals, my financial planner determined that electing the lump-sum option would allow me to use some of the proceeds to purchase a home near my parents. The remaining money could be invested to provide income to meet additional expenses as needed.

Although I explored the option of having the proceeds go into a special needs trust, I decided to receive the proceeds directly. I am still able to make my own financial decisions and the income would not affect my disability benefits. I discussed this with my accountant, and he determined that owning the assets in my name would result in less income taxes to be paid on the earnings rather than in a special needs trust, which pays taxes at a higher rate. In addition, my attorney suggested creating a revocable trust and appointing a power of attorney in case I am not able to handle things alone. At this point, I have not made a decision about the trust.

It was very helpful to have the insight from all three of these advisors to help me and my family with this overwhelmingly complicated decision.

· · ·   —Edward   · · ·

Structured Settlements versus Lump-Sum Payments Legal settlements frequently specify a certain dollar amount to be awarded. The monetary award received for a disabling injury or medical malpractice case is frequently determined by the outcome of a **Life Plan.** The Life Plan is a comprehensive document that determines the future costs required to support the individual that has become disabled. A judgment will be offered in the form of an income stream (commonly called a **structured settlement**) or a lump sum. The structured settlement will frequently consist of two components, monthly payments and lump-sum payments, made on predetermined dates. For example, in addition to receiving a fixed monthly income, lump-sum payments may occur at various intervals throughout the lifetime of the beneficiary. The payment is usually exempt from income taxes and the beneficiary's life expectancy is factored into the payment.

In many cases people are encouraged to elect the structured settlement option. The main advantage of the structured settlement is that the income is guaranteed. Although lump-sum distributions can be structured into the payment, the amount is based upon current interest rates. The fixed income stream can leave people vulnerable to inflation. Rather than agreeing to take the structured settlement, it is recommended to seek professional help to analyze the merits of each option, in other words, the structured settlement versus the lump sum payment. One of the calculations that should be determined is the **internal rate of return** of the income stream. Again, a professional financial advisor can help determine the best settlement option that will financially support the needs of the child as identified in the Life Plan.

Special Needs Planning Pointer

If you elect either a structured settlement or lump-sum payment, it is important to consider having the proceeds paid to a special needs trust. Because the proceeds were awarded to the individual with special needs, the trust will be classified as a "self-settled trust" or a "payback trust" under the Omnibus Budget Reconciliation Act (OBRA) of 1993 (PL 97-35) provisions (d)(4)(A). See Chapter 9 for information on special needs trusts. This type of trust requires that, upon the death of the beneficiary, the reimbursement of any Medicaid based payments must be paid back to the government from the assets in the trust first. The remaining assets may then be distributed to the successor beneficiaries named in the trust.

Even though the beneficiary of the self-settled trust may qualify for Medicaid benefits, it may be prudent to use the income from the trust assets to pay for private health insurance. In addition to providing more comprehensive health insurance coverage, this would potentially reduce the beneficiary's dependence upon Medicaid reimbursements. This would ultimately reduce the reimbursement required for government services from the trust upon the death of the beneficiary. Remember that the trustee's primary responsibility is to provide for the beneficiary with special needs, not for the remainder beneficiaries.

Government Benefit Factors

All too often, families have had the false sense of security that the government would provide adequate funding to meet every need of an individual with disabilities throughout their lifetime. In the past, even if the individual was not currently receiving services, families were fairly confident that in the time of a crisis (e.g., the parents' death or illness), the state would provide services. This form of crisis management may have worked for families in prior years.

Today, government resources continue to shrink while the population of individuals requiring services continues to grow. This has resulted in a system that will be inadequate to support future generations. Families need to be aware of the changing environment and the critical need to do their own planning while also protecting and supplementing the services and supports provided by public resources.

The never-ending fiscal crisis of the federal, state, and local governments continues to elevate the issues of competing interest for government resources. The fact that the population of individuals with special needs is increasing at a faster rate brings added fiscal responsibility to government agencies. This also brings added fiscal responsibility to families, who need to plan financially to protect eligibility for and supplement government benefits available to their family member.

In special needs planning, there are two distinct planning strategies regarding government benefits. One strategy is to protect eligibility for government entitlement programs. The other strategy is to advocate for increasing funding for programs that your family member may be eligible for.

Services or benefits, such as special education services through IDEA'04 and Social Security benefits, are key public programs for individuals with disabilities for two reasons: 1) they broadly apply to children and adults with disabilities, and 2) they are entitlements.

Special Needs Planning Pointer

For Social Security, you can access more information at http://www.socialsecurity.gov. For education information, see the U.S. Department of Education web site at http://www.ed.gov and the National Dissemination Center for Children with Disabilities web site at http://www.nichcy.org.

Entitlement Benefits In special needs planning, the key factor in determining how to utilize government benefits is to determine if the benefit is or is not part of an entitlement program. There are laws and regulations that dictate the eligibility for **entitlement benefits** or services to an individual with disabilities, as long as they qualify. It is critical that families maintain the eligibility of their family member through proper planning. Although the process of applying for benefits may result in delays for obtaining entitlements, individuals are not supposed to be placed on waiting lists. Once eligibility is determined, services or benefits are provided, even if they take some time to obtain (e.g., 90 days to receive the first Social Security check or health benefits card). Life may not be perfect, but the wheels turn and at least something is received.

It is important to remember that there is a cost to these services funded by taxpayers. Consequently, our national and state budgets are affected by entitlements, and entitlements are affected by national debt and spending decisions. Every year Congress and state legislatures are required to find a way to fund the budget with adequate money to pay for the entitlement programs.

Public Benefits Other services, which can be classified as **public benefits** or services, are provided if proper appropriations in the state and local budgets are made. If a state does not appropriate new funds for an eligible service, then there will be no funding for new people in need of such services. A state may even reduce the allocations to people currently being funded to address the needs of the new people that require eligible services. The following are examples of eligible services:

- Residential services

- Supported employment services

- Day program services

- Family support services

- Respite care services

- Transportation services

These eligibilities are frequently listed as line items in a state's disability agency budget. Determination of an individual's eligibility is one step in the process. The second step is to determine the amount of benefits the individual will actually receive. Your state's budget process determines both of the preceding steps.

Special Needs Planning Pointer

The increasing demand for services means that the government's budget will have to increase, that families will have to go without services, or that the system will have to change in some way to accommodate the growing numbers. More than ever, families need to plan for ways to help supplement what the government will provide.

In Massachusetts, there were approximately 300 individuals with disabilities statewide turning 22 just 8 years ago. That number has consistently grown, to the point where in 2005, there where approximately 600 individuals turning 22 in the Class of 2006 (from Massachusetts State Budget for the Department of Mental Retardation presented to the Governor's Commission on Mental Retardation, Fall 2005). For 2007, this number is estimated to be approximately the same.

Advocacy is a critically important part of the special needs planning process. Many families may never have the financial capacity to privately pay for all of the services that their son or daughter will require in a lifetime. Although this book concentrates on various financial techniques that a family can utilize to provide for their child, without government resources the security and quality of life may be jeopardized for many. A frequent term used in financial planning is the ability to create a future income stream. Government funding helps to provide a future income stream of benefits to your family member. In special needs planning, advocacy is considered another financial tool to help secure your child's future. It should also be considered as a financial planning strategy.

Special Needs Planning Pointer

We often hear, "My child is all set," because parents are currently receiving appropriate services to meet their needs, which are fully funded by government benefits and services. Prior to having a feeling of lifetime security, the question we ask is, "Do you have the full faith and confidence that the government will always be there for your child and do the right thing on his or her behalf?" With the constantly changing political environment, it is strongly suggested that you do not put your child's security solely into the hands of a government that is constantly changing. Proper planning to maximize government benefits as well as doing all that is possible to maximize personal resources will help to ensure success.

· · ·   **Special Needs Planning Story**   · · ·

When our son was 2 years old, we were allocated enough money from a government agency that provided for 5 hours of nursing services per week. Although our son was on medication, he only took the medication in the morning and the evening—and we administered it to him. At that time, we did not need anyone to administer his medicine. We needed someone to be there to care for him so that we could have a break. Instead of the nurse, we simply wanted to hire our next-door neighbor, who was getting a degree in special education, to help. We were excited because we could secure 25 hours of coverage for the cost of the 5 hours of nursing. We were told that this was not the policy. This inefficiency gave us the passion to fight hard to change the system, not only for our family, but also for other families facing the same dilemma. We now have a new statewide family support policy that provides families choices and flexibility in acquiring services.

· · ·   —John and Susan, James's parents   · · ·

Public Programs Public programs define whom they serve through regulations. To obtain supports or qualify for services from public agencies, an individual or family must first confirm the existence of a disability. It is important to know the various types of government supports and funding that may be applicable to your child or family member at each planning pressure point.

Special Education Services Through the Individuals with Disabilities Education Improvement Act IDEA'04 is the nation's special education law. It is federally funded to assist states and local communities in providing educational opportunities for students with varying degrees of disabilities who participate in special education. (See *Individuals with Disabilities Education Act (IDEA) Guide to "Frequently Asked Questions,"* Committee on Education and the Workforce, February 17, 2005.)

Special education is one of two federally funded programs (the other being Social Security) that is an **entitlement** and is broadly applied to all individuals with a disability. In the case of IDEA'04, each state has its own specific laws and regulations. The state law may closely resemble the federal law or may have more benefits and rights for students, but the state is expected to meet the minimum federal standards. Getting a diagnosis that the government accepts for special education services is a complicated and usually not transparent process. But in the case of IDEA'04 and Social Security, there are laws and regulations that you can depend on.

Early Intervention Services Part C of IDEA'04 provides early intervention and other services for infants and toddlers with disabilities (from birth to age 3) and their families. If you become aware of your child's disability prior to the age of 3 years, he or she should be enrolled in an EI program. Infants with a diagnosed developmental disability, or ones at clear risk to experience a developmental delay, are eligible for EI services. For example, infants born prematurely and/or infants living with families in difficult environmental circumstances may be eligible for EI services. Each state has discretion in how it determines which situations or conditions may potentially result in a developmental delay.

To obtain EI services, your pediatrician may be a good resource to begin with. Use the Internet or a telephone book to locate an EI provider. You should contact your state chapter of The Arc to find the gatekeeper, or state agency office, responsible. Often there is a local office within a county that must first determine eligibility for services.

Special Education Benefits Before your child is 3, it is important to begin the application process for school services. Special education is provided through local educational agencies (LEAs). An LEA is really another name for the public school system in your town. That system, however, takes different shapes depending upon the size of a community. The LEA has a process for determining eligibility for special education services. To obtain special education services in your schools, contact the school district's superintendent office and ask for the special education services office number. Often staff in EI programs can help you in this important transition. Even if your toddler's disability is not apparent until his or her second birthday, it is worth applying for EI services. Although you may have missed many services, you will get assistance in your child's transition to a special education program administered by the school, in addition to the therapies and parent support available. Getting help through the transition period from EI to the school system is critically important because this period is a major pressure point in the planning process. Having a smooth transition will relieve much of the anxiety that is a major deterrent to enabling you to continue your planning process.

Social Security Benefits   The second entitlement program for individuals with disabilities is Social Security. Adults with disabilities can qualify for two different Social Security programs, whereas children under age 18 may qualify for one. IDEA'04 considers children through 21 or 22 years eligible for special education services; adult eligibility for Social Security begins at age 18 years.

Social Security provides adults with disabilities a monthly benefit payment and health insurance if they meet a low income and asset threshold. The health insurance benefit, which is Medicaid, is discussed later in this chapter. Children with disabilities under age 18 years are also eligible for Social Security benefits, but the parents' income and assets are considered with the child's in determining financial eligibility. The Social Security program eligibility guidelines are consistent in every state. State agencies are responsible for implementing the disability determination, but they are obliged to use the federal regulations to do so (see http://www.ssa.gov for more information).

Although Social Security is known best for providing benefits to retirees after the age of 65, most children and adults with disabilities also qualify for Social Security benefits through one of two Social Security income benefit programs: SSDI or SSI.

Social Security Disability Insurance   SSDI is a disability benefit income payable to children of parents who have a work history and thus contributed to Social Security; the children are eligible due to the death, disability, or retirement of the parent. When you qualify for Social Security benefits, your children may also qualify to receive benefits on your record if you become disabled or die. Your eligible child can be your biological child, adopted child, or stepchild. To receive benefits, the child must be unmarried and 1) be under age 18, 2) be between ages 18 and 19 and be a full-time high school student, or 3) be over age 18 and have a disability that started before age 22. Benefits typically stop when children reach age 18 unless they are disabled. The specific amount of this benefit is based on either parent's Social Security earnings record. In addition, the beneficiary is eligible for Medicare health insurance. If your family member is an SSDI recipient, make sure he or she is determined eligible for Medicaid to ensure access to public services provided by your state.

Special Needs Planning Pointer

To maintain eligibility for SSI benefits, an individual cannot have more than $2,000 of resources in his or her name. This includes cash, bank accounts, stocks, and U.S. savings bonds. Prior to the child's turning age 18, and before applying for SSI, make certain that the child meets this requirement.

Supplemental Security Income   SSI is an entitlement benefit that is payable to adults or children who have a disability or who are blind and have limited income and resources. Although this is an entitlement benefit, the value of an individual's resources is one of the factors that determine whether he or she is eligible for SSI benefits. Not all resources, however, are included in making the determination of eligibility for SSI. The current limit for countable resources is $2,000 for an individual and $3,000 for a couple (see SSI Resources at http://www.ssa.gov for a summary of countable and noncountable resources).

If you receive SSI, you usually receive food stamps and Medicaid. States have different names for their Medicaid program (e.g., CAL-Med for California, Tenn-Cares for Tennessee, MassHealth for Massachusetts). Children under 18 years may also be eligible for SSI. Their parents' income and assets, however, are factored into the eligibility. For more information regarding your state specifics, see http://www.ssa.gov.

The Medicaid Program   Title 19 of the Social Security Act established the Medicaid program. Medicaid is a joint federal–state program that provides the majority of funding for long-term care services for individuals with disabilities (see the Medicaid Reference Desk for information about Medicaid for people with cognitive disabilities at http://www. thedesk. info). Medicaid benefits reviewed later in this book should not be confused with Medicare. Medicaid is a valuable resource for individuals with disabilities. It is a public form of health care insurance that provides standard medical benefits, including doctors' visits, hospital stays, prescriptions, and related medical services. In addition, Medicaid benefits provide access to long-term care services or supports. All states receive partial reimbursement from the federal government for these services. Consumers who obtain Medicaid funding services possess certain rights dictated by federal regulations. Consequently, it is important to know if your services are reimbursed through Medicaid.

How to Obtain Services or Funding for Your Loved One Each state varies in how services and funding to individuals are provided, despite national legislation and regulations that guide the delivery of services such as health care, education, and long-term care. There are two points of contact one can make. One is through an advocacy agency group such as The Arc, UCP, NAMI, or ASA or other support agencies. The other is through the government agency in your state that generally provides the funding of services and support programs for your child's diagnosis. Perhaps the first point of contact should be the advocacy agency that supports your family member's disability. Also, see the Obtaining Services section in Chapter 9.

Special Needs Planning Pointer

Suggested steps to help secure government resources for your family member:

1. Locate possible programs or funding. Depending on the age of your child, your EI coordinator, doctor, school system, and other parents are good resources.

2. In order to determine the most suitable agency that meets your needs, identify the agency that has a mission related to the disability of your family member. In addition, it is important for you to find out which state agencies have the greatest funding. In some cases, your child may have a dual diagnosis and may qualify for services through more than one agency. If this is the case, refer to your state's budget to determine which agency has the largest resources allocated. You may want to request assistance from an aide in your state legislator's office.

3. Begin the application process. As soon as you identify an agency that is relevant and has services you require, ask for an application. If you are uncertain how to complete the application, request assistance from the agency.

4. Proactively address any barriers to the application process. As you fill out the application, if you see gaps in your information, address them through setting up appointments for evaluations or requesting information that is missing from your files.

(continued)

(continued)

5. Monitor the application process to ensure timely completion. Follow up with the agency once or twice to see if there is anything you can do to facilitate the application process. Contact them if a deadline has passed.

6. Be prepared to advocate for specific supports or services that fit the personal vision of your family member and/or family.

Timelines and prompt sharing of records are important to keep in mind when you are attempting to get an application approved. The date of your application triggers all the deadlines for various steps in the process. If you delay on your part of the application, the school or local Social Security office is no longer under the same time obligations triggered by your application date.

Do not hesitate to follow up if a case manager misses his or her deadlines. But make sure you get your necessary paperwork together so you do not miss deadlines as well. You can rely on a certain level of responsiveness, because both programs have federal laws and regulations.

The Difference Between Service and Support   Today, advocates and professionals often use the word *support* to encompass anything that someone may need to live in his or her community. Often in human or disability services, an individual has to accept a change in location or compromise in the type of supports needed. The two examples following describe the differences between support and service.

1. After transitioning from EI into their city's school system, a family was looking forward to having their child attend their local elementary school. In their transition meeting, they were informed that their son would be sent across town to the one after-school program established to accommodate children with disabilities. The family, however, wanted their child to make stronger connections with children at their local school. After a series of meetings, the school district agreed to allocate "supports" through a voucher or other procedure to increase the capability of the local school to meet the child's unique needs. This was accomplished by hiring a part-time staff person and budgeting training for the other teachers at the local after-school program.

2. After years of having a successful job-coaching arrangement while in high school, an individual with disabilities turned age 22 and was told that he had to enter a sheltered workshop for employment services 10 miles away from his home. It was a disappointment for his parents because their son had done so well working in the community. The policy for the adult services system had been to invest resources into

local workshops in an effort to provide services to adults. Feeling that this was not appropriate for their child, the parents had many meetings with the disability agency and contacted their legislator in an effort to develop a job-coaching arrangement similar to what they had before to support their child in the community. Fortunately, they succeeded and were given the ability to interview three agencies that would provide them with the supported employment services that met their son's individual needs.

The preceding examples highlight the differences between cases in which services are standardized to meet the general needs of many and those in which supports are developed around an individual's needs. One must realize, however, that every state will have various degrees of flexibilities built into their support and service delivery system. In planning your child's future, it is suggested that you push to have supports that are built around your child's particular needs. Placing emphasis on supports involves developing a program around the needs of the individual. An environment that is driven by providing services frequently builds standardized programs for all.

The Life Cycle of Services and Supports   Throughout our lives we change and evolve. This is no different for individuals with disabilities. For a child, most of the options are consistent with options that other children face. As your child approaches the teen years, it will be vital to change perspectives and help him or her exercise more control and opinions concerning daily life. This will set a foundation that will assist your child with disabilities to build a life that he or she feels is consistent with inner desires and dreams. Avoid the temptation to accept the first service that is offered to you; instead, go into the process with a clear idea of what you and your child are seeking.

Although the special needs planning timeline covers multiple planning pressure points, there are three major periods when supports and services change regardless of your location. The major ages that trigger a change in services and/or supports are at your child's birth, at age 3, and at age 22. There are additional pressure point ages and changes that trigger key planning considerations. These include transition planning at age 16, guardianship and Social Security or SSI at age 18, as well as the death, disability, or retirement of a parent. These planning pressure points are discussed in more detail in the discussion of the special needs planning timeline in Chapter 1.

Birth to Age 3   When you discover your child has a disability, it is important to obtain EI services as soon as possible. In addition, look for "parent-to-parent" programs where you can connect with another parent who is raising a child with a disability. Other parents can mentor you and share their information and knowledge. Apply for EI services even if you think you are not quite ready to start them, because there may be a waiting period. Research shows that the earlier infants receive stimulation and further professional supports, such as physical, occupational, and speech therapy, the better the child does in reaching milestones.

Age 3 to Adolescence Transition to school is a very important period. At age 3, the school system is responsible for offering educational and related services. In addition, if a child has special health care needs, such as a chronic illness, a disabling condition, or a frequent need for medical technology, check out eligibility for your state's TEFRA program (the Tax Equity and Fiscal Responsibility Act of 1982) or Special Health Care Needs Program (this program is often referred to as the "Katie Beckett" Waiver; see Chapter 9 for more information). EI staff will be of great assistance to explore such options, as well to help with the transition to school.

You may face some challenges during the school year, such as

- Helping your child develop a social network

- Obtaining an appropriate education program while helping your child get included in the everyday life of the school

- Helping your child learn about his or her body changes during adolescence

- Making sure you work with your child, beginning at age 16 years or earlier, to develop transition goals at school and outside school to prepare for adult life

- Eventually developing a plan with your child and others who care that reflects his or her dreams and desires

· · ·   **Special Needs Planning Story**   · · ·

When Jake was 3¹/₂ years old, he attended a preschool program. We were still unclear about his disability, but he had limited interest in verbal communication, and he made little eye contact with his peers and us. The school program is providing him with only one communication activity per week through a speech therapy session. We talked to the special education coordinator, but she stated that only the director of special education can make a change, and that we had to have the change written into his education plan.

After 6 months of going back and forth with no results, we decided to contact the social worker at the EI program that Jake had attended for 1 year. She agreed to meet with us and brought in an educator for part of the meeting who helped us identify missing elements in his present school program. The social worker also connected us with a parent that was involved in educational advocacy within the same school system that Jake attends.

After meeting with the parent advocate, we decided to hire her to assist us at the team meeting, which would review Jake's current educational plan. At that meeting, the director offered us a compromise for his communication goal, which we accepted pending a 3-month review. We also stated that if progress was unsatisfactory by that time, we would then ask for a mediation session with the school district on Jake's plan and push for the activities that we felt would be optimal for him. We were successful.

If it were not for the assistance of this parent advocate, we would not have accomplished so much on Jake's behalf. There are so many factors that have to be considered, and we are still new to this. Her involvement made such a difference for all of us.

· · ·   — Jake's father   · · ·

Age 22 Years and Beyond Becoming an adult is not easy for any of us. If your child needs adult services for any aspect of his or her life, you should start learning about the funding and programs offered by the time he or she is age 18 and still a student. Waiting until the last minute may mean limiting or delaying options in adulthood. Different organizations have materials that you can read to help prepare for this stage, but the foundation of the plan should be developed during the teen years.

· · ·   **Special Needs Planning Story**   · · ·

My sister Marie has lived with my parents for her entire life. She has a developmental disability and has held a part-time job at a nursing home since her 25th birthday. Since my mother's death, my father has found it difficult to take care of my sister alone. Because of this, we began to look into finding her someplace to live that could support her needs. I know that my parents never considered this eventuality. But after seeing my father struggle, I realized that something had to be done as soon as possible. When we were told there was a 10-year waiting list for residential services, we were both surprised and disappointed.

Although I live two states away, I tried to visit every other month to help with Marie and talk about her options with my dad. We happened to meet an old classmate of Marie's, who is now living in a supported apartment with two other roommates. This was encouraging for all of us.

Based on the suggestion of the classmate's parents, who were also told there was a 10-year waiting list for their daughter, we took things a step further and asked for a formal letter identifying Marie's eligibility and status for services. They also introduced us to a family support group at a local agency. We reviewed the letter with a staff person from that agency. They helped us to develop a plan to advocate for Marie, which included Marie's ideas about her future life.

Since then, my Dad has become involved in legislative advocacy for new funding. He has met other parents in the same situation, as well as those who continue to be active after obtaining services for their children. After 2 years of advocacy and visiting different service providers, Marie finally moved into her new apartment. The best part is that it is only 5 miles away from Dad.

· · ·   —Marie's sister   · · ·

Advocacy Over the decades, community services have evolved, resembling a patchwork of assorted options. Legislative advocacy and legal settlements have dictated the growth of services. Government finances are finite, and service expansion has slowed as taxes have been reduced. As this book is published, Congress has voted to allow states more flexibility in limiting Medicaid-funded services, which means our present long-term care models may shrink as the baby boom generation grows in its need for supports and services.

Public funding for services has not kept pace with the need. Parent involvement in advocating for new funding and encouraging efficient use of existing resources is vital. It is important for you to keep in mind that financial planning tools are not the only investments and saving strategies. Advocacy is a critical component of the planning process. Even after you receive funding, ongoing advocacy is needed to maintain the service at a reasonable level. Funding for services requires constituents to say they are necessary so that legislators will hear about their importance. You can participate in legislative advocacy simply by being informed of the funding requests that are being made and sharing your support with your state and federal public officials.

· · ·   **Special Needs Planning Story**   · · ·

My daughter Janet is 15 years old. She has received home health services since she was 10 years old. Janet has a wheelchair, which allows her to get around, and although she can understand me, she has trouble expressing herself verbally. My husband and I are finding it difficult to physically transfer her on a day-to-day basis because we need a second person to assist. The home health agency cannot meet the schedule that was agreed upon. Furthermore, the aides do not have the necessary training to teach Janet how to be as independent as possible.

When I talked to a staff person at our local chapter of The Arc, she told me about the Medicaid personal care attendant (PCA) program. I learned that the family (or the individual) hires the staff person and that they can directly negotiate hours. In this case, since Janet is not able to supervise the attendant, I as her parent would serve as a surrogate supervisor of the PCA. Another benefit is that the PCA, although hired to assist Janet, may also be able to help her to become more independent. The only stipulation is that if Janet does get the PCA services, she will have to give up the home health program.

I went through the paperwork to get Janet her PCA services only to receive a rejection based on the fact that she is under 18 years of age. When I shared this news with a staff person at the local chapter of The Arc, she gave me the name of a parent using the PCA program as well as the phone number of a law center that is working on improving access to services. Not wanting to rock the boat, however, I decided to wait for the service and make due with the home health program.

After 4 more weeks of unfilled aide hours and missed classes for Janet because I cannot get her out of bed when my husband is away on business, I finally called the disability law center and the other family who has a minor receiving PCA services. When I found out that Janet could be served through the PCA program, I got up the courage to appeal the rejection of our application. It took me 4 months, but now Janet is receiving PCA services. My life is so much easier.

• • •   —Janet's mother   • • •

5

Planning for Stage I

CHILD'S BIRTH TO AGE 3

The birth of a child with disabilities will probably change the course, but the destination is the same: creating opportunities for our children, and providing long-term security for our families. —A loving parent

• • • **Thoughts from John** • • •

When my son James was born, we were completely surprised that he had Down syndrome. In fact, the night before his birth, Susan had taught her last aerobic classes and had a pleasant evening out with her friends. James was born right on his due date, and his delivery was quick. As soon as James was given to Susan, she said, "This child has Down syndrome; there must be some mistake." Initially, Susan felt that it could not have been her baby. While in the birthing room, I was totally unaware as to what was happening, other than that something was bad. I was not tuned into what Susan was actually saying but was responding to the serious looks on the physician and nurses faces. When the physician said she had some suspicions, I fainted from the shock of it all and had to be revived by the staff.

When I went home to care for our other two children, I stepped back into our "normal" life. I remember, as clearly today as I did 16 years ago, my thoughts of how I was going to take care of our third child. I thought about converting the barn in the back of our house to a home for him when he became an adult. I went to the hospital library to research the subject of Down syndrome. All that I found were old books on mongoloidism. It was depressing to see the descriptions of the limited possibilities of his life. I finally found a photo of a child with Down syndrome that was dancing.

I made a copy of this photo and kept it on my desk to remind me to think about the positives of what might be.

For Susan, it was different. She wanted out and asked to go home with James immediately, but James needed to be checked out and of course they don't let you just leave. She remained in the hospital, where the staff was indifferent; they, too, were at a loss for words. Susan asked that her hospital door be closed, and the staff limited their contact with her. Perhaps it made them feel more comfortable. It is not that they were not caring; they just simply did not know what to say. If only someone could have just said "congratulations."

. . .   . . .

GENERAL DESCRIPTION OF STAGE I

So let us first say to you, congratulations on the birth of your child! After many months of anticipation, the day has finally arrived, and you are now parents of a wonderful baby. Some parents may have known about their child's special needs in advance, but regardless of how much advanced notice we receive, we are never quite prepared. For others, the realization of having a child born with special needs may never have even been a consideration—there was no family history, it was a normal pregnancy, you had other healthy children, even prenatal testing showed no known indications of complications. Whatever the cause, whether or not there are answers, you still have a new baby to cherish.

Your first contact with professionals will probably be the medical staff at the hospital. In some cases, people will offer well-intentioned advice and guidance, while others may feel awkward and completely unresponsive. The fact is that some professionals may be in a position to offer valuable advice. In other situations, however, you as the parent will know best just by sheer instinct.

Just as every child is unique, the way each parent reacts to the situation will be different. It is common for some parents to think about the immediate impact that having a child with disabilities will have on their lives. In other cases, parents will think about the long-term implications of the future.

Sharing the news with family and friends may be difficult; their reactions may simply be different in the way of sympathy rather than celebration. Some people may be at a loss for words, or feel uncertain of the "right" thing to say. Others may share "success" stories of other special kids they have known in an attempt to provide hope and support.

Perhaps your child's disability was not immediately diagnosed at birth. You may have had concerns that he or she was developing a bit "differently" than other children, but were afraid to ask. Or if you did ask your pediatrician, he or she may have tried to soothe your worries by saying that every child develops at his or her own pace. Today, pediatricians typically provide a referral for EI services if there is any question about the child's development. Childcare providers are also more aware of the stages of development and can encourage parents to seek early support services as well.

UNIQUE PLANNING STEPS FOR STAGE I

First see the core planning points outlined in Chapter 2:

- Ask your pediatrician about EI services in your area.

- Identify local support agencies that specialize in providing information and services for your child's specific needs.

- Do not assume that the government will fully provide for your child's lifetime needs. Begin learning how to advocate for your child's services.

- Maintain a balance in your overall planning, to include needs for other children as well as your own needs (both personal and financial).

- Determine an adequate amount of life insurance needed in the event of a premature death of a caregiver or primary wage earner.

- Do not establish savings or investment accounts in your child's name. These include custodial accounts of Uniform Gifts to Minors Accounts (UGMAs) or Uniform Transfer to Minors Accounts (UTMAs). You should save in accounts in the name of the parent(s) that could be "earmarked" for the child.

Special Needs Planning Pointer

The most recent 529 College Savings Plans (529 Plans) provide a number of advantages to use for a college savings vehicle. Interpretations of the ownership and/or beneficiary designations, however, must be carefully reviewed to determine if this type of asset is a countable asset that will disqualify your child for SSI and government benefits eligibility.

The 529 Plan's definition of qualified distributions (e. g., distributions for the beneficiary's qualified educational expenses at an eligible educational institution) will determine the tax consequences but will not necessarily guide you as to your child's eligibility for government benefits.

(continued)

(continued)

Currently, there are no published guidelines by the Division of Medical Assistance to determine if assets in the 529 Plan will count as an asset of the beneficiary for government benefits eligibility.

The New York 529 College Savings Program *Direct Plan* Program Brochure and Privacy Policy, and Tuition Savings Agreement states,

> The effect of an Account on eligibility for Medicaid or other state and federal benefits is uncertain. It is possible that an Account will be viewed as a "countable resource" in determining an individual's financial eligibility for Medicaid. Withdrawals from an Account during certain periods also may have the effect of delaying the disbursement of Medicaid payments. You should consult a qualified advisor to determine how a 529 Plan account may affect eligibility for Medicaid or other state and federal noneducational benefits. (2006, p.17)

Depending on the laws of your state of residence, favorable tax treatment for investing in a 529 Plan may be limited to investments made in a 529 Plan offered by your state of residence. If your state or your designated beneficiary's state offers a 529 Plan, you may want to consider what, if any, potential state income tax or other benefits it offers before investing. Consult with your tax advisor or contact your state of residence college savings plan sponsor to learn more about any state tax or other benefits that might be available in conjunction with an investment in your in-state college savings plan. Some state 529 Plans indicate that expenses for a student with special needs may also be considered as a qualified education expense. This assumes the beneficiary is able to meet the acceptance requirements of a qualified educational institution.

FAMILY AND SUPPORT FACTORS

One of the most frustrating things to new parents is the lack of information available to help formulate a general framework from which they can create a vision of their child's future. During much of this early stage, your life is lived on a day-to-day basis. It is only natural to feel overwhelmed with all the added logistics on top of the arrival of a new baby. A basic understanding of your child's diagnosis is often as much as can be expected at this stage. Significant changes may need to be made based upon your family values and the needs of your child with special needs and other children. There are, however, other factors to consider.

- Do you have extended family members, friends, or neighbors who would be willing to help babysit your child and/or other children if needed? Initially, it is a natural reaction for family members to be uncomfortable caring for a child with disabilities, particularly if they have a number of medical issues. In addition, it is quite natural for you to be unwilling to seek the assistance of others in caring for your child with disabilities. Our experience has been that the earlier you get people involved in your child's life, the more comfortable everyone will become. Giving others a chance to develop a relationship with your newborn will help to shape future caregivers.

- Will you have to pay for the additional costs of specialized child care when you need a break? Depending on the needs of the child, a family may consider hiring an au pair, a nanny, or specialized babysitters to help support the caregiving parent at home, as well as the other children. Frequently, you can contact a service provider that has experience dealing with individuals who have needs similar to those of your child, to have them identify an appropriate match.

- Will one parent need to make adjustments to his or her work schedule, resulting in a loss of income? You should not only analyze the economic impact of a job adjustment; you should also analyze the personal impact of no longer being employed outside the house. It is often beneficial for both parents to work at some level to maintain a sense of self and well-being.

- What adjustments in lifestyle expenses are needed to allow for one parent to stay at home if he or she was a joint income earner before? These factors may have a significant impact on your cash-flow needs, and therefore your lifestyle. Perhaps the mother was the primary income provider, but now is required to be the primary caregiver. Perhaps one income was used to provide the "extras" in your lifestyle, such as club memberships, travel and entertainment expenses, the vacation home, or additional savings. Changes to these aspects of your life need to be evaluated carefully.

- Are your employers supportive of your situation? Does your job schedule provide enough flexibility to be available for unexpected events and medical emergencies? If not, it may be time for a change of employers and/or careers. It is possible that your work life will be affected by the demands of caring for a child with disabilities.

- If you are self-employed, will you lose precious billable hours for medical appointments and other consultations for your child? Do you have staff or business partners that can keep the business flowing in your absence? Discuss with your partners your needs and expectations. Determine a plan.

EMOTIONAL FACTORS

Some families may be introduced to a whole new world of medical terms, developmental terms, and definitions of progress—the world of families with special needs. Emotional factors will constantly change as you learn more about your child's abilities.

- If your child with disabilities is your firstborn child, have you taken a moment to congratulate yourselves on becoming new parents? Your lives, as those of all parents, will be filled with both challenges as well as rewarding moments. Do not forget to appreciate the joys of bonding with your new baby.

- Do you have a good understanding of your child's diagnosis? Increasing knowledge of the diagnosis will help to formulate your vision for your child over time. It is possible that it may take years to find a specific diagnosis.

- Have you sought out a positive support network of other parents and/or professionals? People's opinions and comments, positive or negative, have a way of affecting one's emotions, and it is helpful to find others who support you emotionally.

- Are you frustrated because there is a lack of accessible information about your situation? The greatest changes in the world have been made because parents have questioned the existing system at some point, and forced a change. Do not be afraid to be advocates and trail blazers for yourselves and your children.

- Are you emotionally prepared to plan ahead? It is understandable to become overwhelmed by the day-to-day issues and crises or to be unable to identify planning needs. It may not even be possible to plan every detail for the future. It is critical, however, that you take some immediate steps to develop a plan to cover any short-term financial catastrophe that can affect your family today, such as the premature death of a parent.

FINANCIAL FACTORS

Although this book is based upon the understanding that you have to plan for the long term, there is enough going on in your life at this point that you may become fearful of planning for the future. This is understandable. We encourage you to live in the present and seek strategies to help plan for the future, which is why we have written this book. Some of the most critical financial factors to consider are those that would influence the immediate and long-term security of your family.

- Have you taken the time to determine the amount of money you need for you and your family to meet basic monthly expenses? Once this is determined, it will allow you to get a better handle on making financial decisions. Refer back to Chapter 3 for more information on budgeting.

- If both parents were working when your child was born, were you planning that one parent would stay home to be the primary caregiver? Or is this now an option that needs to be considered due to your child's disabilities? You should examine whether it makes financial sense for both spouses to continue working, or whether it is more economical for one spouse to stay at home. Sometimes there may be no choice; one parent may have to stop working outside of the home.

- Have you reviewed your present life insurance policies (both group insurance and personal insurance), to make certain that premiums are up to date and beneficiary designations are current? This is the time to determine an appropriate amount of life insurance needed. This is the planning stage where your need for protection is greatest.

- Have you reviewed your present long-term disability insurance policies (both group insurance and personal insurance coverage)? This may be a good time to consider the importance of such coverage. One of the most frequently overlooked financial needs is providing for yourself and your family in the event of an extended disability. Financially, the total cost of a permanent disability of a parent can have a greater financial impact than the death of a wage earner.

- Are you taking advantage of, or do you clearly understand, all of the benefits that your employer is providing for you? This is the time to call your human resources representative to get a better understanding of available options.

- Are you having difficulty meeting your monthly expenses and finding that your credit card debt is increasing because of daily expense charges? Review the interest rate charges to reevaluate the true costs of using this kind of debt to meet your expenses. You should also determine if there are spending patterns that need to be changed immediately.

- Are you currently in, or planning to be in, a litigation process with the potential to receive a financial settlement? You should compare and contrast the use of a structured settlement versus a lump sum settlement. You should consult with a CFP® practitioner or other advisors who are knowledgeable in special needs planning prior to accepting any terms of settlement and/or receiving money. If you are in the beginning phases of litigation, it is important to realize that it often takes years to settle a case; it is not uncommon for it to take greater than 6 years. Be prepared; you may need to make adjustments to accommodate the additional time and money needed to pursue a legal settlement.

> ### Special Needs Planning Pointer
>
> For self-employed individuals, an accountant will often suggest a means to reduce taxable income in an effort to minimize Social Security contributions. Reducing your contributions to FICA, however, will have an effect on your child's future income from SSDI benefits. Explain the importance of the Social Security system to your advisors.

Although the level of income and your family's net worth are important, the key to financial security is to have the ability to live within your means. Regardless of the age of the parents or the age of the children, the fundamental steps of financial planning are the same. A family's ability to achieve financial security depends upon their ability to manage their debt as well as their capacity to save. These are the most basic elements.

The first issue is to have the discipline of managing debt. Those individuals or families that are living beyond their means and finding that they have excessive credit card debt, loans on retirement plans, and/or very little equity in their home may need to explore options to pay down debt and build savings. A simple test to determine if this is an issue for your family is to look at your short-term debt obligations, such as credit card debt, to determine if interest payments are consistently greater than any earnings that you may be receiving on savings and investments. In the event that this occurs, it is suggested that you immediately begin to reduce debt and decrease spending.

The second issue is to have the capacity to save. A common question that families ask us is whether or not they have enough money saved to achieve their goals. We have found that many families do indeed have the capacity to save; however, they may not realize what they should be saving for. The needs are often so overwhelming that it becomes paralyzing to figure out where and how to begin.

After identifying the goals and quantifying the needs, you may realize that it is virtually impossible to have and/or to accumulate the personal financial resources needed to provide all the supports for your child's lifetime needs. If this is the case, your goal should be to at least supplement what the government provides. Once the needs are determined, it is often a matter of prioritizing your goals and redirecting your savings to achieve these goals. This is why it is critical to maximize any and all eligibility for government benefits and supports.

Another consideration in financial planning is income tax planning. Often people depend on a large refund in April to help pay off debt or contribute to savings; for others, it is considered as "found" money and used for vacations and other recreation. This is often referred to as "a tax-free loan to the U.S. government." If you have difficulty budgeting, however, this may be an easy way to have forced savings. If, on the other hand, you could adjust your tax withholdings throughout the year, you could use the additional money on a monthly basis to build savings. Certainly the key is not to get into tax liability, but to manage tax payments. Special needs planning builds the foundation for planning for your own personal security, the lifetime security of your child, and striking a balance.

You could have two next-door neighbors with similar houses and very similar incomes. But one family might be struggling financially because they do not have any discipline in savings and cannot resist the urge to spend, while the other family might be disciplined in their savings habits and are financially comfortable. This is why the actual dollar amounts may not be as important as the percentage of your income that is spent.

LEGAL FACTORS

Prior to a child turning age 18, eligibility for government benefits is based upon the parents' income and assets. In many cases, the parents' level of income and assets will disqualify the child's eligibility for benefits such as SSI and Medicaid. Although your child is only a newborn, it is important to follow proper planning techniques now, to avoid the potential of disqualifying him or her for benefits at age 18. Although you may not currently qualify for SSI, maintaining eligibility for these benefits should be paramount in your estate plan, regardless of your child's current abilities and/or your current financial status. In planning at this stage, flexibility is critical. It is important not to eliminate any options or jeopardize the potential receipt of benefits by improper planning.

- Do you have a legally written estate plan? If not, the state in which you reside will create one for you upon your death. It is important to consult with a qualified estate planning attorney who is knowledgeable in planning for individuals with special needs.

- Have you identified an individual that is willing and able to take care of your child if you are no longer able to do so, in the event of your own disability or premature death? This is the person you would refer to as a *guardian.*

- Do you have current wills to name a guardian for your minor children? If you do not name a guardian in your will, the family probate court in your state will determine this individual for you.

- Have you coordinated the ownership and beneficiary designations of your life insurance, retirement plan accounts, and annuities with your overall estate plan? Unless your wills and trusts are properly coordinated with your life insurance and other assets, the money you intend to be available to support your family may not be accessible to them.

- Have you considered the use of a special needs trust as the recipient of an inheritance for your child with disabilities? A properly drafted and adequately funded special needs trust is the key to your child's future security. It will provide the resources required to supplement your child's needs and protect their eligibility for many entitlement benefits.

- Are you currently in, or planning to be in, a litigation process with the potential to receive a financial settlement? Before accepting the terms of the settlement and/or receipt of the money, you should consult with a qualified attorney to establish a special needs trust, if appropriate, in order to protect your child's future eligibility for government benefits.

Special Needs Planning Pointer

Gifts from family and friends should not be made directly to the child, to custodial accounts (i.e., UTMAs), or college savings accounts (i.e., 529 Plans) in the name of the child.

GOVERNMENT BENEFIT FACTORS

It is a known fact that the government is a bureaucratic system that can be very difficult to navigate—even for the most experienced and educated family. One of the most frustrating experiences you may have is trying to identify one person that has the knowledge of all of the programs, services, and funding available for families. What makes it more difficult is that the needs of your child may frequently cross various government agencies and departments.

- Has your medical practitioner referred you to EI services? If not, ask for a referral immediately.

- Do you know which government agency (or agencies) your child will be receiving services and/or resources from? If you do not know, you need to identify the primary government agency that will be responsible for meeting the needs of your child.

- Does your child have multiple disabilities? If so, this will increase the likelihood of having to deal with several government agencies. Identify and begin to work with the agency that has the largest budget first.

- Does your local government provide services directly, or do they hire local agencies to provide such services? There may be various providers of services you can choose to work with in your local area.

- Have you explored your family's eligibility for government benefits? Based upon your family's total financial income and assets, you may be eligible for financial assistance through government programs. These include SSI and health insurance benefits (Medicaid benefits), among other governed by your state of residence.

Special Needs Planning Pointer

Do not be intimidated by what may seem to be a large and impersonal system. Get on the telephone, search the Internet, and talk to people that have gone through this experience before. Keep a diary of all contacts you make, including
- The name and telephone of the person you reach
- The date of the conversation
- The person's title
- The agency and department the person works for
- The name and title of the person's boss

· · ·   **Thoughts from John**   · · ·

One of the most frustrating experiences for Susan and me was our inability to find someone that had any authority to help us. It appeared that whomever we called, that person's job was to take information from us and about our son, rather than to give us information about the services available to help us. Trying to deal with the bureaucracy of how the system worked was much more challenging than dealing with our own personal situation. The breakthrough came when we realized that we had to understand how the government works. Without that understanding, we felt that we were continually in a maze. Our goal was simple—to get some help. We made it our mission to understand how the money and resources were allocated to families. To do this, we built an organizational chart, which included the person who picked up the telephone all the way up to the governor. This experience taught us that you must identify the person who has the decision-making ability that will have the most impact on you and your family. Once we were able to identify the right people, we found people who truly cared and stepped forward to help. The preceding experience not only helped us break the barriers of what felt like a huge system, it made us realize that the people within the system really do care. They are in this business because they care. Many have become friends and supporters for the rest of our lives.

. . .   . . .

USING CASE EXAMPLES AS A HELPFUL GUIDE

Because every region of the nation has a different standard of living, it is not possible to use specific dollar amounts in the case studies that will be applicable to families throughout the United States. Even within the same geographic area and the same level of income, a lot depends on the family's value of money and how they spend it versus how they save it.

The principals of financial planning are the same if a family is of moderate income and net worth, or high income and net worth. The key to achieving personal goals is dependent upon your ability to save a certain percentage of your income on a regular basis. Without a doubt, the specific dollars are important in planning to determine what the needs of the family are. When working with a financial planner, tax preparer, or attorney, the details of your personal financial resources and information will be most important in driving recommendations. For purposes of this book, we try to be as general as possible so that we may provide the guidelines for your personal planning and illustrate the techniques behind the special needs planning process.

Our objective in sharing real case examples is not to categorize families based upon levels of income or levels of net worth. It is instead to show the various strategies based on the different factors and how they affect a family's ability to plan.

CASE EXAMPLES FOR STAGE I

The Brown Family: Building Security

Family and Financial Profile   Richard (age 29) and Patricia (age 28) have been married for 5 years. They have two sons, Patrick (age 3) and Joseph (age 1). Joseph was diagnosed at birth with special needs.

Before Joseph was born, the Browns purchased a new home. At the time, both Richard and Patricia were earning approximately the same annual income. They each contributed to their employer's 401(k) plans. They chose Richard's health insurance plan rather than Patricia's because it included dental coverage. Patrick was in a child care program five full days per week, which he really enjoyed. Richard and Patricia's mutual lifetime goal was to have two or three children and both continue with their careers.

Their total assets including their home are $457,000, and total liabilities from their mortgage and automobile loans are $195,000, resulting in their net worth of $262,000. Richard has a total of $350,000 in life insurance coverage; this includes his group life insurance from his employer for $150,000 plus a personal term life insurance policy for $200,000. Patricia has a total of $250,000 in life insurance coverage, which includes $150,000 of group life insurance from her employer plus a personal term life insurance policy for $100,000.

Their primary concern in having these amounts of life insurance was to pay off the mortgage and have some extra savings to help with the living expenses. Because Patricia's salary was not needed to meet their monthly expenses, they were able to save most of her monthly income. They paid the full balance due on their credit card bill each month. Since they have been married, they have saved enough money over the 4-year period to put a 10% down payment on the purchase of their first home. Although the bank was willing to give them a much larger mortgage than they applied for, they decided to make sure that their monthly mortgage payment was going to be less than or equal to 20% of their monthly gross income.

They were taken by surprise when Joseph was born with Down syndrome. After extensive tests to determine whether Joseph had any health issues, it was determined that he was a healthy child. Patricia took a 6-month leave of absence. They found a very caring home daycare person for Joseph when Patricia returned to work. After a few months, Patricia found it very difficult to balance her professional life with her family life. Because of this, they decided together that it would be best for the family if Patricia stayed at home for a while until the children began school.

Richard recently received an increase in his salary. Previously, Richard's income alone was sufficient to meet the cash-flow needs of the family. Child care costs would be reduced because Patrick could begin attending preschool part time and Joseph could be at home with Patricia. Because other expenses did not increase as much as his salary, Richard's raise could be earmarked towards saving for future family goals. They want to do what is necessary to achieve their financial goals and wanted to know how their decision for Patricia to stay at home would affect them financially. They also wanted to know what they should be doing differently to provide for Joseph's special needs.

Goals and Objectives They developed primary goals, including the following

1. *Cash management:* Maintain an emergency cash cushion of 3 to 6 months of expenses.

2. *College funding:* Have adequate resources available to enable Patrick to attend the college of his choice.

3. *Joseph's financial independence:* Have adequate resources available to supplement Joseph's needs and maximize eligibility for government benefits.

4. *Retirement:* Have the financial option for Richard to retire at age 68 with a retirement income equal to 80% of their current gross income.

5. *Family protection at death or disability:* In the event of the premature death or disability of either parent, the plan is

   To enable the surviving spouse and family to continue to live in the family's present home debt free

   To maintain the lifestyle to which they have grown accustomed

   To allow Patricia the financial option to continue to stay at home with the children

   To have funds available for Patrick's college

   To provide for Joseph's long-term security

   To provide for financial independence at retirement for the surviving spouse

Family Timeline of Goals The Brown family timeline (Figure 7) shows the unique needs of their family's special needs planning timeline and how the needs of the parents and the children are incorporated with the planning pressure points. Even though the needs have been placed along a timeline, they may have to make adjustments periodically, as income, expenses, and goals change.

Family and Support Factors Both Patricia and Richard have large families that live near their home. Patricia's mother helped to care for Patrick when Patricia worked longer hours, but was not certain that she could handle both children after Joseph was born. Patricia has a married sister who is a special education teacher with two young children. Richard has a sister who is divorced with a 2-year-old child. Richard's sister is also close to Joseph and Patricia.

Brown Family Timeline

		2007	2009	2022	2024	2026	2028	2035	2046	2063
Parents' ages	Patricia:	28	30	43	45	47	49	56	67	84
	Richard:	29	31	44	46	48	50	57 (mortgage paid)	68 (retirement)	85 (death of parent)
Children's ages	*Joseph:*	*1* (EI)	*3* (public school)	*16* (transition)	*18* (SSI eligibility, guardianship)	*20*	*22* (adult program begins)	*29* (residential option)	*40* (SSDI begins)	*57* (lifetime supplemental needs)
	Patrick:	3	5	18 (college begins)	22 (college ends)					

Figure 7. The Brown family timeline shows the Browns' planning pressure points, the dates associated with them, and each family member's age at that date. (*Note:* The italicized name, ages, and goals represent the individual with special needs.) (*Key:* EI = early intervention; SSI = Supplemental Security Income; SSDI = Social Security Disability Insurance.)

Richard has great flexibility with his work schedule. This allows him to be involved with his family's daily activities. The fact that Joseph was born healthy means that Richard has not had to take time off frequently for trips to the doctor or hospital.

Special Needs Planning Assessment

The Browns have a very strong family support network that has been incredibly supportive with Joseph. What they did not have was a strong network of other families with special needs, which was to be expected at first. They were referred by their pediatrician to EI services, and connected with several other families and provider agencies to build their support network.

Emotional Factors   Joseph's diagnosis soon after birth was a surprise. Both Richard and Patricia continue to adjust to the fact that their lives may bring challenges that they did not anticipate. In addition, Patricia expressed some concern that she was feeling isolated and missed the social interaction that she enjoyed from her work.

They are also concerned that Patrick and Joseph share as typical a sibling life together as possible. Because Joseph is still an infant, Patrick does not sense any difference between Joseph and his friend's younger brother. Their concern is what it will be like when greater differences in abilities begin to surface. They have considered having additional children, but have put this decision off for a bit.

They have always felt very confident about their financial decisions because they were always able to talk about money with their friends and family. In fact, they had a neighbor who was very successful and had children the same age. When he set up a 529 Plan for his son, the Browns did the same for Patrick. Now they are worried, because they do not know what they should be doing about saving for Joseph's future and are afraid to make any mistakes.

Special Needs Planning Assessment

Discussing their financial goals and concerns helped them to feel less anxiety over their decision to have Patricia stop working. We introduced the Browns to their local Down syndrome congress and their local chapter of The Arc. Connecting with other families and getting involved helped Patricia feel less isolated. She was able to have a play date for Joseph and Patrick together. They did attend one of the sibling support group activities with Patrick, and they hope to continue doing so. The more families they meet, the more comfortable they begin to feel.

Financial Factors   The original plan was for both Richard and Patricia to continue with their careers on a full-time basis. They now need to factor in the loss of income associated with Patricia's stopping work to be at home with the children. She would like to someday continue with her career plans, but is not sure at this point.

Richard and Patricia have been disciplined in their spending and always saved a portion of their pay. They have both historically contributed to their company's retirement plans on a pre-tax basis. Richard continues to fund his employer's retirement plan at the level needed to receive the employer's full matching contribution. They have minimal debt, other than their mortgage and only one auto loan. They have sufficient cash in their money market savings account for emergencies and a cash cushion.

Patricia lost her group life insurance coverage when she stopped working. The premiums on their term life insurance policies continue to increase each year. Richard's employer continues to provide long-term disability coverage, which provides for 60% of his gross pay in the event of his disability. His employer also provides the family's health insurance coverage.

Both Patricia and Richard are very goal oriented. It was frustrating for them not to be able to develop a plan of action for Joseph, as they did for their own retirement and for Patrick's college. It was important for them to realize that they have positioned themselves in such a way to be able to begin planning for Joseph's needs. As his needs and abilities develop over time, the planning strategies can be modified if necessary.

Special Needs Planning Assessment

Although Patricia and Richard were initially concerned about their ability to achieve their financial goals, overall they had a solid financial base and good saving habits upon which to build. They were able to meet their monthly expenses and to continue their savings for Patrick's college education and their own retirement. They were also able to begin saving

(continued)

(continued)

money in a joint account each month that they have earmarked for Joseph's long-term needs.

They transferred the beneficiary of Joseph's 529 Plan to Patrick's name. In order to avoid any penalties and tax implications, expenditures from the 529 Plan must be considered as a qualified expense (i.e., a payment for the beneficiary's higher education expenses). At this point, it is questionable whether Joseph will attend a qualifying institution for higher education. In the event that he is able to attend a qualifying institution, they will be able to change the beneficiary on Patrick's account to Joseph at that time.

Richard's current life insurance coverage was less than adequate to allow Patricia to stay at home until the children completed school. It was determined that they needed to have $950,000 of life insurance protection on Richard's life and $700,000 on Patricia's life. In addition to his group coverage, Richard purchased an additional $700,000 of life insurance. He purchased $500,000 of 20-year level term coverage, which provided protection to the family at least until Joseph was age 21. Because Patricia lost her group coverage when she stopped working, she needed to purchase a total of $700,000 of life insurance coverage. She purchased a $500,000 20-year level term policy. They were both able to replace their annual renewable term policies with policies that had level premium rates for 20 years.

In addition, Richard purchased a $250,000 universal life insurance policy and Patricia purchased a $200,000 universal life insurance policy. Because they had the ability to pay the higher premiums of the universal life insurance without compromising their other financial goals, they were able to purchase these permanent life insurance policies. Because of their relatively young ages and excellent health, they were able to get very low rates. When their 20-year level term policies expire, they will still have protection from their permanent life insurance policies to provide for their family, and ultimately for Joseph.

Legal Factors Richard and Patricia had prepared their estate plan when Patrick was born. They each had a will, a health care proxy, and a POA. They did not feel that the person they had selected as guardian in their wills would still be appropriate for Joseph as well. They had named each other as primary beneficiaries on their life insurance policies and retirement plans, and Patrick as the contingent beneficiary.

Special Needs Planning Assessment

The Browns met with the attorney who first drafted their wills and also helped with the closing on the purchase of their home. She suggested they meet with another attorney who is a specialist in the area of disability law, so that they could make appropriate provisions for Joseph.

After discussing their goals with Patricia's sister, she agreed to assume the responsibility of guardian for both of the boys in the event that Patricia and Richard both die. The new documents made provisions for the guardian to care for Patrick until he became an adult at age 18. They also provided for Joseph's lifetime guardianship needs if necessary.

They also drafted a children's trust that had special needs planning provisions to protect Joseph's eligibility for government benefits as well as provisions for Patrick's needs until he was financially responsible to make his own choices.

They changed the contingent beneficiary designations on their retirement plan accounts and their life insurance policies, to coordinate with their new estate plan, to be the children's trust. The primary beneficiary designations remain as each other. They began to complete their Letter of Intent.

Government Benefit Factors   Currently, because Richard and Patricia have assets greater than $2,000, the family does not qualify for government benefits under SSI or Medicaid. Because Joseph is under age 18, SSI eligibility is determined by the parents' assets. They did want to take care to maintain his eligibility for government benefits in the future.

Special Needs Planning Assessment

Their pediatrician has referred the Browns to EI, so they have begun receiving services for Joseph.

After researching supplemental health insurance, it was determined that it was not economically feasible for them to contribute to supplemental health insurance, as the premium was more expensive than any of Joseph's medical needs not covered by Richard's group health insurance policy provided by his employer.

They did not establish a 529 Plan or a UTMA account for Joseph. They instead established a joint account with both Richard and Patricia's names on it, and earmarked this for Joseph's future needs.

The Murphy Family: Gifting from Grandparents

Family and Financial Profile   Sophia and Ben are in their mid-30s and have three children. Ben Jr. is 8 years old, Sara is 5 years old, and Elizabeth is 3. Elizabeth was born with fairly significant developmental delays and medical issues. They still do not have a definitive diagnosis for her. Both Sophia and Ben were employed as teachers in the public school system until Elizabeth was born. Sophia now stays at home to care for the children.

Due to the loss of Sophia's income to the family, they do not have the ability to save for long-term goals. They are able to meet their monthly expenses without building credit card debt. They have a small amount of money in a savings account and CDs at the bank that they had saved before Sophia stopped working. They consider this sufficient to be their cash cushion in the event of an emergency or unexpected expenditure. They own their home with a manageable monthly mortgage payment. Overall, they live comfortably, but at the end of the month they do not have any extra cash to put towards savings. Their inability to save is one of their primary concerns. Although they finished EI, they are not yet familiar with the way their state works to provide long-term supports.

Ben's father, Mr. Murphy, is age 83, financially secure, and wants to help them out financially. He is a widower, and Ben is one of four children. Although his other daughters have promised to care for him if he needed long-term care assistance to prevent him from going to a nursing home, he is reluctant to intrude on their lives and plans to remain as independent as possible. He has enough money to pay for his care. With his estate planning attorney, he was advised to make annual gifts to his children and grandchildren to reduce his estate tax liability upon his death, because he did not do any estate tax planning prior to the death of his wife.

Goals and Objectives   They developed primary goals, including the following

1. *Cash management:* To find a way to reduce expenses and begin saving for long-term goals.

2. *College funding:* They would like to have some money set aside to help pay for Ben Jr. and Sara to attend college. Their goal is to pay for both of them to attend a public university as they each did.

3. *Elizabeth's financial independence:* They do not know enough about Elizabeth's long-term abilities and needs to be able to predict her financial needs with any certainty. Their overall objective, however, is that she will be able to be as independent as possible.

4. *Retirement:* Ben wants to be able to retire at age 62 and maintain their current lifestyle.

5. *Family protection at death or disability:* If either Ben or Sophia were to become disabled or die prematurely, they feel that it would be traumatic to the family. They want to make sure that if something were to happen to one of them, the family would not suffer financially.

Family Timeline of Goals   The Murphy family timeline (Figure 8) shows the unique needs of their family's special needs planning timeline and how the needs of the parents and the children are incorporated with the planning pressure points. As with the Brown family (and any family), they may have to make adjustments periodically, as income, expenses, and goals change.

Family and Support Factors   When Elizabeth was born, the Murphy family did not receive a great deal of support from their extended family. Ben's brothers and sisters who live nearby all have children of their own and little time to lend any extra help. Sophia's family lives out of state; her mother came to help for a few weeks when Elizabeth was born, but has not been able to help since then because of her own health issues. Because of her disabilities, Elizabeth requires a great deal of attention. Finding help with the children has not been easy.

Clearly, the Murphys do not have a strong family support network to turn to. Nor do they have a network of other families with similar issues, because they do not have a definitive diagnosis for Elizabeth and are not certain what agencies they should consult. Ben's father wants to help financially, but he is not sure how he can.

Because Ben is a teacher, he is home most afternoons before dinner and bedtime to help with the children. During the summers, he works as the director of a day camp to earn extra income.

Special Needs Planning Assessment

The Murphys should have become more assertive with their social worker contact from EI to connect them with any agencies that might provide respite hours. Because they do not have any family support network, there is the possibility that their family may be treated as a priority in the allocation of resources for respite and/or family support.

It is important to look at opportunities where Elizabeth may be included with typical children. Ben's camp appears to be a possible opportunity for that needed social interaction.

Murphy Family Timeline

	2007	2017	2020	2021	2022	2024	2025	2026	2029	2034	2056
Parents' ages											
Sophia:	35	45	48	49	50	52	53	54	57	62	84
Ben:	35	45	48	49	50	52	53	54 (mortgage paid)	57	62 (retirement)	84 (death of parent)
Children's ages											
Ben Jr.:	8	18 (college begins)		22 (college ends)							
Sara:	5		18 (college begins)			22 (college ends)					
Elizabeth:	*3 (public school)*		*16 (transition begins)*		*18 (SSI eligibility; guardianship)*		*21 (adult programs)*		*25 (residential options)*		*52 (lifetime supplemental needs)*

Figure 8. The Murphy family timeline shows the Murphys' planning pressure points, the dates associated with them, and each family member's age at that date. (*Note:* The italicized name, ages, and goals represent the individual with special needs.) (*Key:* SSI = Supplemental Security Income.)

118

Emotional Factors   Although there is no definitive diagnosis for Elizabeth, the Murphys are still hopeful that a diagnosis will be made. It is difficult for them to think about planning for Elizabeth's future because they are emotionally drained from dealing with the day-to-day medical issues related to her care. Even though they met many families at the EI program, they still felt isolated because all of the other families had a diagnosis for their child.

Special Needs Planning Assessment

The Murphys should not keep themselves isolated simply because there is no diagnosis for Elizabeth. They needed to connect with other families that are dealing with similar characteristics and issues that Elizabeth experiences. They were able to connect with other families through the hospital where Elizabeth receives her specialized care. This helped the whole family, because they found that other families from the hospital were dealing with many of the same issues and uncertainties.

Financial Factors   On the surface, because they are not saving money on a regular basis, it might appear that they will never achieve any of their financial goals. Because, however, the state teachers' retirement system provides a guaranteed lifetime income to Ben and Sophia, and their mortgage will be paid, they should feel comfortable about their long-term retirement needs. Ben's goal is to retire at the age that he will be eligible to receive the maximum level from his state teachers' retirement pension plan, age 62.

Although they are not currently able to save extra money, they have been diligent in making sure that their expenses are fixed and manageable. Historically, in their state, teachers' salaries have continually increased over time. Ben plans to continue to teach in the public school system until he retires. Although they no longer have Sophia's income, the combination of having low fixed expenses and Ben's increasing income puts them in a position to be able to begin saving.

They only have group insurance benefits from Ben's employer, which are very minimal. The health insurance coverage is paramount for their family's security, but it does not cover all of Elizabeth's needs. His group life insurance coverage only provides for a $5,000 death benefit. His long-term disability insurance coverage is tied into his pension benefits. Sophia does not have life insurance or disability insurance coverage. They have wanted to buy additional life insurance on Ben, but have not been able to find the extra money to pay for the premiums. They have not started any savings for Ben Jr.'s and Sara's college tuitions. They are very grateful that Ben's father is willing to help them financially, but they do not know how to best take him up on his offer.

Special Needs Planning Assessment

The Murphy family initially met with a life insurance agent who advised them to purchase term life insurance protection that insured just Ben. He also advised them to purchase a second-to-die life insurance policy, mainly because they could buy a large death benefit amount for a low premium. If Sophia were to die first, however, Ben would not be able to continue to work; if he did continue to work, he would have to hire someone to care for the children.

It is not recommended for the Murphys to purchase a second-to-die life insurance policy at this point in their lives. To collect the death benefit from this insurance policy, both Ben and Sophia would have to die. There would be, however, a significant financial hardship if either Sophia or Ben died. Therefore, they should each buy a life insurance policy covering their individual lives. To keep costs as low as possible, while buying an adequate amount, they should buy term life insurance now while they are healthy and relatively young. They can then convert some or all of this term coverage to a permanent policy, as their budget permits and as Elizabeth's long-term needs are defined.

We met with Mr. Murphy and his estate planning attorney to discuss gifting options. Before we could advise Ben and Sophia, it was important to know the dollar amount of each gift and whether he planned on giving on a regular basis to each grandchild. He was fairly certain that he would be able to make gifts on an annual basis, up to the maximum exclusion amount (currently $12,000 annually in 2007) for a number of years, without jeopardizing his own financial security.

The annual gifts to Ben Jr. and Sara were used to fund a 529 Plan account for each of them. They also kept aside a portion of the gift to help pay for summer camp and after-school activities that the family was not able to pay for from their income.

The annual gifts to Elizabeth helped to establish and fund a special needs trust for her. The trust was recommended because Ben's father has committed to make annual gifts for a number of years. If the gift was a one-time gift, it would not have been recommended to fund the trust; doing so would have created additional administrative duties and expenses that would outweigh the benefits of funding the trust today. A simpler recommendation for a one-time gift would have been to gift the money to Ben and Sophia directly to keep in a joint account earmarked for Elizabeth.

They used a portion of Elizabeth's gift to purchase supplemental health insurance for her from their state plan, to bridge the gap on uncovered medical expenses. This helped to decrease the Murphys' out-of-pocket expenses by allowing them to increase the co-payment amount on the family's health insurance, because the rest of the family was healthy and very rarely went to the doctor's.

The annual gifts to Ben were used to help build liquid savings in a joint bank account. A portion of the gift was used to pay for the premiums on the life insurance policies on both Ben and Sophia. Instead of purchasing all term life insurance today, the gift enabled them to add some permanent life insurance to the term insurance that they purchased and will maintain.

Legal Factors   Ben and Sophia have not made any wills or done any formal estate planning. They may feel better prepared to begin this process after the financial changes they have been able to make with the assistance of Ben's father.

Special Needs Planning Assessment

Ben and Sophia should meet with a qualified estate planning attorney who is familiar with disability laws in their state of residence. At the very least, they should each have a will, POA, and health care proxy. They should also establish provisions in their planning to protect Elizabeth's eligibility for government benefits. This involves creating a family trust that contains language to protect Elizabeth's eligibility for government benefits and provisions for Ben Jr. and Sara. They should also coordinate the beneficiary designations on their life insurance policies by designating the family trust as the contingent beneficiary. Because Ben Jr. and Sara are both very young, they split the assets equally between both children. The separate special needs trust that Mr. Murphy created and funded will help to provide for Elizabeth's supplemental needs while maintaining her eligibility for government benefits.

Government Benefit Factors   The Murphys had a fairly positive experience with EI services. They are not yet familiar with the way their state works to provide long-term supports. Nor do they know what Elizabeth will require at this time.

Special Needs Planning Assessment

Even though they are not able to think long term for Elizabeth, Ben and Sophia need to be mindful that they should begin their planning in such a way as to protect her eligibility for any and all government benefits. Basically, they should not save any money in her name. The special needs trust is one way that they can save to supplement what she does not receive in government benefits.

6

Planning for Stage II

CHILD'S AGE 3–15

GENERAL DESCRIPTION OF STAGE II

EI services end at your child's third birthday, as specified in Part B of IDEA'04. When your child is 2 years and 6 months old, EI typically makes a referral to the public school system if your child has a clear diagnosis and/or an established need for services. Along with this referral comes all of the testing and evaluations that have been done for your child to this point. The school district may request additional evaluations prior to finding your child eligible for public school special education services.

Assuming that your child is eligible, on or around his or her third birthday, special education services will be available through the public school system. This is the first major transition—or planning pressure point—that you will experience. The key difference is that the services will no longer be focused on the family (working from an IFSP). EI services are all about home-based supports and family-centered supports. The focus now will shift to the child and his or her IEP. Services up to this point have most likely been provided in your home and/or the community. After age 3, the bulk of the services are provided to the child in a classroom environment in a public school or in the least restrictive environment determined appropriate for the child.

Your role as a parent also changes somewhat at this point. You will no longer be participating at the same level as you did during EI. Where you were once encouraged to participate in your child's therapies and services, your participation is now defined by school and classroom policies and procedures. This is governed by the same law (IDEA), just a different part (Part C). Parents are still part of the process but may need to participate in different ways. Communicating effectively with the people providing for your child during the school day is essential in addressing any concerns you may have; you want to be certain to relieve your own anxiety concerning this change in order to make it a positive experience for you and your child. Knowing what your child's day is like will also help you to feel more connected and involved. Therefore, you need to be able to feel like you are getting all of the information that you need about your child's school day. Establishing an effective way to communicate with teachers should ease any anxiety surrounding this transition.

Now is a good time to begin your role as advocate for your child's educational rights. Connecting with other parents of children with special needs is most helpful in navigating your way through the system. You should check your local school for parent support groups and/or parent advisory councils. Typically, most states also have a parent information center to help train parents about the laws of public education services and to help them understand the rules and regulations. Knowing what your child is entitled to, and what he or she is eligible for, is essential to maximize your child's ability to make effective progress in school.

In many instances, you will be learning a whole new language. While your child is attending a new school and gaining a new experience, you may also feel as though you are gaining a new education. The terminology of IEP team meetings will be different from the previous terminology in EI team meetings.

If your child was diagnosed after the age of 3, you would not have received services from EI. If you missed EI services for any reason, your child will now be in the public school system, and you will become familiar with the necessary issues. Of course you should listen and pay attention to your own instincts as the parent, because you know your child best. Follow through on your instincts, addressing all of your concerns and trusting yourself to recognize what your child needs. The sooner you define your expectations for your child's education, the more opportunities you can create for him or her.

Over the years you will be introduced to a whole new world of local, state, and federal agencies that provide supports and services to children and adults with disabilities. As you become more aware of your child's abilities, you may find that you redirect your focus towards seeking out those opportunities that help to build his or her skills towards independence.

· · ·   **Special Needs Planning Story**   · · ·

When James moved from EI services to the public school system, it felt like we had moved from a cruise ship to a dinghy. We had so appreciated the services coming to our home and the family-centered approach of EI. Our opinions, schedules, and plans for James mattered.

When he entered the school system, our experience was very different. The IEP team immediately directed us to a segregated classroom for James. We knew that he belonged with his typical peers. We needed the teachers to support us in our vision for James. What we always tried to do with James was to surround him with people who thought he had limitless potential. If they looked at only his diagnosis, they would deny him of opportunities we thought he should have. We had to work to create a team of "believers."

We continue to have to search out believers and people who can journey with us and imagine the possibilities. James continues to surprise us and remind us that his potential is limitless.

• • •   —Susan, James's mother   • • •

UNIQUE PLANNING REQUIREMENTS FOR STAGE II

First see the core planning points outlined in Chapter 2.

- Learn as much as possible about your child's diagnosis.

- Build and maintain relationships with physicians, schools, therapists, teachers, provider agencies, and your neighborhood community.

- Get to know who your local officials, legislators, representatives, and senators are and how to contact them. Investigate how programs are funded.

- Register with your local police and fire departments, and let them know you have a child with special needs living in your home. Obtain and complete a child's identification kit, and include a current picture.

- Get to know your state's laws on public education; make sure you have a clear understanding of your child's entitlements and your rights and responsibilities as the parent.

- Check your local school and provider agencies for parent support groups, educational workshops, and/or parent advisory councils.

- Make sure that your budget includes family vacations, evenings out, time away, and activities that you enjoy.

- Review your current financial and estate plan at least every 3 to 5 years, as well as any time your situation changes.

FAMILY AND SUPPORT FACTORS

At this stage, you may need to work a bit harder to communicate to others that your child, even with special needs, is beautiful and valued. You may find that you are spending an incredible amount of time to understand and educate yourself about your child's behavior and/or diagnosis. You may even find that you lose touch with other friends or people with whom you were once close. Your definition of a friend may become more solidified. It is possible you may seek support from different people now more than you did before. In some cases, parents find it difficult to communicate with close relatives, including grandparents, aunts, and uncles.

- Can you identify family members, friends, or neighbors that appreciate and love your child and family the way they are? Are there individuals that you anticipate being an integral part of your child's life and who want to help? Find ways to encourage your family and friends to build a relationship with your child; then give them the opportunity, time, and space to do so. Share successes and milestones, no matter when they occur. These efforts will help to create a circle of support. Some of the individuals who are concerned and involved now may be potential caregivers and/or guardians in the future.

- Do the people in your neighborhood and community understand the unique behaviors of your child? Be clear with others about what your child's needs are, including safety issues. Also be clear about what they can and cannot expect based on your child's abilities. Explain how your child communicates his or her needs, and how others can respond.

- Are grandparents or relatives interested in helping with the day-to-day activities of your family? Are they able to treat all of your children equally or fairly? It is important for you to communicate to others what is most helpful to you. If they do not know what your needs are, they will not be able to help.

EMOTIONAL FACTORS

In many instances, other families could not imagine having a child with a disability. They might not even imagine that your child could be in the same classroom as their child. In spite of other's opinions, you can continue to have a positive vision for your child's future. This will help to provide a basis on which to build and to plan.

Special Needs Planning Story

When one mother told me that she did not want her child sitting next to my child in the classroom, we wrote a letter to the entire class. Our intention was to share our basic beliefs that what we wanted for Travis was also what they wanted for their children, and that he wasn't so different. We wanted him to be a contributing member of society, to be a good citizen, and to have friends. We explained to them a little bit about autism spectrum disorder, with the hope that they would accept and understand Travis as their children had done so naturally. I let the other parents know that if they had any questions, they could find me at the playground.

· · ·   —Travis's mother   · · ·

Your life circumstances are what they are. Parenting a child with disabilities has all the potential of being a wonderful experience, especially if you develop a support network. Your problem-solving abilities will surprise you in overcoming various obstacles and challenges. Parenting a child with or without disabilities can sometimes be a little embarrassing, always a bit humbling, but ultimately a triumph.

Parents of children with disabilities can feel isolated at times, imagining that no one could possibly feel or understand some of the issues that go on in your home. For example, changing diapers on a 9-year-old may be very natural for you, but the idea may be startling to another parent. Parents of children with disabilities often experience stages of grief, sadness, and anger. Moving through these stages takes courage. You will soon find that you simply will do what needs to be done for your child without even stopping to think about it. Toilet training at age 10 might be a significant milestone for your entire family. If it is, be certain to celebrate it.

- Are you tending to the needs of yourself, your spouse, and your entire family? Are you receiving professional support when needed? Keeping a healthy family requires that everyone appreciate and support each other, addressing the needs of the mother, the father, and the other children. Reinforce the idea that everyone in the family matters, including their opinions, their accomplishments, and their support.

- Has one spouse been required to stay at home? For that spouse, realizing that family responsibilities overshadow every other aspect of life often may take some time to accept. The loss of a job can also create a loss of social network, income, and purpose. Finding a balance and regaining a sense of self may take time and effort. The arrival of a child with significant disabilities can bring many changes, but it does not mean that life cannot be fun and worthwhile. We encourage you to recapture the things that are enjoyable and make time for them.

FINANCIAL FACTORS

At some point during Stage II (ages 3–15), most families will have a specific diagnosis for their child. More than likely, they will also have a better sense of his or her abilities for the future. The primary focus during this stage, however, is to maximize the entitlements of public education services. This could require significant effort on your part each year, upon review of your child's IEP; your continued efforts in advocacy are paramount during this stage.

- Do you need to have the assistance of a special education advocate and/or an attorney to help obtain an appropriate education in the least restrictive environment for your child? If this is the case, you should be willing to spend the money to hire such a professional. It may seem like a lot of money to hire someone, but this is well worth the investment. An appropriate education can maximize your child's abilities and potential for independence. Having a comprehensive education that builds life skills and helps to develop relationships in the community will provide valuable opportunities. The more independent your child can become, the less costly it will be for you to financially supplement his or her lifetime needs.

- Are you losing time at work to tend to your child's needs, medical appointments, evaluations, and meetings? If both parents are employed outside of the home, you should carefully review your income and expenses to determine whether it is economically feasible for one parent to stop working. There are many instances in which, after reviewing the income and expenses of the family, it has proven to be economically beneficial for one parent to stay at home. If one parent needs to stop working, consider what other employer-sponsored benefits would be lost, such as contributions to retirement plans, health insurance, disability insurance, and other employee benefits.

- Do you find that you are volunteering your time to help other families understand the "system" and advocate for their child's entitlements? Many parents find a way to earn additional income by contracting with a local provider agency as a paid advocate or family support person.

· · ·   **Special Needs Planning Story**   · · ·

After my son was diagnosed with autism, and after years of struggling with the school for the most appropriate educational environment for him, I was very frustrated because I was getting nowhere. My husband and I had many long discussions and shared the same frustrations. We finally determined that we were in a financial position that would allow me to quit my medical practice and devote my time and talents to our son's education. After spending approximately a year researching various education options for children with autism, we decided to start our own school. I was able to involve several other families that were in the same position as our family. We combined our expertise and were eventually able to obtain a grant to develop a school that met the needs of our children. We now have state accreditation and are currently exploring residential options as our children get older.

· · ·   —Jeffrey's mother   · · ·

- Have you begun a savings and investment plan for your child's future needs, as well as college funding for other children and your own retirement? One of the most important financial principals enabling you to develop wealth is the power of compounding interest. By beginning to save money early, regardless of the amount, you can accumulate more wealth over time instead of waiting to begin saving money at a later date. Figure 9 illustrates the impact of this concept.

- Are you reluctant to save money because you are unsure of the amount of money that you will ultimately need for your child's care and your

Save Now versus Save Later

Save $3,000 per year for 30 years   **Save $9,000 per year for 15 years**

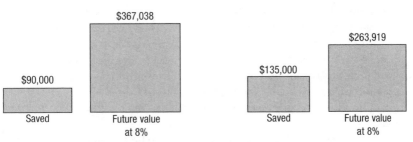

Figure 9. The above illustrates the time value of compounding interest over time. The sooner you begin to save, the less money you will have to save over time. This is a hypothetical example and is not representative of any specific situation. Your results will vary.

family's goals? It is not uncommon for families to be uncertain at this point in determining where and how they should save their money. It is most important that you begin to save money on a regular basis, either through payroll deduction or systematic savings from your checking account. Having a joint savings and investment account between both spouses will provide the most flexibility to your plan.

- Are you increasing your amount of debt through credit cards, mortgages, home equity loans, or 401(k) loans? If so, you need to revisit your cash flow and spending patterns and make immediate changes. Review the interest rates being charged on your credit cards and transfer balances to lower rate cards, being certain to understand the terms of any credit card charges and "teaser" rates. Review any adjustable rates on your mortgages, and the terms and conditions under which they will increase—try to lock in fixed rates when appropriate. If you have a loan against your company's 401(k) plan, it is important to pay this off as soon as possible. If your employment by that company should end, you would be required to pay off such a loan immediately.

- As your child grows older, it is also likely that you are maturing in the workforce and in your career. This is a key point where you should reevaluate the planning strategies that you implemented in earlier years. If you have had increases in your pay, you should make a point to increase your savings amounts. You should be maximizing contributions to all eligible retirement plan accounts. If your family has become accustomed to a more expensive lifestyle, you should reevaluate the amount of life and disability insurance coverage amounts. In addition, you should consider the type of life insurance protection that you have and be sure to have some permanent life insurance coverage.

Special Needs Planning Pointer

If you initially purchased all-term life insurance, you may now need to include some additional permanent life insurance coverage. Permanent life insurance protection is important for two reasons: 1) Your health may change in later years, which may prevent you from purchasing more life insurance or prevent you from renewing level term insurance after the guaranteed period is over; and 2) your child with disabilities may need a guaranteed source of money when he or she gets older and you are no longer alive.

If your health status has changed since you first purchased your term life insurance policy (or policies), and buying additional permanent insurance is prohibitive (either due to costs or insurability risk), you may be able to convert a portion of your present term life insurance policy to a permanent life insurance policy. You should check with your insurance agent and/or your life insurance company, to determine what conversion options are available to you.

LEGAL FACTORS

In a perfect world, you would have already taken the time to have the necessary legal papers in place to provide legal guidance and structure in the event that either or both parents were to die prematurely. Because managing your day-to-day life is extremely time consuming, however, it is understandable that some families may not have carved out the time to take these simple but necessary steps to protect themselves and their families. A good question to ask yourself is, if you had died last night, would you want someone else to relearn all that you go through daily, but without any guidance or protection? There may be many friends and/or family members who have promised you that they would take care of your family if something were to happen to you. Unless you have the proper legal documents in place, they will not have the authority to do anything for your child. The court will decide your child's guardian and place of residence, as well as the distribution of your assets. These facts should be motivation enough for you to contact a disability law attorney today and make an appointment.

- Are grandparents or relatives interested in helping with the financial security of your child? Do they have intentions of transferring their wealth to your children to minimize estate taxes or for other reasons? Take care that they do not leave a direct inheritance to your child with special needs. They should direct their inheritance to a properly executed special needs trust, which will protect your child's eligibility for government benefits in the future.

- Have other individuals established savings accounts or trusts in your child's name? If so, this is the time to review the options to spend down those assets and/or to transfer them to a payback trust (see Chapter 9 for more information on this and other types of trusts).

- In the event of a divorce, have you clearly defined the need for lifetime financial support? Is the language used for child support appropriate to protect his or her eligibility for government benefits? In many instances, both parents will need to contribute to the lifetime financial needs of the child. Because of this, the typical child support should not end at the child's age of majority or when the child completes school. In addition, you should be very clear concerning the definition of child support in your divorce agreement, because the receipt of such benefits can potentially jeopardize the child's eligibility for government benefits upon turning 18.

- As a divorced or single parent, have you coordinated your estate plan with your child's other parent? You should communicate how each parent plans to provide for the child with disabilities upon death. The use of a special needs trust (see Chapter 9) along with life insurance should be used to protect the lifetime supplemental and support needs of the child.

GOVERNMENT BENEFIT FACTORS

If your child qualifies for special education services, he or she is guaranteed by law to receive those services. Your role is to be your child's advocate to maximize those entitlements on his or her behalf through the IEP process. Your personal planning should also include protecting his or her future eligibility for government benefits before turning age 18.

- Do you have a good understanding of your child's entitlements for education? Knowing your rights and responsibilities as a parent is paramount at this stage. Contact your state's department of education to get a clear understanding of this information and to keep up with any changes.

- Have you explored the most appropriate options available to help meet your child's needs, including Medicaid services through TEFRA? This waiver may allow your child to receive Medicaid services, while still living at home with the family, without counting parents' income or resources. States can decide whether they want to offer TEFRA. See the Family Resource Guide available at http://www.thearc.org/familyguide.

CASE EXAMPLES FOR STAGE II

The Stein Family: Financial Independence and Legal Settlements

Family and Financial Profile Harry (age 50) and Sally (age 48) have two children: Mark (age 17) and Joanna (age 14). The family is awaiting a financial settlement from a lawsuit as a result of a head injury to Joanna. Because of her injury, it is anticipated that she will never be able to live independently. In preparation for the case, a life plan was developed as part of the litigation process. Initially, the purpose of the life plan was to identify all of the potential lifetime expenses required to care for Joanna and support her needs, which were a result of the head injury. This information was used to create the financial basis to determine the dollar amount of the settlement. The proceeds (of $1,200,000) from the settlement will be paid to a special needs trust, with Joanna as the primary beneficiary (see Chapter 9 for additional information about trusts).

Harry's successful career as a director of sales and marketing has allowed the family to be financially secure. His job does require that he travel throughout the United States on a regular basis. His annual base salary is approximately $200,000, with additional bonuses of up to $100,000 per year. His employer benefits are very generous, including covered family health insurance, short- and long-term disability insurance (66% of his base salary with a monthly maximum of $5,000), life insurance of 2 times his base salary, and a flexible spending plan for medical expenses. In addition, his employer provides an employee stock option plan and a stock purchase plan. If he were able to exercise all of his stock options today, the current market value would be approximately $750,000. His stock purchase plan has a current market value of approximately $250,000. His employer provides matching contributions to his 401(k) plan, which has an approximate market value of $300,000. Harry has always maximized contributions to his employer-sponsored retirement plans.

Because of Joanna's head injury, Sally had to leave her full-time position as a college professor. She hopes to return to teaching, at least on a part-time basis, once they are able to identify adequate supports to help care for Joanna. She had always maximized her contributions to her 403(b) retirement savings account, which has a current market value of approximately $90,000. She lost her group life insurance and disability insurance benefits when she quit. She does not have any personal insurance policies.

When Mark was born, they made their wills to name a guardian for him. The beneficiary designations on their retirement plan assets name each other as primary beneficiary, and the children equally as the contingent beneficiaries.

Mark is a good student and athlete, and he has a very active social life. He will begin his freshman year at a private college next year. He received a small academic scholarship from the college. The family had originally anticipated that Mark would attend the university where Sally taught, because tuition is free to children of certain full-time faculty members. Once Sally left, they were no longer eligible for this benefit. His college tuition will cost approximately $30,000 per year.

Joanna was 7 years old when she had the accident that resulted in her head injury. She attends an integrated program at her local public school. Her parents plan on her remaining in the same school system until she graduates at age 22. Her doctors believe that Joanna should have a normal life expectancy. Her medical and support needs, however, are likely to increase as she gets older. The family pays privately for an occupational therapist, as well as for help when Joanna is home. As she is getting older, it is becoming more difficult for her to maneuver her way around the house safely.

Their total assets, including their home, are approximately $1,825,000. The estimated market value of their home is $650,000. Their mortgage has a balance of $250,000, which is their only debt. In addition to Harry's stock options and stock purchase plans, they have liquid savings of approximately $35,000. In addition, they have a 529 Plan for both children, with Mark's balance at approximately $35,000 and Joanna's at approximately $25,000.

Goals and Objectives Their primary goals include

1. *Cash management:* To be able to supplement the expenses for Joanna's care that they are currently paying for out of the proceeds of the settlement.

2. *College funding:* To have adequate resources to pay for Mark's tuition out of their savings and Harry's monthly income.

3. *Joanna's financial independence:* In order for Joanna to live as independently as possible, they want to maximize her eligibility for any government benefits and select the settlement option that best meets Joanna's current and future financial needs.

4. *Retirement:* To have the financial option for Harry to retire from his present position at age 60, to pursue other career options until his full retirement at age 66 (the age at which he will begin receiving Social Security retirement income).

5. *Family protection at death or disability:* In the event of the premature death or disability of either parent

   To enable the surviving spouse and family to continue to live in the family's present home and maintain their current lifestyle

   To have enough money to pay for Mark's college tuition

   To provide for Harry or Sally's retirement security

   To make sure there is enough money available to meet Joanna's lifetime needs

Family Timeline of Goals The Stein family timeline (Figure 10) shows the unique needs of their family's special needs planning timeline and how the needs of the parents and the children are incorporated with the planning pressure points. Even though the needs have been placed

Stein Family Timeline

	2007	2008	2009	2011	2012	2015	2017	2019	2023	2039
Parents' ages										
Sally:	48	49	50	52 (works part time)	53	56	58	60 (retirement)	64	80
Harry:	50	51	52	54	55	58	60 (decreases work hours)	62	66 (retirement)	82 (death of parent)
Children's ages										
Mark:	17	18 (college begins)	19		22 (college ends)					
Joanna:	*14*	*15*	*16 (transition begins)*	*18 (SSI eligibility, guardianship)*	*19*	*22 (adult programs begin)*	*24 (residential options)*	*26*	*30 (SSDI begins)*	*46 (lifetime supplemental needs)*

Figure 10. The Stein family timeline shows the Steins' planning pressure points, the dates associated with them, and each family member's age at that date. (*Note*: The italicized name, ages, and goals represent the individual with special needs.) (*Key*: SSI = Supplemental Security Income; SSDI = Social Security Disability Insurance.)

along a timeline, they may have to make adjustments periodically, as income, goals, and needs change.

Family and Support Factors   Since Joanna's injury, the family has been through a great deal of changes and challenges. Joanna has continued to grow and develop as a teenager; however, her cognitive abilities have not kept pace. As a result, family members and friends have not been able to easily identify with her injury and have had a difficult time accepting it. Sleepovers and typical teenage activities with her friends and favorite cousins are no longer possible. Small changes in her routine always seem to present problems and create a great deal of stress for Joanna as well as those around her.

Mark has had a difficult time dealing with Joanna's injury, and does not have patience in dealing with her mood swings. Before the injury, they had a nice relationship as brother and sister and shared many of the same interests and circle of friends.

Mark now has his own group of friends and is very busy with his own school and social activities. He has very little interest in being with his sister. The family is concerned that they are growing apart as siblings. At this point, they are worried that if something were to happen to either parent, Mark would not be attentive to his sister. They also do not know whom else they could depend on to care for Joanna's needs.

Before Joanna's injury occurred, the family did not have a close relationship with anyone with a child with special needs. Nor did they have any understanding of how the service system worked. Sally has gained a great deal of insight through her own research and meetings with other parents of children with head injuries.

Special Needs Planning Assessment

When Mark turns age 18 next year, he would have the legal authority to act as successor caregiver, guardian, and/or trustee for Joanna in the event of Harry and Sally's deaths. They should not, however, give him any legal authority over her. They should support the sibling relationship as best they can. Family counseling may help bridge this gap.

Sally should complete the Letter of Intent, which would make all of Joanna's pertinent information available in one place for Harry and/or successor caregivers in the event of her premature death. This would be important because Harry travels often and is not aware of the details of managing Joanna's needs. Harry should try to arrange his schedule to attend IEP meetings with Sally so that he can become familiar with the system.

Emotional Factors   It is frustrating for Joanna to see her peers participating in activities that she can no longer participate in because of her injury. She continues to try to fit in with her peer group, but it is becoming increasingly difficult as they no longer share the same interests and activities as Joanna. As a result, she is becoming lonely, frustrated, and angry. She has difficulty expressing her emotions.

Sally and Harry are having difficulty adjusting to Joanna's limitations. They differ tremendously on how they treat Joanna regarding discipline. With Mark, they were often able to agree on parenting issues. Because Harry is frequently traveling for business, he finds it frustrating when he returns home because he is not successful in connecting with Joanna or Sally.

Because there are frequent changes in Joanna's abilities and personality, they are uncertain as to how to plan for her future. They do agree that they do not want Mark to be solely responsible for his sister.

Special Needs Planning Assessment

They have maximized Harry's medical insurance coverage for the family's mental health benefits. Because Joanna's behavioral issues contribute to her inability to focus on her school work, they should advocate for additional supports such as a behavior specialist to be included in her IEP.

Financial Factors   In addition to Harry's generous compensation package, the family has been successful in maintaining low expenses while maximizing savings. One of the cornerstones enabling them to reach this financial position was their insistence that their monthly mortgage payment and real estate taxes always remain at less than 20% of their monthly income.

Since Joanna's injury occurred, the family has lost Sally's income and has had increased expenses for Joanna's needs. They have been able to meet these expenses from Harry's income, but have jeopardized their ability to increase savings outside of the company-sponsored retirement and saving plans. They had hoped to save the full amount for Mark's tuition expenses prior to needing it.

They were presented with three different settlement options for Joanna's lawsuit. The first option was to receive a lifetime annual income based upon Joanna's life expectancy. This annual income would increase by 2% each year. The second option consisted of fixed monthly payments, with a lump-sum payment every 5 years. The monthly income remained the same, but the lump-sum payment increased by 3% compounded annually. The third option, which they chose, was to receive a lump-sum payment of $1,200,000 all at once today. Their overall concern was not just to meet Joanna's expenses for today's needs, which they are capable of paying from Harry's income, but to meet Joanna's financial needs when she becomes an adult. This lump-sum settlement option, if invested properly, would allow them the flexibility to meet Joanna's needs as they change and evolve over her lifetime.

The settlement proceeds were deposited directly into a special needs trust set up for Joanna. Having the funds go into a trust was a critical requirement, not only because she was a minor in age, but also to protect her eligibility for government benefits during her lifetime. The special needs trust contains payback provisions to the government upon her death, for reimbursement of benefits received from the government (see Chapter 9 on OBRA'93 Trusts).

Special Needs Planning Assessment

For retirement planning goals, Harry should continue to maximize contributions to his employer's 401(k) plan in order to receive their matching contributions. As cash flow permits, he should also elect to contribute the "catch-up" contribution amount that he is now eligible for at age 50. (Individuals who are age 50 or older may increase their contributions above the regular limits in IRAs and employer-sponsored retirement plans.)

Sally should consider rolling over the money that is currently in her old retirement plan (a 403[b] plan) to a personal IRA rollover account. She should be careful when completing the forms so that she will maintain the tax deferral status of the account. Moving the money to a self-directed IRA account will allow her greater control of her retirement savings.

Harry should consult with his financial planner and accountant to determine a strategy to address his stock options and stock purchase plan while minimizing tax implications. Although the stock option plan is a generous benefit for Harry, he must keep in mind that having so much money invested in his employer's stock creates additional risk of market value fluctuation.

Approximately 70% of the family wealth, excluding the home, is tied to Harry's employer through his stock purchase plan and his stock option plan. Because of this, it is recommended for Harry to implement the recommendations from his advisers to further diversify his stock portfolio.

Harry receives the basic group long-term disability insurance for which his company pays premiums on his behalf. The maximum monthly income amount is $5,000 before taxes. In the event of Harry's disability, the family would have financial difficulty maintaining their current lifestyle with this income. Harry should elect the long-term disability insurance buy-up option from his employer, which would allow him to increase his monthly income benefit amount. Because they will deduct the premiums from his paycheck on an after-tax basis, the income he would receive while disabled would not be taxable to him.

Sally does not have any long-term disability insurance coverage, because she does not have any earned income, insurance companies will not offer her disability income insurance. In the event of Sally's long-term disability, however, the family would have difficulty maintaining the household while caring for Sally and Joanna at home. If she needed to go to a long-term care facility, this too would create a financial hardship for the family. As cash flow permits, they should explore options of long-term care insurance for both Sally and Harry.

In the event of Harry's premature death, the family would suffer from financial hardship. The only protection on Harry is $400,000 of group term life insurance coverage. After researching the provisions of his employer stock option plan, Harry found that his $750,000 of stock option values would expire upon his death, and Sally would not receive the value of them. Harry's intent is to enable Sally to stay in their present home and provide for Mark's college expenses. To accomplish this, Harry should purchase an additional $1,000,000 of life insurance, including a combination of term coverage and permanent coverage.

In the event of Sally's premature death, Harry would need some additional income protection to continue his career. They should purchase $250,000 of permanent life insurance for Sally in order to cover the mortgage balance at least, as well for potential estate tax planning needs.

Prior to receiving the settlement, they were paying for Joanna's needs from Harry's income. The settlement proceeds in the special needs trust should be invested to meet current and future expenses for Joanna. Because she is only 14 years old, it is not possible to precisely define the amount of money necessary to pay for her residential and support needs for her lifetime. The plan is to hire an independent consultant when Joanna reaches age 20 to help the family determine the best living arrangement for her. The life plan developed as part of the legal process also provides some general guidance to the trustee(s) to help determine appropriate expenses and distributions of the trust assets. A prudent

(continued)

(continued)

investment plan would ensure that there is money available to meet her short-term, intermediate, and long-term needs.

The proceeds of the settlement were timely, because the portion of Harry's income that covered expenses for Joanna can now be used to help pay for Mark's college tuition in addition to his 529 Plan savings account. It is unlikely that Joanna will be attending college. Therefore, they should change the beneficiary on Joanna's 529 Plan to Mark to use for his tuition needs.

Special Needs Planning Pointer

Beneficiary designations on 529 Plans can be changed without tax implications. In the event that there is a 529 Plan set up for a child with special needs, the owner can change the beneficiary to another child or individual to use for qualifying higher education expenses.

Legal Factors   The Stein family's current estate plan consists of a will for each of them, naming a guardian for their minor children. Mark will soon be age 18 and no longer need a guardian. They are uncertain whether Joanna will require full guardianship at age 18. The individual named as guardian in their current will would not be an appropriate person for Joanna at this time, so they need to update this information. They do not have any health care proxies or POA in place.

One of their concerns is that Mark should not become the sole trustee, guardian, or caregiver of his sister in the future. They do want him to be involved with Joanna's life; however, at this point they are concerned that he may not be able to fulfill one of the more primary roles adequately.

Special Needs Planning Assessment

Harry and Sally should meet with an estate planning attorney who is also knowledgeable in disability law in their state. At the very least, they should prepare a will, a POA, and a health care proxy for each of them. In addition, they should include provisions to protect Joanna's eligibility for government benefits by incorporating a special needs trust into their estate plan for her share of their inheritance.

They need to name a new guardian for Joanna in the event that they should die prior to her turning 18. They should consider the need for guardianship, or most likely, a less restrictive alternative to guardianship at Joanna's age 18. (See section on guardianship and less restrictive alternatives in Chapter 4.)

Harry and Sally should name a corporate trustee as the primary trustee of Joanna's special needs trust. They could also include Mark as trust advisor. This would allow him to participate in his sister's life and support her needs without having the fiduciary responsibility of it all. He would be able to oversee the trustee.

They should also stipulate in their estate plan that Mark's share of the inheritance will be held in trust for him and distributed to him over a number of years rather than in one lump sum. A common practice is to allow trust money to be spent for a child's education and basic needs. Depending on the amount of the potential inheritance, additional distributions could be made at different ages and at different percentages based upon the parents' views of Mark's financial responsibility. The Steins have directed the trustees to distribute 20% of the trust account per year from the time Mark turns 25 until he turns 30.

For income tax purposes on retirement plan accounts, they should name the spouse as the primary beneficiary and Mark directly as the contingent beneficiary. This will enable him to take advantage of the tax laws that will allow him options to continue tax deferral on a portion of the retirement plan assets. Harry and Sally should rename the contingent beneficiaries listed on their life insurance polices, removing the designation of "children equally" and having Joanna's share directed to her special needs trust. They should discuss the option of utilizing an irrevocable life insurance trust with their attorney when purchasing additional life insurance, to remove the proceeds from their taxable estate (see the trusts section in Chapter 9).

Special Needs Planning Pointer

Confirm that the attorney with whom you are preparing your estate planning documents understands the different regulations within your state regarding payback provisions of special needs trusts. In some instances, it may be advisable to have two special needs trusts. The trust that was established to receive proceeds from a settlement would be a payback trust (i.e., one that requires, upon death of the beneficiary, that the government be paid back for benefits provided during the lifetime of the beneficiary). A trust that you establish to receive money from gifts and inheritances for your child's supplemental needs may not require payback provisions, depending upon your state of residence.

Government Benefit Factors Joanna currently receives services for her education entitlements, which will end when she turns age 22. The family has no idea at this point whether Joanna will be eligible for residential or day services upon turning 22. They have not yet been able to identify a state agency that will provide adult supports and services for Joanna. Because of the uncertainty of any government programs available for Joanna, Harry and Sally feel that they should preserve the proceeds from the settlement to provide for Joanna's lifetime needs when she turns 22.

Special Needs Planning Assessment

Harry and Sally should coordinate their financial and estate plans in a way that protects Joanna's eligibility for government benefits both during their lifetime and upon their death.

When Joanna turns 18, they should apply for SSI benefits for her. The primary benefit would not be the income but the services that she may be eligible to receive. They should also review the issues of guardianship or some alternative that they feel is most appropriate for her needs prior to her reaching age 18.

The Smith Family: Maximizing Government Benefits

Family and Financial Profile Bob (age 43) and Mary (age 45) have three children: Paul (age 15), Stacey (age 12), and Justin (age 11). Paul has an autism spectrum disorder but no significant medical concerns. Mary works part-time as an administrative assistant. Her flexible work schedule allows her to care for the needs of her family, which is most important to her. Bob has worked as an employee in a large company that has a good retirement plan and health insurance benefits.

They have limited assets other than owning their home. Mary has saved almost $20,000 in an IRA account. Bob has saved $50,000 in his company's 401(k) plan, in addition to the pension plan that his employer provides for him. Bob receives full family health insurance coverage, which covers adult dependents with disabilities. This coverage will continue to provide health insurance for Paul as long as Bob is living.

Their total assets including their home are $351,000. This includes the total value of their home of $275,000, plus retirement funds of $70,000, and a savings account of $6,000. Their liabilities are a mortgage of $75,000, car loans of $13,000, and credit card balances of $2,000, resulting in their net worth of $261,000.

Bob has total group life insurance of $150,000. This includes $75,000 paid for by his employer and $75,000 in supplemental group life insurance that Bob pays for directly from his paycheck. They feel that this is an adequate amount of insurance to enable Mary to pay off the mortgage and provide a little extra in the event that Bob were to die. Mary does not have any life insurance protection on her life. They have not yet made their wills.

After they pay their monthly bills and make the $65 weekly contribution to Bob's 401(k) plan, they potentially have $150 per month left over for savings. They are frustrated that they do not know where that extra money goes. If Mary were not able to work, it would be a financial hardship to the family, and Bob might need to find a second job to support the needs of the family.

Paul is doing fairly well at school, but they are uncertain about his abilities to live independently. They have mixed feelings, however, about whether they even want Paul to move away from their home when he gets older. Currently, they are not able to leave Paul home alone for extended amounts of time. Although they are not receiving respite or any other support services to help them on a regular basis, they both feel that, in the event of an emergency, Bob's brother and sisters who live nearby are available to help. There are very few resources and services available for children with autism in their state.

Goals and Objectives   Their primary goals include the following considerations:

1. *Cash management:* To be able to increase their monthly savings by $100.

2. *College funding:* College planning is not a high priority, because neither of them attended college. Stacey thinks she wants to be a hairstylist. They feel that Justin is still too young to know what he would like to do. If he does attend college, they would depend on financial aid. At this point they are not certain whether Paul will pursue any school or training beyond high school.

3. *Paul's financial independence:* They would like to have enough savings that if something were to happen to them, Paul could be safe. They are not sure what types of benefits or services Paul will receive when he completes school. They do want to maximize his eligibility for any government benefits.

4. *Retirement:* To have the financial option for Bob to retire at age 65, and be able to live off the income from his pension, Social Security, and retirement savings.

5. *Family protection at death or disability:* In the event of the premature death or disability of either parent, they want to enable the surviving spouse and family to continue to live in the family's present home. Upon the death of both parents, they want to make sure that Paul would be taken care of.

Family Timeline of Goals   The Smith family timeline (Figure 11) shows the unique needs of their family's special needs planning timeline and how the needs of the parents and the children are incorporated within the planning pressure points. Even though the needs have been placed along a timeline, they may have to make adjustments periodically, as income, goals, and needs change.

Family and Support Factors   There is a large extended community of family and friends that live near the Smiths. They all rally around Paul, and he seems comfortable with most of his cousins. His siblings are very patient with him, and they all seem to get along fine. Mary's sister has told her that she would take care of the children if Mary became unable to care for them herself.

Special Needs Planning Assessment

Although there are many family members who love Paul, Bob, and Mary should begin to think about the best person for each of the roles of successor caregiver, guardian, and/or trustee for Paul in the event of their death. Once they decide on who would be their successors, they should discuss the vision that they have for Paul with those individuals. It would also be helpful to complete the Letter of Intent, with all of Paul's pertinent information available in one place.

One gap they should consider addressing is to connect with other families that have children with an autism spectrum disorders. Because there are few services for individuals with autism spectrum disorders available in their state, advocacy could make a tremendous difference in improving options; if they located other families who have children with autism spectrum disorders, they might be able to form an advocacy group to try to begin to make some changes. Paul is currently age 15 and will soon begin his transition from the public school system. The special education administrators and staff should be a good resource to help them connect with other families, state agencies, and organizations that serve individuals with autism spectrum disorders. They should connect with the Autism Society of America at http://www.autism-society.org.

Emotional Factors   Both Bob and Mary have a strong marriage and family community. They feel they are at a good place emotionally regarding Paul's situation. Although Paul can be challenging at times, they have a lot of fun with him and see no urgency to having him move from the family home. If a residential placement does open up when he is older, however, they would be willing to give it a try if they thought it was best for Paul.

Smith Family Timeline

	2007	2008	2010	2013	2014	2024	2029	2046
Parents' ages								
Mary:	45	46	48	51	52	62	67	84
Bob:	43	44	46	49	50	60 (mortgage paid)	65 (retirement)	82 (death of parent)
Children's ages								
Paul:	15	16 *(transition begins)*	18 *(SSI eligibility and guardianship concerns)*	21	22 *(adult program begins)*	32	39 *(SSDI begins)*	54 *(lifetime supplemental needs)*
Stacey:	12	13	15	18 (high school ends)				
Justin:	11	12	14	17	18 (high school ends)			

Figure 11. The Smith family timeline shows the Smiths' planning pressure points, the dates associated with them, and each family member's age at that date. (*Note:* The italicized name, ages, and goals represent the individual with special needs.) (*Key:* SSI = Supplemental Security Income; SSDI = Social Security Disability Insurance.)

Special Needs Planning Assessment

Things seem to be going great. Bob and Mary should continue doing what they are doing to keep it that way.

Financial Factors   Bob and Mary have a fairly good handle on their expenses. They are frugal in their spending, and they are disciplined in adding to their retirement plans. They would like to save more, but this is not possible based upon their current income and expenses. Because their mortgage will be paid at Bob's retirement, unless something dramatic happens with Bob's job, they should be able to achieve their own retirement goals. Bob's pension and their diligence in adding to their retirement savings provide them with a level of security.

Special Needs Planning Assessment

Overall, the Smiths are on target to reach their retirement goal. They pay 18% interest on their credit card balances, or $360 per year on their $2,000 balance that they have had for several years. They should use $2,000 from their passbook savings account, which earns only 1% interest, to pay off their credit card loan. The savings they will gain in reduced interest payments alone could be used towards achieving other goals.

Bob receives group long-term disability insurance from his company. Mary does not have any. Although this is an important concern, they currently do not have the extra money available to purchase an individual long-term disability insurance policy on Mary. They should try to build up their savings account as much as possible as an emergency cash cushion.

They are financially vulnerable if either Mary or Bob dies prematurely. Although their extended family will gladly care for the children, they cannot count on the extended family to pay for Paul and the other children every day. Based upon their current expenses, it is recommended that they purchase a minimum of $250,000 in life insurance on Mary. This will enable Bob to hire someone to help with Paul and the children after school, while they are still at home and he continues to work. This will also help to replace the income lost from Mary's earnings to meet the family's expenses.

The current coverage of $150,000 on Bob is not adequate to meet the long-term needs of the family. They should also purchase an additional $500,000 life insurance policy on Bob. This will help to replace the income lost from Bob's earnings. This would also help pay for the family's health insurance coverage through Mary's employer.

Because they have limited surplus in their monthly budget, they should purchase term life insurance policies at this time. Term life insurance is more affordable for them to provide the protection they need for their family. It is recommended that they purchase at least 15-year level term on Mary and 20-year level term on Bob. Bob's 20-year coverage will provide an additional safety net until Bob's pension becomes available at his age 65. If Bob dies before he is eligible for his full pension, Mary's retirement security will be jeopardized. This insurance plan would allow the family to continue to live within their means.

Cash flow today limits the Smiths' ability to implement a comprehensive life insurance plan. When Paul begins to receive SSI at age 18, there will be some extra cash available. The monthly income from his SSI will help pay for Paul's fair share of expenses. This will enable them to afford to convert some of their term insurance to permanent life insurance, to fund Paul's long-term needs.

A major concern is that the family's retirement security is dependent upon Bob's pension income. They plan to elect the reduced income benefit option that will provide ongoing income to Mary upon the death of Bob. Upon Mary's death, however, the income to the family will stop. Therefore, the Smiths need to monitor and reassess their life insurance plan periodically.

Legal Factors   Currently, the Smiths have not done any of their estate planning. They need to make this part of their special needs planning a priority to ensure the family's quality of life if something were to happen to one or both of them.

Special Needs Planning Assessment

Bob and Mary should meet with an estate planning attorney who is also knowledgeable in disability law in their state. At the very least they should write a will, a POA, and a health care proxy for each of them. In addition, they should include provisions to protect Paul's eligibility for government benefits by incorporating a special needs trust into their estate plan. The wills can allow them to name a guardian for Paul and their other children.

They should not fund Paul's special needs trust today. The surviving spouse should be named as the primary beneficiary on their life insurance policies and retirement plans. The children's trust, which has provisions for Paul's special needs trust, should be named as the contingent beneficiaries.

(continued)

(continued)

Bob and Mary should consider the need for guardianship, or a less restrictive alternative to guardianship, at Paul's age 18. They should discuss guardianship options with their lawyer, and consider Paul's abilities based on feedback from his teachers and doctors.

They should share their plans and their vision with the future caregivers, guardians, and trustees that they have selected. This should include the guardians named for their other minor children as well as Paul. They should share their Letter of Intent with those individuals, and provide them with updated copies on a regular basis.

Government Benefit Factors   Paul currently receives services for his education entitlements, which will end when he turns 22. Paul is currently not eligible for SSI, because he is under age 18 and his parents' income and assets exceed the threshold for qualifications. They are uncertain about his eligibility and the availability of transportation, employment, and residential services after he turns 22. Most likely he will live at home with the family until they can no longer care for him, or until the ideal residential placement comes his way.

Special Needs Planning Assessment

The Smiths should work with Paul's IEP team to increase his life skills while still under education entitlement benefits. This should be the focus while transitioning to adult services. Because Paul's parents are not able to save for his future supplemental needs, they should make certain to protect his eligibility for any and all government benefits for which he may qualify. He does not have any savings in his name, and his parents should maintain the qualifying asset limits at all times (currently $2,000), both during their lifetime and upon their deaths.

At Paul's age 18, they should apply for his SSI. They should also put into place a guardianship, or some alternative that they feel is most appropriate based upon his abilities. They should attend transition workshops for parents as often as possible to learn more about the services and agencies available to Paul after he turns 22. They should prepare for the eligibility intake process to determine whether Paul would qualify for services. If available, they should engage in a person-centered planning program to help them identify a vision for Paul.

7

Planning for Stage III

Child's Age 16–21

GENERAL DESCRIPTION OF STAGE III

At age 16, your son or daughter is probably established in an appropriate school setting, and you have worked to help develop appropriate social opportunities. Now is the time to think ahead to the day your young adult turns 22, when the bus no longer arrives to take him or her to school. What do you want that day and the days after that to look like? What does your young adult child need to succeed? This is the stage where you should be focusing on the future and what you want that future to be.

Planning for Stage III primarily deals with your child's transition from adolescence to adult life. Up to this point you have been working to support your child's academic goals. The focus shifts now towards helping him or her to achieve the greatest possible level of independence. This will include building his or her skills for potential employment opportunities, leisure and recreational activities, independent living skills, and a full life. By age 18, your direction will include maximizing the education process to understand and maintain eligibility for government benefits and adult services.

In addition to planning for and moving into your child's adult services, you may also be planning for college education for your other children, and possibly for your child with disabilities. Researching and visiting potential schools will be an additional demand on your time. Your financial resources will be directed towards college tuition payments in addition to your daily family expenses. This should also be a period of transition to college planning and assessing your financial abilities to pay for college expenses.

During this transition stage, more than ever, you will need to maximize services obtained through the entitlement benefits of special education. You should take an assessment of what skills are necessary for an independent adult life and what skills need to be developed and/ or strengthened. It is important to explore various interests for employment, social, and recreational opportunities to help develop a sense of your child's likes and dislikes. Your son or daughter needs to be connected to the community and able to get around safely. Managing money, shopping, preparing meals, caring for health and hygiene, managing time, establishing relationships, and having fun are essential skills required to have a quality life.

You need to use every aspect of the education system to look at what your child requires to live as independently as possible once he or she turns 22 (or age 21 in some states). The goals in the IEP need to reflect the goals and the vision for your child's life after public education. The overall work of the IEP should be to support these goals and teach skills to help your child to achieve his or her independence and find joy in life.

Prior to your child reaching age 18, the age of majority, you need to have a clear understanding of his or her abilities to make sound decisions. The age of majority varies from state to state. Most states place the age of majority at 18 or 19. The age of majority, however, is 21 in Washington, D.C., and in Mississippi. The age of majority is the age at which an individual is considered an adult and responsible for his or her actions in the legal sense. At this point you will need to determine whether legal guardianship is necessary (see the sections on guardianship and less restrictive alternatives in Chapter 4).

You should understand what you need to do to apply for government benefits, including SSI and Medicaid, prior to your child reaching age 18. The most important planning strategy is to make certain that your child is financially eligible for these benefits by the time he or she is age 18. (That means he or she should have less than $2,000 of savings/investments in his or her name, including joint accounts and custodial accounts.)

You should get to know which, if any, state agency will provide adult services for your child. Get to know the appropriate agency or agencies, and understand how they administer funding for adult services and supports, including vocational, residential, and transportation. Learn about the eligibility process, what steps you will need to take, and when to pursue eligibility for services.

You, too, are transitioning, from being a parent who has gained confidence in understanding how the public school system and entitlement services are administered, to being a parent of a young adult entering a new arena of adult services. Your years of experience with IEPs, education, and health care may not directly apply to a new world of services and supports that are driven by a different set of criteria. The first point of entry into the system will occur primarily upon your child's turning 18, when you will encounter issues concerning guardianship, SSI, SSDI, ISPs, and a whole new "alphabet" of acronyms to learn; you will also need to master a system where entitlements to services are no longer mandated by law, but advocated for by families. Gaining a solid understanding of how your state's adult services and supports are funded and administered will help you to be the best advocate that you can be for your adult child. Learn as much as possible through workshops, family support programs, teachers, and other parents. Don't hesitate to ask questions and make use of the resources available!

This may also be the time to engage your child and his or her siblings in conversations about the future, although it may be a new experience for your family. Often a young adult has a clear vision of what he or she wants to do and where he or she wants to live or work. You will need to find ways to help your son or daughter with disabilities communicate his or her vision as well.

This is a major transition period for families, which is why we suggest you begin the process at your child's age 16. Starting early will help you to prepare for the planning pressure points at age 18 and again at age 21 or 22 (depending on your state). Many states have implemented transition plans and training to help families begin to understand the changes ahead. Seek out these educational services.

UNIQUE PLANNING STEPS FOR STAGE III

First see the core planning points outlined in Chapter 2.

- Your child's abilities may be more defined by this stage, and you may be able to have a glimpse of his or her future abilities as well.

- Now is the time to explore options and alternatives for when your child reaches the age of 21 or 22 (the age at which your state no longer provides public education services). This is called **transition planning,** and focuses on residential and vocational opportunities for your child when he or she reaches adulthood.

- Get involved in any person-centered planning programs that may be available to your family.

- Obtain eligibility information for any and all government agencies in your state that may potentially provide funding and services for your child after turning age 22.

- Interview and ultimately identify the most appropriate agency to provide residential and/or vocational services based on your child's abilities. Vocational services may also include a day program for your child to attend, again depending upon his or her abilities.

- If you feel that your child will not be able to make decisions on his her own behalf upon reaching age 18, you should consider the possibility of filing for guardianship (see the sections on guardianship and less restrictive alternatives in Chapter 4).

- Prepare your child to financially qualify for SSI and/or Medicaid benefits. This means that assets in his or her name, including custodial accounts, should be less than $2,000 (based on 2006 asset limits).

- In the event that your child's assets are in excess of $2,000 and he or she would not financially qualify for SSI and/or Medicaid, you should contact a CFP® professional and an attorney knowledgeable in government benefits eligibility, to discuss options of spending down the assets or transferring them to a special needs trust (OBRA'93 Payback Trust) prior to applying for benefits.

- Assess your overall financial situation to help determine your ability to achieve your financial goals, including college funding for other children, financial requirements to fund the supplemental needs of your child with disabilities, and your own retirement goals.

- Review your estate planning documents to be mindful of estate tax planning considerations, ownership and beneficiary designations of assets, retirement plans, and life insurance policies.

- Talk to your other children about your plans and your vision for your child with special needs; they may have input to share as well.

- Communicate with extended family members, including grandparents, aunts, uncles, and other friends and relatives, who may be interested in transferring wealth to you and your child. Tell them that you are in the process of planning for your child's future security.

- This is the ideal stage to begin planning for the future for your child. You still have time to make changes and to explore options if you have not done so already.

Special Needs Planning Pointer

At this stage, it is recommended that you consider hiring an independent consultant to work with you in identifying the supports and programs available to meet your child's needs. Although you will probably be assigned a service coordinator by a state agency to help in the transition process, you must keep in mind that this person can be responsible for serving a very large number of families. In addition, your state's service delivery system is complex and constantly changing. Your child may be eligible to receive services and supports by more than one government agency or program, which creates even more challenges. It is always best to get a second opinion and have a knowledgeable advocate working with you.

FAMILY AND SUPPORT FACTORS

By this stage, you probably have a good idea of your child's abilities. You may also have established a network of supports that includes other parents, teachers, respite providers, and friends. Even at this stage, there can still be day-to-day uncertainties that need to be addressed. Your energies still focus on educational supports, and perhaps respite services. If your child has significant medical needs, you may be working on finding qualified nurses to provide respite supports. This is also a time of transitioning supports from educational services to adult services.

- Have you begun to think about a vision for your child's future, when he or she is no longer in the public school system? It is a good idea to imagine the future—where do you see him or her living, working, or socializing each day?

- Have you participated in the person-centered planning process? This process will help you identify the friends and family members you can count on for your child's supports and who are willing to participate in his or her adult life.

- Have you connected with a family support agency that serves your child's disability? If not, you should do so at this point. Learning how to advocate for adult services will be important as you plan ahead.

- Have you shared your vision with your other children and family members? This is a good time to let others know what your thoughts are. They may be able to help build upon your vision.

- Have you listened to your other children and learned how they envision their involvement, if any, with their sibling with special needs? Too often parents take a strong lead in determining the direction of all of their children. This may not result in the healthiest situation for all family members. It would be unfortunate to suddenly find out that a son or daughter you were assuming would be involved in the life of your child with disabilities tells you that he or she has other intentions.

• • •   **Special Needs Planning Story**   • • •

My family is not the typical American family. I have a younger brother named James who has a disability that only one in one thousand people have. James has Down syndrome. This affects my family in many different ways. Having James as my brother impacts my behavior and my character.

There are so many positive things that come out of having a brother with Down syndrome. We have so many fun times together, such as batting practice with the whole Red Sox team! My brother and I have been to many sporting events, such as seeing the Bruins, Lowell Spinners, Loch Ness Monsters, Red Sox, and much more. Believe it or not, I have been on the news during the Red Sox game because James and I got to sit in the Dunkin Donuts Dugout. The most impressive thing was that my family got to be in the *USA TODAY* newspaper. My brother has such a huge impact on my life that he even decides which girl is a keeper. I have the ultimate test that I do with almost every girl. When I bring her over to my house for the first time, I introduce her to my brother. If she acts comfortable and fine, then I know that she is the right girl for me. If she acts weird and doesn't know what to do, I know that she is not my type. It means a lot to me when people treat my brother respectfully. Having a brother with Down syndrome is just like an action movie—always an adventure.

When I really think about having a brother with special needs, there are really no negative sides about it. He means so much to me. When I contemplate it, about the only negative thing is that he doesn't go to high school with me. I can't stop in to see him in class and hang out with him when I have had enough of all my teachers. He goes to a special school 25 miles away where he has a full day.

My brother James means so much to me that I would do anything in the world for him. We share so many good times; if you gave me 30 seconds, I could come up with at least 200 fun things we have done. I will never forget the day I got my driver's license. I had planned this day for as long as I can remember. I sat and waited for James' bus to pull into the driveway after coming home from taking my driver's test. I wanted James to be my first passenger, and our first experience together without our parents was to his favorite place, McDonalds.

James really is the nicest kid I know, and even though he can't talk, I understand everything. It's a brother-to-brother instinct. James has taught me a lot. He has made me more patient; I have to be in order to figure him out. He has made me more responsible; I take good care of him. James has taught me that it is not what's on the outside that matters most.

• • •   —Ben, James's brother   • • •

EMOTIONAL FACTORS

Since Stage III acknowledges the reality that your child will soon be leaving the public school system of entitlements. It can be quite overwhelming. Just as you have begun to navigate the maze to advocate effectively for your child's education, you will soon need to learn about a new maze of adult services. You are leaving a system of entitlements to enter into a system where most services are provided based upon available resources. This can be challenging and emotionally overwhelming. Many parents find that they are not able to envision their child living outside of their home. They may not, however, be able to continue to have their child with disabilities live with them into adulthood, for either physical or emotional reasons. To have an adult child with disabilities graduate from school to stay at home each day can create additional stresses and responsibilities.

- If your child does not have a day program to attend upon graduation, will you need to change your work schedule to stay home with him or her? Since day program services are not an entitlement, in some situations a child has no place to go each day like he or she did when in the school system. Your efforts to advocate during this transition phase should be to connect with businesses in the community and other vocational service providers.

- Have you thought about where your child will live when he or she is no longer in school? Are you emotionally able to continue having him or her remain at home with you, or are you looking forward to seeing your child move to a more independent residential setting?

- Remember that having your child at home with you may be a real pleasure for yourself, but it is important for you to provide opportunities for your child to gain independence. This may not happen immediately upon the child's turning age 22, but it will at some point be inevitable.

- Have you spoken to other parents with older children who have gone through this transition stage already? Seek out those you respect and with whom you share similar values. Also consult parents who have children with disabilities similar to those of your child.

FINANCIAL FACTORS

As your child leaves the school system, you are more than likely getting closer to your own retirement years. You may also have other children who are college bound. You may have elderly parents to look after, either financially or in other ways. You may also be inheriting wealth. There are various financial factors that need to be coordinated during this phase. These issues are best coordinated with a professional CFP® practitioner or other advisor who is knowledgeable in special needs planning. The most important financial factor in this stage is to make sure that your child is financially eligible for government benefits, such as SSI and Medicaid, before turning age 18.

- Have you assessed your financial situation and determined how you are positioned to achieve financial goals for yourself and for your family? Now is the time to be proactive, either by making changes to your spending and saving habits or to your portfolio. You might also adjust your personal financial goals to be more in line with your financial resources.

- If you have been saving money in your child's name, you should stop and redirect the savings to accounts registered in your own name. Another option is to begin to fund a special needs trust. Before doing so, see the section in Chapter 9 on funding a special needs trust.

- Review your life insurance policies to make sure that there is adequate protection in the event of a parent's premature death. Make sure that you have a base of permanent life insurance coverage that will not expire but instead last for your lifetime. This will be important in order to fund the supplemental needs of your child, or for estate tax planning purposes. As you get older, any changes in health could make life insurance more difficult to acquire and more expensive to purchase.

- Review the beneficiary designations on your life insurance policies and retirement plans. Although it is usually recommended to have your spouse listed as the primary beneficiary, you should review the contingent beneficiary. If your other children are older and independent, you may consider making changes so that a larger portion of the life insurance proceeds goes to a special needs trust for your child with disabilities.

- Review your disability income protection—long-term disability insurance and/or long-term care insurance are important financial considerations. See the section in Chapter 9 on risk management for more details.

LEGAL FACTORS

The key planning pressure point during this stage occurs at age 18. This is the age of majority from childhood to adulthood in most states. You will always be your child's parent, but legally you have no right to make decisions on his or her behalf without authority as legal guardian, a POA, or a health care proxy.

- Have you considered the possibility of obtaining a full guardianship for your child when he or she reaches the age of majority? In general, if a child with disabilities is not able to communicate his or her needs effectively, or if his or her cognitive ability impedes appropriate decision making, it makes sense to obtain full legal guardianship.

- Do you know the steps necessary to obtain a court-approved legal guardian for your child? Prior to obtaining a guardianship, you will be required to prove the need for guardianship to the court. This is done by providing evaluations and expert opinions from professionals, including doctors, teachers, and therapists, in addition to any specific evaluations mandated by your state. You may need the assistance of an attorney, either one you hire privately or one who is employed by a state agency. You should work with a professional who understands the issues of guardianship.

- Do you have a clear understanding of your role and responsibilities as a guardian? If not, you should seek advice from a disability law attorney or the probate court. Make sure to pass this information along to successor guardians.

- In the event of your death, have you identified who will be the successor guardian for your child? Often one or both parents will serve as a coguardian or successor guardian.

- Perhaps you named a guardian in your will for your minor children. Is this the same person that you would like to have as guardian for the lifetime of your adult child with disabilities? When was the last time you reviewed these decisions? If you have not revisited these decisions recently, you should do so and update your will with any revisions.

- If you do not feel that a full guardianship would be required for your adult child with disabilities, have you considered a less restrictive alternative, such as a medical guardianship, POA, or health care proxy (see the Guardianship section in Chapter 4 for more information)?

- Confirm that all of the professionals involved in your child's life, including medical doctors, service providers, educators, state agency workers, and others, know of your legal guardianship.

- Have you updated your Letter of Intent? Although it is not a legal document, it will help future caregivers and guardians have a clear understanding of your child's abilities, important information, and your vision for his or her future.

- If you have prepared a special needs trust, have you identified a trustee who could work along with the guardian that you have selected? These individuals also need to have a clear understanding of your vision and values for your child in the event that you are no longer able to be there for him or her.

- Is the trustee of your special needs trust still the most appropriate person, or should you consider an alternate such as a corporate trustee?

The individual you once intended to be the trustee may be more suitable to serve as a trust advisor to a corporate trustee (this could be a financial institution, bank, or law firm). A trust advisor can help provide direction to the trustee on how resources can be used, but does not have the fiduciary responsibilities and obligations of a trustee. Take care that the legal document provides a means to remove the corporate trustee if it has been determined that they has not been acting in the beneficiary's best interest.

GOVERNMENT BENEFIT FACTORS

The key planning issue at this stage is to maximize your child's eligibility to receive and maintain government benefits at age 18 and beyond. He or she will be eligible for SSI benefits at age 18. We can't stress often enough that you need to ensure that your son or daughter qualifies for benefits based upon disability and financial income and assets (i.e., by having no more than $2,000 in assets) before you apply for SSI. If he or she is eligible for SSI, then he or she will also be eligible for Medicaid services. These are two key components that can help provide for current and future needs for food, clothing, shelter, and health care.

- Have you made certain that your child will not be disqualified for government benefits because of assets in his or her name? Make certain that all savings bonds, custodial accounts, and potential inheritances are not placed in his or her name directly. If the total assets in his or her name exceed $2,000, eligibility for SSI benefits will be compromised. Prior to applying to the Social Security Administration, you should take an inventory of all of your child's savings and investment accounts, including those set up by relatives and friends.

- If the assets of the child exceed the $2,000 threshold, you should develop a strategy to spend down the assets or transfer them to a special needs trust with payback provisions (see Chapter 9 for more information on payback trust provisions).

- Have you discussed with other family members the importance of proper planning to protect your child's eligibility for government benefits today and in the future? You need to communicate to others that if they currently have savings for your child, or intend to leave an inheritance to your child, they should consult with your attorney to check that any gifts or inheritances are directed to a properly executed special needs trust.

- Is one parent disabled, retired, or deceased? If so, your child might be eligible to receive SSDI benefits under that parent's Social Security work record (see http://www.ssa.gov for details).

• Were you previously denied services or supports from a government agency? If so, find out why. Was it because your child did not meet eligibility requirements at the time? Perhaps he or she does now, or perhaps the eligibility requirements have changed. What can you do, if anything, to help with your child's eligibility? Inquire about your child's eligibility for the "Katie Beckett" Waiver in your state. This waiver may allow your child to receive Medicaid services, without counting parents' income or resources, to address his or her needs while still living at home with the family (see the Family Resource Guide available at http://www.thearc.org/familyguide, which is available by state).

Special Needs Planning Pointer

When you apply for SSI, if your child is living at home with you, you will be asked by the Social Security representative if your child will be sharing any of the household expenses. You should add up your total housing expenses to include a reasonable rent, utilities, food, clothing, medical expenses, and other miscellaneous expenses. Identifying the expenses that will be shared with your child will help to maximize his or her monthly benefit received from SSI.

CASE EXAMPLE FOR STAGE III

The Cooke Family: Planning as a Single Parent

Family and Financial Profile   Lisa is a widow (age 52) who has two children: Brian (age 20) and Alyssa (age 18). Brian is legally blind, very intelligent, and extremely independent. When Brian turned 20, he was able to graduate from high school. Alyssa is approaching her first year of college. Lisa works full time as a registered nurse and carries the family's medical insurance. Lisa's mother often helps with the children's expenses and has expressed an interest in helping to pay for some of their college educations.

When Lisa's husband, Roy, died suddenly 4 years ago at age 50, he had two life insurance policies with proceeds of $650,000: one group policy from his employer, and one that he purchased separately. He had $310,000 in retirement plan accounts that were rolled over into an IRA in Lisa's name as spousal beneficiary. Currently, Lisa has $50,000 in her personal savings account, in addition to a checking account with the life insurance proceeds. She also has approximately $55,000 in her company's retirement plan, to which she continues to contribute. The market value of her home is $480,000, with a $60,000 mortgage balance that will be paid off in 10 years. Brian, because he was disabled before the age of 22 when his father died, will continue to receive his father's SSDI benefits. Brian has a Uniform Transfer to Minors Account (UTMA) that his parents saved for him, which has $55,000. As a result, he is not eligible for SSI or Medicaid services.

Alyssa no longer receives survivor benefits since she turned age 18 and graduated from high school. She also has an UTMA account with $46,000 in it, which she plans to use for her college tuition expenses. Brian and Alyssa will both be entering their first year of college in the fall. Brian's tuition will be $18,000 per year, and Alyssa's will be $25,000 per year.

Roy's death left the family devastated, but financially secure, with savings, investments, and life insurance proceeds of approximately $1,065,000, excluding their home. As a result, they were not forced to make major changes to their lifestyle for financial reasons, but Lisa felt it was necessary to return to work full time. Her goal was to earn enough money to meet their current monthly expenses and to keep the inheritance for the financial security of the family's future needs.

After paying the monthly bills, Lisa is able to contribute to her employer-sponsored retirement plan, with matching contributions from her employer. She also has group long-term disability coverage equal to 60% of her salary, and life insurance of $50,000. In addition, she carries the family's health insurance. Lisa has not updated her estate plan since Roy's death. Her group life insurance and retirement plan beneficiary designations are directed to the children equally.

Goals and Objectives Lisa's primary goals for herself and her family are as follows:

1. *Cash management:* To save more towards her long-term retirement goals and future financial security.

2. *College funding:* To determine how Brian's IEP will help to support his college tuition expenses until he turns age 22. Also to use Brian's funds in his UTMA account for college expenses without jeopardizing his eligibility for Medicaid. Lisa does not want her children to have any college loans to repay upon graduation.

3. *Brian's financial independence:* To provide the supports that would allow Brian to live as independently as possible. Also to maximize Brian's eligibility for government benefits.

4. *Financial independence at retirement:* Lisa hopes to retire from full-time nursing at age 60.

5. *Family protection at death or disability:* In the event that Lisa dies prematurely, she would like the children to have the opportunity to continue to live in the family home if they wish. She would like to distribute her estate equally between Brian and Alyssa. In the event that Lisa requires care assistance as she ages, she would like to remain at home as long as possible without depleting her assets.

Family Timeline of Goals   The Cooke family timeline (Figure 12) shows the unique needs of their family's special needs planning timeline incorporating Lisa's goals with those of her children, being mindful of the planning pressure points. As with any family, they may have to make adjustments periodically, as income and needs change.

Family and Support Factors   Lisa's mother is quite supportive of her, both emotionally and financially. She has always been a help with the children, who have a very nice relationship with their grandmother. Lisa does not have any other brothers or sisters.

Brian plans to attend the same college as his close friend from high school, who is also legally blind. Together they have developed a nice network of supports and friends. He will continue to live at home and commute to college.

Alyssa will be going to college out of state, but will only be a 3-hour drive from home. She struggled with the idea of moving away to college, because she always wanted to be available for Brian. Although Lisa thought that this was very thoughtful of Alyssa, she encouraged Alyssa to live away from her family while at college. They both agreed that she would still be a part of her family's life even though she is away from home.

Special Needs Planning Assessment

Over the years, the family has developed a nice network of family and friends who are very supportive of Brian. Because he will be going to school locally, he will be able to maintain the friendships that he has developed. He has become increasingly independent over the years, and better able to seek out supports and resources as he needs them. Lisa does not have to be as involved in finding resources and supports for him. This is enabling Lisa to attend to her own personal needs.

Emotional Factors   Since Brian was born blind, the family has learned together how to encourage his abilities. As a result, Brian is a very independent 20-year-old with a great deal of self-confidence among his

Cooke Family Timeline

Parent's age	Lisa:	52	54	56	60 (retirement, mortgage paid)	84 (death of mother)
		2007	2009	2011	2015	2039
Children's ages	*Brian:*	*20 (transition to college)*	*22 (adult program begins)*	*24 (supplemental needs)*	*28*	*52 (lifetime supplemental needs)*
	Alyssa:	18 (college begins)	20	22 (college ends)		

Figure 12. The Cooke family timeline shows the Cooke's planning pressure points, the dates associated with them, and each family member's age at that date. (*Note:* The italicized name, ages, and goals represent the individual with special needs.)

friends and family. It has been very difficult for Brian to effectively communicate his abilities to others, however, and he gets frustrated when they only see his blindness rather than his abilities. At times this concern has left him very discouraged, especially when he had difficulty finding part-time jobs after school, because he had heard of so many other friends getting jobs easily.

Since Roy's sudden death, the family has continued to stay strong and to find support through one another. Lisa and Alyssa continue to be concerned about caring for Brian, but Brian continues to push them away in an effort to maintain his independence. Alyssa wants to be there for her brother even after her mother is gone, and has made that clear to both of them. Lisa is concerned that Alyssa will sacrifice too much of her own life for her brother's needs and does not want her to feel so much responsibility at such a young age.

Special Needs Planning Assessment

Brian should continue to grow as independently as possible, and seek job opportunities at his college, where they may be more accommodating to his needs. The family should try to maintain the open communication they share now even when Alyssa is away from home.

Financial Factors   Lisa feels that she is able to maintain the family's household expenses, including the mortgage payment, from her income. She has not had to use any of the proceeds from Roy's life insurance policies, and they remain in a checking account with the insurance companies. She intended to use some of these proceeds for college expenses rather than invest them in long-term investment vehicles.

Instead, Lisa's mother has offered to pay for the children's tuition expenses each year. She is willing to pay the balance due for each child if Lisa contributes $5,000 to each and/or if they receive scholarship money.

Special Needs Planning Assessment

Lisa is currently receiving survivor benefits based on Brian's disability and his living at home as a dependent adult with disabilities. She has been adding this money to his UTMA account rather than using it to meet the family's monthly expenses; she should consider using the survivor benefits to help make extra payments towards the principal on her mortgage. This will allow her to have her mortgage paid by her desired retirement age of 60, when Brian will be living independently. Lisa wants to be able

(continued)

(continued)

to supplement his needs from her income and savings to support his independence. To pay both a mortgage and a portion of Brian's expenses would create an excessive financial burden on Lisa's cash flow. When Brian is no longer living with her as her dependent, she will no longer receive Social Security benefits on his behalf. Neither will she be entitled to full Social Security survivor benefits until her retirement at age 66.

Lisa continues to negotiate with the school district to have them pay for Brian's tuition. They have agreed to pay for his transportation expenses. Therefore, she will have to pay for the college tuition expenses.

The children's grandmother should make the college tuition payments directly to the college rather than to the children or Lisa. Paying money directly to the college does not count towards the amount that she can gift each year without having to file a federal gift tax return to the IRS.

Lisa should use the money in Brian's UTMA account first to pay for his college expenses. Since the grandmother planned to pay for his tuition, she could instead help to fund a special needs trust with that money. When the UTMA funds are depleted, she could then make tuition payments directly to his college.

After analyzing Lisa's retirement goal of age 60, given her monthly expenses, including supplementing Brian's needs, it has been determined that Lisa should consider working until at least age 63. At age 63, she will be eligible for at least a portion of her Social Security benefit, or at age 66, she will be eligible for full retirement benefits.

Lisa should maximize her contributions to her employer's retirement plan. She should also include the catch-up amount that the IRS allows for individuals age 50 and older. Even if she cannot afford to have more money taken out of her pay to make the maximum contributions, she can use the money from her life insurance proceeds to make up the difference. Making maximum contributions will help to reduce her current income taxes and help her save towards retirement.

With the proceeds from Roy's life insurance policies, she should annually fund a Roth IRA. She should also reallocate those funds from the checking account to a more balanced allocation to help meet her long-term goals.

Lisa should purchase an individual long-term care insurance policy to help pay for any expenses that may be the result of an extended illness and/or disability. In the event of her death, Lisa's current assets plus her life insurance proceeds will provide for her children's financial security.

Legal Factors   Lisa has not updated her estate plan since Roy's death. All of her beneficiary designations are to the children equally. She does not want them to receive a lump sum of their inheritance, but to be able to receive various amounts of money at different ages. She is concerned that Alyssa should not be solely responsible for meeting all of Brian's needs, including his financial security. Since Lisa does not have any brothers or sisters, and Lisa's mother is aging, she does not have anyone else to name as a trustee for her children's inheritance.

Special Needs Planning Assessment

Lisa should meet with an estate planning attorney who is also knowledgeable in disability law in her state. At the very least, she should create a will, a POA, and a health care proxy. She should also help each of her children to have a POA and health care proxy written. This would be a less restrictive alternative to guardianship, especially for Brian.

In addition, instead of leaving Brian's inheritance outright to him, she should designate a special needs trust to receive his inheritance as part of her estate plan. This will help to protect Brian's eligibility for government benefits if and when they are needed. Because each state has different laws regarding the distribution of assets remaining at the death of the primary beneficiary of a special needs trust, it is important that she understands the laws of her state and how they might affect her goals.

Although the special needs trust may be funded to supplement government benefits, the trustee will have the authority to distribute income and assets to Brian even if he does not qualify or need assistance from government benefits. At the very least, it will provide a safety net for Brian's inheritance.

Lisa should name a corporate trustee as the primary trustee of Brian's special needs trust. Alyssa could be named as the trust advisor, which would allow Alyssa to still be involved in Brian's life without having the fiduciary responsibility of it all. It is important to clarify in the trust that Alyssa would be able to replace the named corporate trustee with another corporate trustee if she has concerns in the future.

Lisa should change her beneficiary designations on her retirement plan accounts and group life insurance policy to be coordinated with her revised estate plan.

Lisa needs to check that her mother's estate is set up so that any inheritance to Brian will not disqualify him for government benefits. Any share of her inheritance intended for him should be directed to his special needs trust. Her attorney could speak with her mother's attorney to discuss the proper planning techniques.

Government Benefit Factors Lisa was able to secure funding for Brian's transportation as part of his IEP until his age 22. Upon his turning 22, she is uncertain about which government benefits he would be eligible for. The state does have a commission for the blind and an employment assistance program. The college also has a career center that supports employment of individuals with various disabilities. The advantage to this particular college is that they continue to support their alumni.

Special Needs Planning Assessment

Lisa is very optimistic about Brian's chances of finding gainful employment and living independently. Her planning, however, should protect his eligibility for any and all potential government benefits in the event that his needs change in the future. If an individual is eligible for both SSI and SSDI benefits, the SSI benefit is reduced dollar for dollar by the SSDI received. In this case, the SSDI benefit would exceed the SSI benefit, and therefore Brian will only receive the SSDI benefit and Medicaid benefits. Even if Brian is gainfully employed, his income may qualify him to receive subsidized housing benefits.

8

Planning for Stage IV

CHILD'S AGE 22 AND BEYOND

. . .   **Thoughts from Cynthia**   . . .

It wasn't until my late twenties that I had the opportunity to join a sibling support group sponsored through the Greater Boston chapter of The Arc. I don't know how I heard about it or why I even decided to attend and commit myself to 12 weeks of talking about what it was like growing up with a brother with developmental disabilities. It certainly was not a topic that I discussed very openly at that point in my life.

I had been through various dates—with Ron always being the final verdict on whether I would continue to date the guy. If he treated Ron well and agreed to take him to Ron's favorite summer event, the Marshfield Fair, the relationship was good to go. With every relationship, I had to answer about Ron and who he was and who he would become. And it was always a daunting reality to speak about who would care for him after my parents were gone. I would subtly outline to the current boyfriend that if he were to get involved with me, he would have to get involved with Ron too, because I would be responsible for caring for Ron. I was the youngest—and the only girl—therefore, I was the future caregiver. I assumed that I would be living in my parents' house so Ron would not be disrupted. But I never allowed myself to think about my own needs.

Attending the sibling support group provided me with a completely new picture of what my options were—and what kind of life I could allow for myself. WOW! It was quite the eye-opener. For starters, I found other siblings like me struggling with the same issues that I had. And I found that there were solutions to residential options, estate planning options, social and recreation groups, even genetic testing for me! I found myself looking forward to the next Tuesday session. There was always an informative speaker or topic to discuss.

Shortly after that session, I was dating someone that my parents were not too happy about. All of the unspoken plans of me being Ron's future caregiver were now being challenged. We had to discuss them since they seemed to think that I might marry this guy (which I didn't) and he wasn't too keen about Ron. He wasn't one of the guys that agreed to take Ron to the Marshfield Fair. That said a lot. The plan at the time was simply understood that I would inherit Ron's share as a morally obligated gift to keep aside for whatever he needed. But the reality was that if I divorced, or I had financial difficulties, Ron's inheritance could potentially be jeopardized. We clearly needed to do something better for everyone. We met with an estate planning attorney that said he knew a lot about Medicaid planning and he said that was the same planning we had to do for Ron. He was only somewhat correct, it turned out, but we did not know this at the time. It was so painful to discuss these issues that we never had before. He wrote a trust for Ron's benefit. We then decided to fund the trust with life insurance on my father. To me, this made a lot of sense. The trust gave me the marching orders that I needed—essentially my parents could speak to me from the grave. It also helped to clarify their wishes for my brothers and me. The life insurance provided the financial resources for me, as trustee, to have available to supplement Ron's needs after my parents were gone. Now we had a safety net and means to provide for Ron's financial security. I suddenly felt relieved of a tremendous burden—it would not be a financial burden to care for Ron. Essentially, I could live my life the way I wanted and needed. No longer did I have to plan for Ron's needs alone.

. . .   . . .

When does planning for the future of our adult children begin? It begins on the day they are born, if not before. At this stage, all that planning comes to fruition.

GENERAL DESCRIPTION OF STAGE IV

When parents are faced with the future of a child with a disability, they pass through uncharted territory, often without a peer group to share experiences and without role models to offer examples through their successes and failures. At this age, an adult child without a disability offers strong indications to his or her parents, either by rejecting their guidance at a certain point, or by showing clear preferences concerning ways to be supported in future directions.

A child with a disability may offer similar cues when approaching adulthood. Due to a lifetime of caring, guiding, and advocating, however, parents may not be used to paying attention to those cues. Parents may be accustomed to being involved in a more direct way with their child with disabilities than they are with their other children. It is no surprise that one of the critical parts in planning for the future of a child with a disability requires the parents to examine their expectations, their readiness to let go, and their willingness and ability to listen to their child, both directly and indirectly. As a first step in this process, a parent must be ready to accept that the future starts now. A parent must define *now* as to the best time to get serious in order for adult planning to begin. Our recommendation is that this process begins as soon as possible. Preparation beginning in the early teen years allows a family to do the research and thinking necessary, so that when the time comes for the child to leave school and its supports, the family is ready to put a new plan into action.

The life stages of a person with a disability are similar to those of the person without a disability. In some instances, the timing may be delayed, and the sequence may be a little out of the ordinary, but the stages are similar. It is important to realize that the planning you begin at age 16 or 18 will not remain stagnant and remain your plan indefinitely. What decision do we ever make for ourselves or others at age 18 that still applies at age 35, or 50, or 70, or 90? Yet families often feel paralyzed by the enormity of having to make a perfect decision that will last a lifetime. When you remind yourself that a decision can only be made with the information and knowledge available at the time, planning becomes more manageable and less daunting. Your adult child will gather life experiences and skills along the way, which will help guide decisions for later stages of life.

Families should go through a series of questions, and carefully consider the answers, among all significant members of the family who will play a role in the future of the member with a disability. Bear in mind that the adult child with disabilities may also have an opinion, which can influence the long-term success of any residential arrangements made for him or her as an adult. To the greatest extent that is appropriate, the adult child with disabilities should be included in the process.

The first step in the process is to understand your own readiness for seeing your child as an adult on his or her own. The definition of *on his or her own* does not mean without assistance, but it does mean your child with disabilities will not be under your constant protection and supervision. Again, think of your other children. Could you have imagined them handling their own affairs, doing their own laundry, and making the right social choices as long as they were living under your roof? With some children and their parents, the time for separation cannot come soon enough. For others, it seems to never be the right time. But in all instances, the separation involves an emotional readiness to accept the risk of independence.

The same is true with a child with a disability, although some families may have fewer answers, more questions, and more insecurity about the decisions that are being made.

In trying to determine what kind of home you envision for your child with disabilities as an adult, one of the main criteria that differentiate one type of setting from another deals with how much assistance your child needs to manage the daily needs of life. This type of assistance should be broken down by the basics of food and meals, personal grooming and daily hygiene, money management, and social activities and connections. How much physical assistance does your child need in order to handle these tasks? Does he or she need someone physically present in order to accomplish these tasks, or only reminders through visual cues and organization of the environment to limit confusion? Does your child need intermittent support from people outside of where he or she lives, or does your child need the supervision of someone living in the house? Has your child ever been left alone for any period of time, or for an overnight period? If he or she has not been left alone, what do you worry would happen? Can your child be taught skills to address your concerns? You may want to ask yourself whether your fear for your child is the same as what you experience for your other children, in terms of making the right choices as a young adult.

After you have considered these issues, the next step might be to rank what is most important to you and to your child from the following concerns. Remember, there are no right or wrong answers; the questions following are simply offered to help you clarify your expectations.

- Do you see your child living in an urban, suburban, or rural setting? The answer to this question is often dependent on the individual's ability level, and therefore the importance of having access to stores, public transportation, and jobs.

- Does it matter whether your child lives with others of the same gender, or mixed genders? To whom does it matter? There are advantages to both arrangements, and in most cases either situation is fine as long as rules of privacy and space are clearly defined.

- Location is a variable that sometimes stands in the way of finding the perfect housing arrangement. Often families will insist on a location in one of a few towns, typically near where they live. Bear in mind that restricting the options too much may well eliminate a housing opportunity that offers very compatible roommates and is perfect for your child.

- How insistent will you be about the level of cleanliness, the nutritional content of meals, the organization of the room, the neatness of the apartment or the house, the bedtime hour, and so forth?

These questions may seem like minor issues when you are thinking about them in the abstract. They, however, address some of the details that may cause you to second-guess your decision for independence, unless you have come to terms with the value you place on each variable. Ask most parents what they want for their children, and they will answer, "I want them to be happy." It is the definition of happiness—your definition and your adult child's—that makes for peace and satisfaction with the decision of where he or she lives as an adult.

Your family member's ability level, the state where you reside, the funding status of the public department responsible for your child's disability, and your own financial situation will determine whether you receive full, partial, or no public funding for the residential services in the adult years.

If you receive public funding, you will have more limited choices in creating your own vision of residential services, unless your state is committed to, and willing to, fund such programs either directly to families or through an intermediary agency. In either case, you should develop a rank order of priorities, and decide which are non-negotiable, because they are the essence of your definition of happiness for your child.

The variables include the following

- Number of people who will live together

- Location of the residence

- Gender of the roommates or housemates

- Proximity to the individual's job site

- Ownership or rental of the living quarters

- Number of staff and support people needed

- Religion of housemates and staff, or the home's involvement with any religious affiliation

- Aesthetics of the physical setting

- Intelligence and cognitive ability of the housemates

- Behavior problems of the housemates

- Medical issues of the housemates

- Cost

All of the variables preceding may be important to you. It is unlikely that you can meet all the variables satisfactorily; therefore, determining your priorities is important in order to move ahead with planning for your child's residential future.

You may find that you are working with an agency and fitting into an existing residential arrangement that has an available opening. Even if that is the case, shop around, ask about the agency's track record, speak to other families who are familiar with the agency, and visit at dinner time. You may want your child to accompany you on these visits. You are the best judge of the appropriate time to introduce the concept of moving out to him or her.

If your child is high functioning and can manage independently without live-in support, you may want to work with other families in creating your residential vision. The reason for limiting this option to individuals who can live more independently is because the most difficult part of operating a successful long-term residential arrangement is the staffing and support. In the beginning, it may seem like an interesting challenge that can be accomplished through volunteers, family members, goodwill, and hiring connections; in the long term it is very difficult to sustain the staffing needs. Employment and labor laws are quite specific and complicated. Students and volunteers are transitional. Most employees want an organization that can hire, check references, and provide relief and substitutes on short notice.

The energy of a group of families can create wonderful services. As with any cooperative venture, however, you must have a source that represents the collective voice and ensures that the cooperative is not merely a collection of individual needs, but instead a group committed to the same overall goals.

Many interesting models of residential arrangements for people who are moderately high functioning exist. For purposes of clarity, we are defining *high functioning* as someone who can independently take care of his or her personal needs. We are thinking, for example, of someone who does not need assistance with showering, dressing, or eating, can safely stay at home without setting the house on fire or creating other emergencies, and can evacuate at the sound of an alarm. Safety skills can be taught if someone has the prerequisite ability to follow directions that are offered clearly.

· · ·   **Special Needs Planning Residential Model:**   · · ·
Transitioning to Independence

There are numerous innovative housing projects either functioning or in the development phase. The organization, Moving Forward Towards Independence, located in California's Napa Valley, was originally established by a group of parents in order to help individuals between the ages of 18 and 35 transition into living independently. One example is a two-phase program that was established with the goal of teaching individuals who are learning disabled and developmentally delayed the skills necessary to live independently. The first phase of the program is a 2 to 3-year time period where individuals live in a group home setting and learn the skills necessary for independent living. The second phase has the individual living in an apartment community within 6 blocks of the original group home. Staff working in the program help each individual maintain the relationships he or she developed while living in the group home. The funding for the program is primarily generated by parents, but there are some public subsidies. The state pays for vocational rehabilitation services and some individual support services in the second phase. The individuals usually receive SSI, SSDI, Section 8 housing, or other rental subsidaries. The apartments are owned by private investors that are not affiliated with the program. The program is currently working with parents to explore the possibility of families co-owning housing for their children with the program to continue providing the needed support services (for more information, visit http://www.moving-forward.org).

• • •   • • •

• • •   **Special Needs Planning Residential Model:**   • • •
                              Condominium Homeownership

The first housing program in the United States that enables adults with special needs to own their own homes while receiving professional support was developed in 1983 by Specialized Housing, Inc. An individual, a family, or a trust owns a condominium unit within a home. The unit can be resold as any ordinary unit of real estate. Residents and families are involved in the planning of each new household. The adult occupying the unit is supported so that he or she can live as independently as possible. During the day, most individuals work in a competitive or supported work environment. Residents meet regularly with house staff and clinicians to discuss household policy, problems, needs, chores, and maintenance, and to plan celebrations and participate in staff hiring. Families connected to each household meet on a regular basis with key administrative staff and continue to be involved in the household to maintain the standards initially developed for the model.

Specialized Housing works with families to address the Five Factors of special needs planning during an often emotional time and coordinates the legal, financial, and government benefits that help to secure the residence for the individual.

Specialized Housing has pioneered in developing the model of private pay homeownership for this population. Over the years, Specialized Housing has gained experience in tending to the unique needs of aging parents as well as aging adults with disabilities. This expertise assists younger families embarking on this unique residential process. Specialized Housing helps families plan for the continuity of care of the resident upon the death of the parents or other relatives by supporting the next generation in its successor role or by helping families to create alternative arrangements for successors (for more information, visit http://www.specializedhousing.org).

• • •   • • •

The cost of residential settings depends on several factors, particularly the level of assistance needed to

- Self-preserve by evacuating in an emergency (the amount of assistance needed to do so will determine the amount of overnight staffing required)
- Handle personal grooming and hygiene needs on a daily basis
- Deal with the chores required around shopping, cooking, and serving food
- Handle required medication intake, if any
- Maneuver in the home environment effectively (ambulation and mobility needs); limitations in this area could be due to visual, physical, language, or hearing deficits
- Manage one's temper and deal with delayed gratification, as well as other behavioral issues

• • •   **Special Needs Planning Story**   • • •

Joseph, a widower and parent in his early 70s, spoke passionately about his worst nightmare of dying before his only daughter, Julia, got settled to live in a supported environment away from him. Joseph attended conferences and training workshops and planned. What Joseph did not plan on was sitting in his easy chair one evening, closing his eyes, and not waking up. Everyone scrambled to pursue what was best for Julia. His worst nightmare happened. Agencies stepped in, but the transition was traumatic. The loss of her father and her lifetime home was not supposed to be the plan. We would all like to live forever, but proper planning, and acting on those plans, ensures smooth transitions and pleasant dreams.

• • •   • • •

UNIQUE PLANNING STEPS FOR STAGE IV

First see the core planning points outlined in Chapter 2.

- At this point, since your child is now leaving the public school system and services, you should have already gone through transition planning. A day or supported employment program, as well as residential eligibility, should already be established.

- If you have not yet identified local support agencies that specialize in providing information and services for your adult child's specific needs, you need to do so as soon as possible.

- Do not assume that the government will fully provide for your child's lifetime needs. Find your voice for advocacy.

- Maintain a balance in your overall planning, to include the needs for your other children and yourselves—both personal and financial.

- Determine an adequate amount of life insurance needed in the event of a premature death of a caregiver.

- If the individual with disabilities is able to express his or her own personal vision of the future, he or she should be included in discussions at this point.

- If the individual with disabilities is gainfully employed and able to earn an income, he or she may also have an appreciation for and understanding of money. If so, he or she should be encouraged to participate in the planning process.

FAMILY AND SUPPORT FACTORS

Making the transition from public education services to adult services will be different for everyone and for every family. In the past, your role as the parent has been to advocate for services based upon the vision that you have had for your child to help him or her achieve IEP goals. For his or her entire life to this point, you have been the primary source of support and voice for advocacy for your child with disabilities.

Throughout your child's adult life, your role will shift from primary caregiver and coordinator of services towards supporting his or her abilities to shine and encouraging him or her to express wants and desires on his or her own behalf. No longer is it all about the vision that you have for your child, because your focus will shift to incorporating his or her own opinions concerning wants and needs. In some cases, your child might want to live with you forever; in other cases, your child might want to live as independently as possible with his or her own supports in place. The transition at this stage requires that you listen to what your adult child with disabilities has to say.

Make sure that your family member is surrounded with people who support his or her abilities and vision. The support networks and peer networks that you have created over time are changing. No longer is it a natural occurrence in daily life that your child will travel or interact with the same peers. The world is now bigger than the classroom that he or she once knew. Your adult child needs other people to be involved in his or her life—to help with job searches, residential options, and social and recreation activities. It takes more than a parent; it takes more than a neighborhood; it takes more than a village to expand your adult child's network far and wide to people who are more than willing to help.

In some cases, it might mean that a child that has intense medical needs or significant behavioral issues will no longer receive the daily supports that he or she was entitled to receive throughout the school day. Unless you are able to secure adequate funding for adult services, which would include a day program, you might find yourself being the one fully responsible to meet the day-to-day needs of your adult child. For this reason, you need to be diligent and adamant about securing resources. Remember that you too are getting older, and there may be a long road ahead of you. Preserve yourself for your adult child and other family members, who need you to be healthy.

If your child has more severe disabilities and is not able to express choices and needs, you will most likely continue to be his or her primary source of support. You can, however, still promote his or her independence, likes, and dislikes in an environment that would be most appropriate. You may eventually need to relinquish the day-to-day duties, but you will still need to remain involved to a degree, to provide oversight so that your child will always receive the best and the most appropriate supports available.

Now that your child has reached adulthood, your other children may have reached this stage as well. If you have made plans for one sibling to follow through with the caregiving duties of your child with special needs, it is time to be clear concerning your expectations and your plans for that individual's role.

You may also have aging parents that you need to care for while you are providing for your adult child. Some families may find that they are arranging for assisted living for their parents and a residential program for their child in the same timeframe. The support that once existed from your own parents may no longer be the same; they may now need you to be their support network.

- Have you created a circle of supports for your adult child? These individuals share your values and contribute to your child's success. They may include family members, friends, neighbors, co-workers, therapists, educators, staff, and others involved in your child's life. The more people that are around your son or daughter, listening and spending time with him or her, the more positive the difference in his or her life. There are informal and formal processes of creating a circle of support for your family member. Your local chapter of The Arc or other family support agency may have information about creating a circle of support.

- Have you recently shared your vision with other family members and your expectation of their roles? Are they still able to fulfill your wishes? Or do they have other family or career obligations? Even if you have made provisions for your other children to be involved, their lives today may not allow them to be as involved as you or they once hoped. You need to provide options for them, so that they know they do not have to do it all.

- Have you asked your other children how they feel about being involved with the responsibilities of guardianship, trustee, advocate, or caregiver of their brother or sister? The arrangements you make for today may be unrealistic to accommodate the future needs of your child. You should have a contingency plan in place that will cover your child's needs throughout his or her lifetime.

- Do your future caregivers and guardians, including siblings, know the important people in your son or daughter's life? This is a good time to engage them in meetings, to introduce them to residential and/or vocational staff, and to help them connect with your child's friends.

- Do future caregivers know how to take care of the day-to-day needs of your adult child? Keep your Letter of Intent current, updating needs and daily schedules on a regular basis. Identify those individuals and agencies that you feel support your child. Make sure that future caregivers and providers have this information. A good technique to keep the information current is to update the Letter of Intent every year on your child's birthday.

· · ·　　　　　**Special Needs Planning Story**　　　　　· · ·

I never envisioned anyone other than me to take over my parents' role of caring for my brother Ron when they were gone. My dreams for my future always included a place for Ron to be a part of my life. I never realized that he could live independently or work independently. Although Ron is still a part of my life—and always will be—he now has his own life that includes his own vision. It is a life that he is tremendously proud of, as we all are.

· · ·　　　　　—Ron's sister, Cynthia　　　　　· · ·

EMOTIONAL FACTORS

As your child gets older, you too will get older. The reality of your own mortality needs to be addressed, as well as the likelihood that your child may have a full life ahead of him or her even after you are gone. It is common for parents to feel that no one can care for their child better than they can, and indeed no one will have the same level of love and passion for your child that you do, but this should not stop you from planning for the best possible care for your child after you are gone.

When your child turns 22, or enters the adult service system, you may find that you are not emotionally ready to have your child move away from home. This is a common feeling, similar to the feelings parents experience when their children move away to attend college. You may also be fearful, however, that if you do not accept a residential placement for your adult child with disabilities, you will forego the potential for residential funding in the future. This is not always the case, but should be investigated before you make your decision. You need to ask your state agency about their policies and prioritization process for residential services.

Letting go and taking the risk of letting your child have a full life apart from you is different for everyone. Supporting your family member to determine what is right for him or her takes active listening and engaging the help of others. Even if your child lives independently from you, you may still need to manage certain aspects of his or her life and continue to advocate for services.

- Are you happy with the services provided by your state? Perhaps you cannot envision your family member in a standard residential program funded by the state. There are more and more options available today to create housing opportunities specifically to meet the individual needs of adults with disabilities. Explore as many options as possible, and speak to as many families and provider agencies as you can until you find or create the most appropriate setting.

- Are you still waiting to plan for the future until you find the "perfect" person or persons to care for your child when you are not here or are unable to care for them? It is common to find that parents do not plan for the future because they do not know whom to turn to. If you are having trouble finding the right person in your family or extended network of friends, there are a number of agencies to consider that provide guardianship services, trustee services, residential care, social and recreational supports, and other services to help individuals with disabilities to lead full and independent lives.

- Is your adult child emotionally prepared to live away from you and the rules of your household? Your adult child with disabilities may feel ready because he or she has left the school system and sees other friends and siblings moving off to college, into their own apartments, or getting married. Evaluations and assessments by professionals will help you to determine when and if a move would be emotionally appropriate. Good staffing will be beneficial to help make a smooth transition for the entire family.

- Is your child still living at home with you because you depend on him or her for your own companionship? Although it may be difficult to let your child move out of your home, he or she may need to find other companionships with peers. It may also be helpful to other siblings that you can see your child with disabilities develop and establish independence while you are still living.

- Is your child capable of understanding your own mortality? Has he or she expressed concerns about your death? If so, you may need to share your plans in a positive sense, or seek professional counseling to help address these concerns.

- Are you making future plans today based on a crisis due to the death or disability of a parent? If so, you should seek the advice of professionals who are knowledgeable in disability planning, including social workers, therapists, financial advisors, and attorneys, who will not be as emotionally involved in the decision-making process. Be sure to include and listen to the opinions of all family members involved.

FINANCIAL FACTORS

Now that your child is leaving the school system, it is likely that you are beginning to think about both your child's long-term security and your own personal financial security. You are perhaps nearing the end of your peak earning years, or possibly anticipating a time when you can slow down. This is the time to assess your personal financial situation and make sure that you have done everything possible to have the appropriate savings available to first meet your own needs during retirement. You should also assess your financial resources available to supplement your child's lifetime needs while you are living and after you die.

- Have you been monitoring your debt to be certain that you will have limited debt service to pay when your income reduces during retirement years? Now is the time to review your mortgage schedule to at least ensure that your mortgage will not be a large percentage of your fixed monthly expenses. Also review your monthly expenses and budgeting needs.

- Do you have a current list of all of your assets and liabilities, including insurance policies, annuities, and pensions? You should maintain a current net worth statement, along with a listing of the location of all of your important documents (including marriage certificate, veteran's papers, prepaid burial arrangements, and other important items). The ownership of assets and beneficiary designations of retirement plans, annuities, and life insurance policies should be properly coordinated with your overall estate planning documents.

- Have you made appropriate provisions to protect your assets in the event that you require long-term care assistance either in your home or in a long-term care facility? The expense of providing long-term health care needs for a parent can deplete assets that had been intended to supplement their child's needs. You should review the benefits as well as the costs to purchasing long-term care insurance (see the section in Chapter 9 on long-term care insurance for more information).

- Is your current life insurance program designed to meet your long-term family needs? When parents are in their prime working years, the priority in life insurance planning is to make sure a surviving spouse will have the resources available to raise the children and cover for any loss in the primary wage earner's salaries. The recommended solution for this need is to have separate life insurance policies that insure each parent. When you get closer to retirement and have accumulated adequate savings for your personal retirement needs, the need for life insurance often changes. An additional goal is to have enough money available to supplement your child's needs at the death of the second surviving parent. Second-to-die life insurance, or survivorship life insurance, is frequently used to guarantee that there will be money available to supplement your child's needs (see the section on life insurance in Chapter 9).

- Do you know the amount of money required to provide for your child's lifetime needs? Calculating the amount of money needed is an art, not a science. This process requires input from a professional that has experience with residential programs, day programs, and/or supported employment opportunities. You may have been fortunate to be able to fund your other children's college educations, and in order to do so you needed to know the tuition in advance. In order to plan for supplemental needs of your child with disabilities, you need to at least estimate the costs for various options. Once you identify the costs, you can incorporate these costs into your overall financial and estate plan.

Special Needs Planning Pointer

If your intention is to help pay for your child's supplemental needs throughout his or her lifetime, you need to know what the potential residential costs are. Hire an independent consultant to first assess your child's abilities and support needs. This assessment will identify the various options and associated costs. A good starting point to find such a person is to contact a reputable not-for-profit organization that develops residential and support programs for individuals with disabilities (similar to those of your family member). Do not, however, forget to ask whether it is possible to engage their services without having to make a commitment to use their program.

- Have you set reasonable retirement goals? Parents often plan on working well past age 65, and are counting on this income to cover their expenses as well as their child's supplemental expenses. Due to the changing employment environment, no job is considered secure. There are also many questions and concerns about the stability of Social Security benefits for retirees. In addition, changes in your own health may require you to stop working sooner than you would like. Because of these uncertainties, you should make saving for your retirement a priority and establish a disciplined savings strategy.

- Have you engaged the services of your certified public accountant or financial planner to help determine the most appropriate strategies to withdraw money from your savings and investment accounts? There are different tax consequences involved in taking distributions out of retirement accounts as well as from other types of accounts. You should consult with professionals prior to taking any distributions.

- Have you factored in the cost of inflation into your retirement plan? Although many expenses may be reduced while you are in your retirement years, the cost of health-related fees is increasing at a rapid rate. Review your investment allocation with your financial advisor to protect your savings from the impact of inflation.

- Do you want your child to always be able to live in your home? Leaving your home to your child, or even to his or her special needs trust, may create a problem if the transaction is not properly executed.

Although your heart may envision your child always enjoying the comforts of his own home, you really need to ask yourself whether this is the most appropriate setting for his or her lifetime. If it is appropriate, there needs to be enough money in the special needs trust to support the maintenance costs, as well as taxes, insurance, and utilities. This expense would be in addition to providing for the residential supports and caregiving needs for your child's personal well-being and independent living. The cost of supports can range from $12,000 per year to $80,000 per year and up, depending upon your child's needs. These costs will also increase as your child ages and his or her needs increase, as well as due to inflation.

- Do you plan to fund a residential program for your adult child, either fully or partially? If so, you need to make sure that you have adequate money in his or her special needs trust. This will enable future caregivers to continue to pay for the expenses of the program. It is important for you to plan not only for the duration of your lifetime but also in the event you die prematurely or develop a disability.

Special Needs Planning Pointer

The economics behind developing a private-pay residential model with many families is based upon the fact that all families will contribute their fair share. If one family does not continue to pay, for whatever circumstances, it is likely that that family will jeopardize the residential model. Because of this, you need to have a procedure in place where you can validate another family's capacity to continue to pay their expected expenses throughout the lifetime of the resident.

Although discussing one another's personal matters may make you uncomfortable, it is very important that everyone's financial commitment is as strong as yours. It is a common practice for an assisted living facility, or even a nursing home, to validate a family's financial ability to pay for the expected costs of care for the resident's lifetime. This too should become a common practice for private pay residential models for individuals with disabilities.

LEGAL FACTORS

Unlike the legal planning pressure points of your child turning age 18 (the age of majority), it is the personal and financial circumstances of the parents and other family members that is the driving force in planning for this stage. This stage of planning is about transferring wealth to your child while maximizing his or her eligibility for government benefits for the rest of his or her life. As we have emphasized throughout this book, this is planning for two generations.

Hopefully at this point you already have the basic legal documents and estate planning tools in place. The issues of your child's need for guardianship should have also been addressed; although keep in mind that your child's abilities will continue to change, and the need for guardianship may change as well.

Remember that even the most perfectly drafted documents do not provide security for your child's lifetime. Properly coordinating and funding these documents is essential to establishing your child's security.

- Have you reviewed your legal documents to be certain that the trustees and guardians are still suitable? In the earlier stages of your life, it is likely that you selected guardians and trustees that were similar in age to you. If your other children are responsible adults, you may consider choosing them for appropriate roles in your estate plan. Consider whether the people you identified in your documents will be able to serve their roles for an extended period of time. To assist in the continuity of your plan, you should select a co-trustee or an alternate trustee that is appropriate in age to sustain your planning for two generations.

- Are your assets protected if either spouse needs long-term care assistance, either at home or in a long-term care facility? Review the benefits and costs of purchasing long-term care insurance (see Chapter 9 for more information on long-term care insurance). Also consider the planning strategies for Medicaid eligibility if your child continues to live in your home. Currently, in many states, if there is a disabled dependent living in your home and you require nursing home care, you will not be required to sell your home to pay for the cost of the care. There may be some actions required on your part for this type of protection to occur. Therefore, you should consult with a disability law attorney who is also familiar with elder law and Medicaid planning in your state.

- Do you have the financial independence required to fund a special needs trust today? Funding a special needs trust during your lifetime would remove these assets from your taxable estate, and they would not be subject to your creditors, which would include estate taxes. Because funding a special needs trust during your lifetime is an irrevocable decision, it is not always appropriate to do so unless you have achieved your own personal financial security. The money transferred to a special needs trust can only be used to pay for the supplemental needs of your child. Prior to making any contributions to such a trust, you should consult with your advisors to understand the financial, legal, and tax implications of doing so.

- Are the beneficiaries on your life insurance policies and retirement assets coordinated properly with your estate plan? It is likely that at this stage in your life you have accumulated assets in company-sponsored retirement plans, including IRAs. Retirement plan assets, annuities, and life insurance proceeds are distributed according to the beneficiary designations listed on the account and/or policy, and are not directed by your will or trusts. Confirm that the special needs trust is listed as the beneficiary, not your child directly.

- Are the assets that will pass to your child's special needs trust at your death easily converted to cash to help pay for expenses? Many consider a home to be a sound investment. Unless the home is a rental property, however, it will not produce any income to support its expenses. Real estate is a nonliquid asset that is not easily converted to cash unless it is sold. Before the property can be sold, your executors may have to pay for improvements, maintenance, and taxes, as well as realtor fees, all of which will reduce the net proceeds of the sale. When determining the most appropriate assets to leave to your child's special needs trust, you should direct assets such as cash, life insurance, or investments that are easily converted to cash whenever possible.

Special Needs Planning Pointer

When a retirement plan beneficiary is not a spouse, there are various tax implications to the non-spouse beneficiary and/or trust. It is recommended (whenever possible) to direct proceeds from life insurance or other investments, which can easily be converted to cash, to the special needs trust.

GOVERNMENT BENEFIT FACTORS

When your child reached age 18, you were able to determine whether he or she qualified for government benefits such as SSI and Medicaid. If he or she did, you should continue to protect eligibility for those benefits through proper planning. Prior to turning age 22, your child with disabilities received the entitlements of a public education. Upon turning age 22 (or age 21 in some states), individuals are no longer entitled to receive benefits; your adult child now needs to be "eligible" to receive benefits for residential, vocational, and transportation supports. You should carefully read and understand the section in Chapter 4 on government benefits.

This planning stage is a whole new world of advocacy efforts to ensure your child's independence as well as to ensure funding from your state's legislature. Try to get involved in government affairs and take time to know how to contact your state representative for support in your state budget.

- Have you been told that your child is on a "waiting list" for residential placement? Do you understand the process your state uses in prioritizing potential recipients of services? Because the demand for services is greater than the government resources available, most states have established a priority list of those eligible to receive services. Knowing where your family member stands for services will be valuable in knowing how to plan. Your state advocacy support organization or other family support agency can be a good resource for information. States such as Florida and Massachusetts have filed and won lawsuits to address the waiting list issues for residential services in their states.

- Are you tired of waiting for a placement? If government-provided residential services are not the most appropriate for your child and you have resources available, you should explore many of the private pay residential models throughout the country. You can use your child's funding from SSI, Medicaid, housing assistance, other government benefits, and your own resources to put together an appropriate supported living arrangement. The success of this model depends upon finding the right person and/or provider agency to help coordinate these resources.

- Are you concerned that your child's unique abilities are not supported in the residential model provided by the state program? Have your child's needs changed since his or her original placement? If this is the case, you should be sure to articulate what your child needs. Work with your coordinators and staff to develop a program around your child's abilities and needs rather than expecting your child to conform to an existing program, which may not support him or her fully.

- Upon the death, disability, or retirement of a parent, have you applied for SSDI for your child with a disability? The SSDI program pays benefits to adults who have a disability that began before they became 22 years old. The SSDI benefit is considered a "child's" benefit because it is paid on a parent's Social Security earnings record. A parent must be receiving Social Security retirement or disability benefits, or have died after working long enough to receive Social Security benefits, for the adult child to receive benefits (see http://www.ssa.gov for details).

• Even if your child is not currently receiving government benefits, have you properly coordinated your planning to protect eligibility for future benefits? Many individuals that qualify for government benefits by definition may be gainfully employed and currently not eligible for benefits. If this is the case, you should be defensive in your planning, because at some point in the future your child may lose employment or become less independent, and might then need the support of government programs.

CASE EXAMPLE FOR STAGE IV

The Barry Family: Creating Housing Options

Family and Financial Profile Steve is an engineer (age 64) who has worked at a large corporation for 35 years. Donna (age 62) has held a part-time position at the town hall for the last 15 years. They have three children: Nancy (age 32) is an attorney, Alan (age 29) has mental health issues and developmental delays, and Philip (age 21) is a carpenter.

In the past, Steve really enjoyed his job and felt that he would continue to work until at least age 67. His company was recently acquired by a larger corporation, however, and things have just not been the same. Because of these corporate changes, Steve would like to retire if it is financially feasible. Although Donna enjoys her job, she would also enjoy being able to relax.

Nancy worked for a large law firm after getting her law degree. Throughout her high school days and undergraduate college, she was able to spend a lot of time with Alan; however, because she is trying to build her law practice, she just does not have the time for anything else.

Philip has built a steady business. He has a small crew of workers and stays local with his work. His ultimate goal is to own rental income properties. He has not been able to get the money together to put a down payment on a multifamily home. Although both Nancy and Philip have had many challenges in dealing with Alan's behavioral issues, they have become very close over the years.

Alan is still living at home with Steve and Donna. Alan currently receives SSI and Medicaid benefits. He has a part-time job at the local garden center, which he enjoys a lot. He is quite busy during the summer months, but in the winter there is little work for him. This seems to be the perfect job for Alan, as he has been there for 4 years. Prior to this, the longest amount of time he held a job was 3 months. Alan is quite passionate about his hobby, which is listening to music and following his favorite bands. He finds it relaxing to listen to his music collection, and prefers this activity over interacting with others. Although he has proven to be self-sufficient around the home, both Steve and Donna rarely leave him home alone for extended times.

Steve recently asked his company benefits department to provide a summary of his 401(k) profit-sharing account balance, as well as the options available to him under his pension plan. He has $320,000 in the 401(k) profit sharing plan. In addition to the 401(k) plan, he has a pension plan that provides three options to choose from. Option 1 is to elect to receive a single, life-only pension of $5,000 per month ($60,000 per year), with Donna receiving nothing if he predeceases her. Option 2 is to elect to receive a reduced pension amount of $4,000 per month ($48,000 per year), with Donna receiving a smaller lifetime income if he predeceases her. Option 3 is to elect to receive a lump-sum option of $900,000. Initially the lump-sum option appealed to them, because at their death there could potentially be a sum of money available for Alan's supplemental needs.

Because Donna works less than 20 hours per week, she does not have any employee benefits. Steve has $20,000 in an IRA, and Donna has $50,000 in her IRA. They have joint savings and investments equal to $185,000. They own a home valued at $460,000 that they purchased 28 years ago. Their mortgage is currently $500 per month, and will be paid off in 2 years. Because of their low monthly fixed expenses, they feel that they will need approximately $75,000 per year before taxes to continue with their present lifestyle and to do the traveling that they would like.

Steve will receive a Social Security benefit equal to $1,350 per month at age 64, but the amount will increase if he waits until age 65. Donna will receive a Social Security benefit of $600 per month, based upon her wage base, or she can elect to take one half of Steve's benefit as the spousal election. Initially, their concern focused on health insurance costs. Steve was pleased, however, to see that his company currently subsidizes retiree's health coverage by 50%.

Goals and Objectives   Their primary goals include the following

1. *Financial independence:* Steve and Donna would like to retire in the next 6 months. They need $75,000 per year to meet their living expenses to feel financially secure and to travel more. Steve needs to determine the best option to select for his retirement pension. They would like to be able to help Philip pursue his goal of owning real estate.

2. *Alan's financial independence:* Although Steve and Donna would like to retire soon, they need to also supplement Alan's potential future needs. They would like Alan to be living in either his own home or an apartment. They want to take care that he continues to receive government benefits.

3. *Family protection at death or disability:* In the event that either Steve or Donna would die prematurely, they want to ensure that the surviving spouse can maintain his or her lifestyle while continuing to support Alan's supplemental needs. At the death of the second parent, they want to make sure that Alan will be financially secure and will be taken care of. In the event that either of them becomes disabled and needs care in a long-term care facility, they do not want to deplete their assets to pay for that care.

Family Timeline of Goals The Barry family timeline (Figure 13) shows the unique needs of their family's special needs planning timeline and how the needs of the parents combine with the children and are integrated with the planning pressure points. As with any family, they may have to make adjustments periodically, as income, goals, and needs change.

Family and Support Factors Steve and Donna are quite pleased to see that all of their children get along well together. There were some very difficult years while they were going through adolescence, but things have worked out just fine. Although Nancy lives just 30 minutes away, she does not get home very often. In the event that she is needed for anything, however, she has demonstrated on many occasions that she can be counted on for help.

Special Needs Planning Assessment

Steve and Donna should have a family meeting with all of the children to discuss their idea of purchasing a multifamily home. The investment would help accomplish two goals: to provide an opportunity for Philip to ultimately own investment property and to create a home environment for Alan to live independently. Although Alan has demonstrated that he can be independent, Steve and Donna are not sure whether he could handle any unforeseen emergency situations. They feel that some initial supervision is necessary, which Philip could provide. Because Philip is handy with repairs, he could also live in one of the units to save money to buy his own home, while maintaining the property and helping Alan. The other unit (or units) could be rented.

(continued)

Barry Family Timeline

Parents' ages		2007	2008	2009	2013	2023	2027
Donna:		62	63	64	68	78	82
Steve:		64	65 (buy apartments)	66 (retirement)	70 (IRA minimum distributions)	80 (apartments paid off)	84 (death of parent)

Children's ages							
Nancy:		32	33	34	38	48	52
Alan:		*29 (transition to apartment begins)*	*30 (secure residential supports)*	*31 (SSDI)*	*35*	*45*	*49 (lifetime supplemental needs)*
Philip:		21	22	23	27	37	

Figure 13. The Barry family timeline shows the Barrys' planning pressure points, the dates associated with them, and each family member's age at that date. (*Note:* The italicized name, ages, and goals represent the individual with special needs.) (*Key:* SSDI = Social Security Disability Insurance.)

(continued)
> The long-term plan would be to have the mortgage paid for this mul-
> tifamily unit in at least 15 years. In 15 years, the rental income from the
> units could be used to offset any monthly support costs. At that point,
> Steve and Donna may not be able to be as actively involved in Alan's day-
> to-day needs. Nancy is not as easily accessible, but still willing to be sup-
> portive in financial and legal matters where she feels more competent.

Emotional Factors   Steve and Donna are excited about the possibility of retiring. Although they talked for many years about Alan moving
out on his own, the years have passed by without that occurring. Alan continues to express an interest in living on his own even though his brother
Philip also lives at home. Their house is arranged in such a way that the
boys do have their own space.

Because Donna and Alan spend much more time together, the idea of
him moving out is a very difficult decision. She is, however, beginning to
feel that now is a good time for Alan to begin living more independently.
She also senses that when Steve is home more, there may be more tension
in the home. Alan's independence will also allow them the opportunity to
travel more during their retirement years. Donna does not know of many
other families that have adult children with disabilities like Alan, and she
does not know what to anticipate.

Special Needs Planning Assessment

The plan is for both Philip and Alan to move out at the same time. This
will create a great deal of anxiety throughout the family. They should not
move ahead with their plan unless everyone agrees, especially Philip,
because their plain will only work if he assumes a great deal of the
responsibility for his brother.

Financial Factors   This is a critical point for financial planning in
Steve and Donna's lives. In the past, they did not have to make many major
financial decisions. Things were pretty straightforward. Steve contributed
7% of his pay into the 401(k), they never accumulated credit card debt,
and they were able to pay for Nancy's college expenses from their savings
and earnings. The primary question is to determine whether they have
enough money to provide for their financial independence in addition to
supplementing Alan's needs. The next question is whether Steve should

take his pension in a lump sum or choose one of the lifetime income options. Another question is whether they should begin to take their Social Security income now, or defer it until Steve's age 67.

They also would like to figure out how they can afford to have Alan live independently. Steve was considering the option of offering Philip some financial backing to help him purchase a home, but he was not sure how he could do this and continue to help Alan.

Special Needs Planning Assessment

Before they make any commitments to either Alan or Philip, it is important to confirm that Steve and Donna have enough money to meet their needs. After careful analysis of Steve's retirement plan distribution options, it was determined that they should choose the option of a lump-sum distribution of his pension assets. This option may provide sufficient income during their lifetime to meet their needs and allow them to leave an inheritance to the children. Although it is advisable to meet with a financial professional before any decision of this magnitude is made, the following provides a guideline of the steps they took to make this decision.

In order to accurately assess their options, their first step was to determine their combined monthly Social Security income amounts. After completing their retirement needs analysis, it was determined that Donna should choose the spousal Social Security benefit equal to one half of Steve's benefit. At Steve's age 64, this would give them $2,025 per month, or $24,300 per year, from Social Security income.

Another step they needed to take was to determine how much money they would need to take from their investments to achieve their annual income requirement of $75,000. Because Social Security would provide $24,300 per year, they would need to take $50,700 per year from their investments. Based upon all of Steve and Donna's investments, which total $1,425,000 after factoring in the lump sum from his pension, they could take as much as $71,250 per year. This information provides at least a baseline to follow, and gives them the confidence that they will have money available to subsidize Alan's long-term needs.

Special Needs Planning Pointer

A study by Guyton and Klinger (2006) indicated that you can take an inflation-adjusted rate of 5.0% to 5.5% out of a diversified investment

(continued)

(continued)

account per year and have the money last for approximately 40 years. This means, in the case of the Barrys, that a diversified portfolio of $1,425,000 would provide an annual distribution equal to approximately $71,250 for approximately 40 years.

This theory provides only a rough guideline and is based upon historical returns. This is a hypothetical example and is not representative of any specific situation. Your results will vary. It is important to remember that choosing to receive a lump sum from a retirement plan does not provide the same lifetime guaranteed income of a pension. Choosing a lump-sum pension option, however, will allow the money remaining at the death of both parents to ultimately be transferred to a special needs trust. There are also various tax implications to consider. Therefore, prior to selecting a distribution option from your retirement plan, you should work with a financial and/or tax professional to determine the best option to meet your needs as well as those of your family.

After determining that they would be able to achieve their retirement goals, Steve and Donna then wanted to determine how they could create an independent living situation for Alan. Alan is very healthy, and it is likely that he will survive both Steve and Donna by many years. Their situation again illustrates the need to plan for two generations.

Steve and Donna determined that they did have enough money to purchase an investment property. They were able to use a portion of their liquid assets toward a down payment to purchase a four-family house not far from their home and Alan's work. After calculating the numbers, they could achieve their overall goal to support the mortgage and the housing expenses for the next several years until the rental income would be able to provide enough money to help subsidize some of Alan's support needs.

With Philip living in one of the units, he was willing to tend to the property-management needs. He was also able to do some carpentry work to make some minor updates to the property.

Legal Factors The Barrys had not updated their estate plan since the children were minors. Alan is not under guardianship. He does, however, need assistance with making medical decisions and some financial decisions. He is not able to handle money, and therefore the family intends to leave his inheritance to Nancy. They are concerned that he would be vulnerable to others if he had money in his name. She seemed to be the most financially astute child, and they felt she would ensure Alan's needs would be provided for out of his share of the inheritance.

They were also concerned about how to protect their wealth in the event that one of them needs to go into a nursing home.

Special Needs Planning Assessment

The Barrys should meet with a qualified estate planning attorney that is knowledgeable in disability law to learn about the use of special needs trusts. They were intending to leave Alan's inheritance to Nancy, which is ultimately a "morally obligated gift." Nancy could instead be named as the trustee of a special needs trust for Alan. The special needs trust would also protect Alan's eligibility for government benefits (see Chapter 9 for more information concerning special needs trusts).

In addition to creating a special needs trust for Alan's inheritance, they should also update their wills, and obtain health care proxies and POAs for each of them. They should also consider a medical guardian for Alan, to help with his medical needs. If they feel he is competent enough, he should also have a will, POA, and health care proxy for himself. Neither Nancy nor Philip is married. Therefore, they should also have wills, health care proxies, and POAs. They should direct any inheritance to Alan to his special needs trust when it is executed.

Steve and Donna should purchase and own the investment property jointly in order to take full advantage of income tax benefits. In addition, as owners they will receive the rental income that could be used to help supplement Alan's needs. In planning for the future, they can have the property retitled into four individual condominium units. At their death, Philip will inherit one unit and Alan's special needs trust will receive three units. One unit will be Alan's home and two units will be used for rental income to the trust. This income will provide money for Alan's housing and supplemental needs. Because Philip will be an owner of one of the units, it will provide incentive for him to maintain and oversee the property as a part owner.

Steve and Donna should also consider purchasing long-term care insurance to protect their estate in the event of either of them requiring long-term care assistance, either at home or in a long-term care facility. The cost of premiums should be included as part of their retirement income needs as well. They should also consider purchasing a second-to-die life insurance policy to fund Alan's special needs trust.

Government Benefit Factors   Because the Barry family has not been very involved with any type of family support services or provider agency on Alan's behalf, they have not had the opportunity to meet with other families and learn about the various types of housing models and supports.

Alan currently receives SSI and Medicaid. He does not earn enough money to support himself financially. He also needs some supervision if living alone, requiring help with grocery shopping, meal preparation, and banking. Philip is willing to help him with most of these aspects of independent living, at least initially.

Special Needs Planning Assessment

The Barrys should contact the state agency that provides services to individuals with mental health and/or cognitive disability needs. They should inquire about support services to help Alan develop his living skills around meal preparation, shopping, and banking. They should also inquire about any residential supports available to help subsidize his housing expenses. In addition, because Alan meets the financial requirements for low-income housing, they should apply for a monthly rental subsidy (i.e., Section 8 housing subsidy). The Section 8 program provides a rental voucher to a qualified individual or, in some cases, to a number of qualified individuals to live together. The program allows for various living arrangements to qualify. You should seek the advice of a housing consultant to help you identify and apply for the most appropriate program.

When Steve begins receiving Social Security retirement benefits, Alan should also apply for SSDI, which he is entitled to receive upon the retirement of his father. Combining these government benefits of supports and sources of income will help to achieve Alan's independence in the desired residential model.

Alan's independent living was made possible by pulling together all of the Five Factors

- *Family and support factors:* Philip was able to manage the property, and was available to help if Alan needed practical help. The new living arrangement also helped out Philip while he continued to build his business and begin owning his own investment real estate. Nancy is able to provide support in a role in which she is most comfortable, as the trust advisor, rather than supporting Alan's day-to-day needs.

- *Emotional factors:* Steve's retirement created an opportunity for Alan to begin his own independence. Both Steve and Donna were able to feel confident in moving forward with their plan.

- *Financial factors:* Steve and Donna determined that they did have enough money to purchase an investment property. The overall goal was for the rental income to ultimately provide enough money to help subsidize some of Alan's support needs.

- *Legal factors:* The use of the special needs trust allows the Barrys to leave an inheritance to supplement Alan's needs without jeopardizing his eligibility for government benefits. They are also able to avoid leaving a morally obligated gift outright to Nancy, which could have had a negative impact on Nancy's financial situation. Purchasing long-term care insurance allows them to provide for the cost of care for Steve and/or Donna, either at home or in a long-term care facility, without depleting their assets. By also purchasing a second-to-die life insurance policy, they can provide a guaranteed amount of money to fund Alan's special needs trust at the death of the second parent.

- *Government benefit factors:* Alan was eligible to receive a low-income housing subsidy to help pay for his rent, which ultimately helps to pay for the mortgage on the property. Alan will decrease his monthly income from SSI when he becomes eligible for SSDI after Steve begins to receive Social Security retirement income.

9

Important Special
Needs Planning Tools
and Resources

There are a number of financial and estate planning tools and strategies available today to help families achieve their goals and objectives. Some are very effective in special needs planning, while others are not. The appropriate use and coordination of these planning tools is the key to enabling you to achieve your goals and visions. Having a basic understanding of the various tools and terminology, and how they apply to special needs planning, can help you to explore the various options available and determine the best strategy for you and your family.

Because every family situation is unique, it is most important that you consult with your financial planner, accountant, and/or attorney before making any decisions. Proper coordination of financial and estate planning tools is the key to striking a balance. As expressed earlier, be certain that your advisors are both current and knowledgeable in disability law and planning.

The scope of this book is not intended to provide detailed information of each financial and legal tool or technique available for planning. The intent is to introduce the basic planning concepts and how they pertain to special needs planning. There may be some intricacies in your own personal situation or your family situation that will prevent you from using, or benefiting from, some of these techniques. Some planning techniques may not even be appropriate for your family circumstances. Again, because the details vary depending upon a variety of circumstances, you should consult with your own advisors and be sure that all of the five planning factors are coordinated towards achieving your overall goals and objectives.

Special Needs Planning Pointer

You must take care to choose a financial planner qualified to assist you. There are several organizations that are devoted to regulating the qualifications of financial planners and investment advisors. The Certified Financial Planner Board of Standards, Inc., (CFP Board) is the professional regulatory organization acting in the public interest to foster professional standards in personal financial planning. The CFP Board establishes and enforces education, examination, experience, and ethics requirements for CFP® professionals. See the web site http://www.cfp.net for more information.

The National Association of Securities Dealers (NASD) is the primary private-sector regulator of America's securities industry. NASD licenses individuals to be registered securities representatives, admits firms to the industry, writes rules to govern representatives' behavior, examines individuals for regulatory compliance, and disciplines those who fail to comply. See the web site http://www.nasd.com for more information.

The professional association for financial planner professionals, the Financial Planning Association, recommends the use of a CFP® practitioner for your financial planning needs (visit http://www.fpa.org for more information). There are, however, other financial designations denoting professionals qualified to assist you, such as a chartered financial consultant (ChFC) and a certified public accountant (CPA), who hold professional designations developed out of financial disciplines such as insurance and accounting. An attorney who is a member of the professional association of the National Academy of Elder Law Attorneys may also be an asset in estate planning (visit http://www.naela.org to find an attorney in your area). Table 3 shows a checklist of questions useful for interviewing possible financial advisors.

ESTATE PLANNING TOOLS

There are a number of estate planning tools to consider in special needs planning. You should work with a qualified attorney who is knowledgeable in disability laws and government benefits in your state. Your basic knowledge of these tools will be helpful in understanding and implement-

Table 3. Sample checklist for interviewing a financial planner

1. Do you have experience in providing advice on special needs planning? If yes, indicate the number of years.

2. How did you get involved in special needs planning as a profession?

3. Do you know the difference between Supplemental Security Income and Social Security Disability Income? If yes, how does this pertain to my situation?

4. Can you explain the concepts of a special needs trust and the principles behind its purpose? How would this help me in my planning?

5. How long have you been offering financial planning advice to clients?
    Less than 1 year
    1 to 4 years
    5 to 10 years
    More than 10 years

6. Briefly describe your work history.

7. What are your educational qualifications? Give areas of study.
    Certificate
    Undergraduate degree
    Advanced degree
    Other

8. What professional financial planning designation(s) or certification(s) do you hold?
    CERTIFIED FINANCIAL PLANNER™
    Certified Public Accountant–Personal Financial Specialist
    Chartered Financial Consultant
    Other

9. What financial planning continuing education requirements do you fulfill?

10. Are you or your firm licensed or registered as an investment adviser with the
    State(s)?
    Federal government?

11. Will you provide me with your disclosure document Form ADV Part II or its state equivalent? If no, why not?
    Yes
    No

12. How are you paid for your services?
    Fee
    Commission
    Fee and commission
    Salary
    Other

13. What do you typically charge?
    Fee
    Hourly rate $_____
    Flat fee (range) $_____ to $_____
    Percentage of assets under management _____
    Annual retainer fee
    Commission

14. Are you affiliated with any company whose products or services you are recommending? Please explain.
    Yes
    No

(continued)

Table 3. *(continued)*

15. Is any of your compensation based on selling products? Please explain.
    Yes
    No
16. Do you have an affiliation with a broker and/or dealer? If no, why not?
    Yes: Name of broker/dealer_____
    No
17. Do you provide a written client engagement agreement? If no, why not?
    Yes
    No
18. Can you provide three families as a reference that you have provided special needs planning advice to? May I contact them?
19. Can you provide three other professionals in the disability community as a reference? May I contact them?

Adapted from Certified Financial Planner Board of Standards, Inc. (2007). *Checklist for interviewing a financial planner.* Retrieved October 1, 2006, from http://www.cfp.net/learn/knowledgebase.asp?id=8. Adapted with permission.

ing your options. One of the most important aspects of an estate plan is to make certain that all assets are properly coordinated with your overall plan.

Wills

Wills are the basic legal documents that allow an individual to direct to whom their property will be distributed. The executor is the individual that you name in your will to administer your wishes upon your death. This is the basis by which you will leave your assets to your children, grandchildren, charities, or other heirs.

Dying without a will is called *dying intestate.* In the absence of a will, state laws direct the distribution of your assets. This could mean that the share left to your child with disabilities would be distributed directly to him or her. Assets distributed directly to your child will most likely make him or her ineligible for government benefits. Directly receiving even a minimal amount of money ($2,000 in 2006) will jeopardize benefits for the son or daughter with disabilities.

State laws will also determine who will be the designated guardian of your minor children if there is no such person named in your will. Or, if your child is no longer a minor, the state laws will determine his or her need for a guardian and will then appoint one at their discretion. You should name a successor guardian for your child in your will to prevent this responsibility from becoming a court decision.

Keep in mind that not all of your assets will pass directly according to your will. Beneficiary designations for retirement plans, life insurance policies, and annuities will dictate distribution of these assets. Ownership of your assets will also dictate distributions. For example, assets held joint with rights of survivorship will pass directly to the surviving joint owner, not through the provision of your will.

You can also state in your will that a portion of your estate is to be distributed to a trust. You can designate the beneficiary of a life insurance policy to be a trust upon the death of a parent or sibling. You can also name a trust as the beneficiary of a retirement plan (IRA or corporate retirement plan).

Well-meaning relatives or friends can also disqualify a person from benefits by naming that individual in their will; naming that individual as a beneficiary in retirement plans, life insurance, or annuities; or giving that individual an amount of money that is in excess of the qualification limits for government benefits.

The Letter of Intent

The *Letter of Intent* is not a legally binding document, but is an extremely important planning tool. This letter communicates your desires and concerns to future caregivers after your death. It covers vital statistics: your child's personal, medical, and financial profile. It can include details about what works well or not so well for your child, their likes or dislikes, samples of their daily schedule, suggestions about what changes might be needed for the future, a list of pertinent documents and records, and so forth. It provides a means to share the vision that you have for your child with others. Include this with your estate planning documents. But be sure to provide a copy to the future caregivers and update it annually (a good way to remember is to update it each year on your child's birthday). A Letter of Intent appears in the appendix at the end of this book and in the included CD-ROM.

Powers of Attorney

A *POA for property* names an individual to act on your behalf during your lifetime if you become disabled or incapacitated and cannot make decisions on your own regarding your financial affairs. This is an important document in your basic estate plan. Individuals with disabilities who are not in need of full guardianship may also benefit from establishing a legal POA.

A *POA for health care*, also called a *health care proxy*, names an individual to act on your behalf when you are unable to communicate your desires for medical treatment. This is also an important document in your basic estate plan. Often these are required to be signed prior to receiving medical treatment and are provided in a standard format. Individuals with disabilities who are not in need of full medical guardianship may also benefit from establishing a health care proxy.

Trusts

Trusts provide for the orderly administration and distribution of your assets. A **trustee** is the person whom you choose to be responsible to tend to the provisions you have set in your trust documents. The **beneficiary** of the trust is the person who would benefit from the income and principal of the trust assets. The trust **grantor** is the person who establishes the trust.

A **trust advisor** can also be named to provide guidance to the trustee regarding the needs of the beneficiary. He or she can provide oversight without all of the fiduciary responsibilities of a trustee. This is often an appropriate role for a sibling or other family member when a corporate trustee is used.

The special needs trust is used in special needs planning to allow families to leave an inheritance to their child with special needs without jeopardizing their eligibility for government benefits. An important component is to incorporate the proper language in the trust so that assets and/or distributions will not disqualify the beneficiary for government benefits.

Irrevocable Trusts An **irrevocable trust** cannot be changed. Transferring assets to an irrevocable trust during your lifetime prevents you from having any access to these funds. In certain cases, it does have some benefits for estate tax planning purposes that should be discussed with your attorney and financial planner.

An **irrevocable life insurance trust (ILIT)** can be used to remove the death benefit proceeds of a life insurance policy from your taxable estate. Every life insurance policy has an owner, an insured, and a beneficiary. The insurance company pays the benefit upon the death of the **insured.** The beneficiary receives the death benefit upon the death of the insured. The **owner** has the responsibility to make certain that premiums are paid in a timely manner, and can make changes to the policy if needed. If the purpose is to remove the death benefit proceeds from your taxable estate, an irrevocable life insurance trust should be the owner and the beneficiary of the life insurance policy. The trustee, as the owner, must follow the necessary steps to pay the insurance premiums. If one of the beneficiaries of the irrevocable life insurance trust is the child with special needs, the trustee must make certain that they do not jeopardize the beneficiary's eligibility for government benefits when gifts are received into the trust. There must also be specific language similar to that used in a special needs trust to protect government benefits. There are other valuable reasons to use an irrevocable life insurance trust with regard to estate planning as well; these considerations should be discussed with your attorney and financial planner. Establishing and funding an irrevocable life insurance trust can be a complex process with many details that are beyond the scope of this book. Because of this, it is important to work with professional advisors who are knowledgeable in both estate planning and special needs planning.

Charitable Trusts A *charitable trust* can incorporate estate tax planning, income tax planning, and philanthropy into your overall plan. You can designate a charitable organization that is providing services for your child, or another nonprofit organization, to be the beneficiary of a gift of assets by utilizing this type of trust. This can be a very effective estate tax planning tool for certain financial situations where there is significant wealth or highly appreciated assets, and a desire to be philanthropic while decreasing taxes. As with all estate planning strategies, charitable trust strategies should be discussed with advisors who are knowledgeable in this area of planning and can properly advise you on the appropriate applications to your personal situation.

Types of Trusts Used for an Individual with a Disability *A Family Handbook on Future Planning* (The Arc of the United States, 2003), summarizes the various types of trusts used for individuals with disabilities to protect their eligibility for government benefits.

> There are many different trusts for various purposes. Laws that affect trusts can also vary from state to state. However, most states have laws that authorize some form of supplemental, discretionary, or even master "pooled" trust. Experts recommend specialized trusts when parents want to protect government benefits that their child needs. Some of these trusts are called "special needs" trusts. (The term "special needs" trust may have a specific legal and/or technical definition to state/federal agencies, attorneys or others.) (p. 11).

Supplemental Discretionary Trusts *Supplemental discretionary trusts* are designed so that the principal (the amount put in the trust account) and its earnings (from interest or investments) supplement the beneficiary's basic care and do not replace the public funds required to pay for this basic care. This kind of trust is good for the SSI and Medicaid recipient whose assets cannot go above a specific level. The trust grantor can carefully direct that the trust not pay for services covered by Medicaid or other benefits received as a result of the child's disability. Instead, the trust would require the trustee to provide funds for certain items, services, or other expenses not covered by SSI and Medicaid. Supplemental discretionary trusts can also be set up for someone who is not on SSI and Medicaid.

Discretionary Trusts   Some states allow the trust grantor to give the trustee full discretion in how much or how little of the trust to distribute. This kind of trust can also contain provisions that limit distributions so that the person remains eligible for government benefits. The trustee of a discretionary trust must be careful not to distribute money from the trust for goods and services, or outright to the beneficiary, in a way that will disqualify him or her from receiving or remaining eligible for publicly funded services. The trustee must be knowledgeable about the benefits a person is receiving and how to report correctly on the distributions. The trustee has total power over all distributions and may hold back all or some of the trust's distributions. It is important that you choose a trustee whom you trust and who will take the time to learn how certain distributions from a discretionary trust will affect government benefits.

The difference between a supplemental discretionary trust and a discretionary trust is that the supplemental discretionary trust includes language that directs the trustee to use the trust funds to supplement government benefits and not supplant them. The discretionary trust simply states that all distributions are in the sole discretion of the trustee. The qualifying language regarding the grantor's intent to supplement government benefits is not included. Some states have required the trustee of a discretionary trust to pay for basic support when the grantor's intent to supplement government benefits has not been made clear.

In some situations, the child may not be eligible now or in the future for government benefits. In this case, one would question the need for a special needs trust. Individuals with disabilities, however, must often be protected from the possibilities of being defrauded by the unscrupulous. They may need assistance with money management, and sometimes they may need to be protected from themselves and their own habits. Leaving an outright inheritance can further enable a person's drug abuse, alcohol abuse, gambling, or other illnesses.

Unfortunately, there are instances where your child with special needs may have more than the asset limit of $2,000 in his or her name. This will jeopardize his or her eligibility for government benefits. This mistake may have been a result of an error in your planning, an unexpected gift, or a legal settlement. If this is the case, the planning technique to consider is creating a *payback trust*.

OBRA'93 created two types of payback trusts in the Social Security Act section in the federal statute governing Medicaid that can be used in this situation: (d)(4)(A), called the special needs trust, and (d)(4)(C), called the special needs pool trust. OBRA'93 allows that a payback trust which is funded with the beneficiary's own assets permits the beneficiary to qualify or maintain eligibility for needs-based government benefits such as Medicaid or SSI.

(d)(4)(A) special needs trust provisions provide that the trust is

1. Created with the assets of an individual with disabilities who is under age 65

2. Established by the individual, a parent, a grandparent, a legal guardian, or a court appointment

3. Specified that, upon the death of the beneficiary, any remaining funds in the trust will first be used to reimburse the state for Medicaid benefits paid on the beneficiary's behalf

4. Further specified that, if funds remain in the trust after reimbursement to the state, any remaining funds may be passed on to the beneficiary's family or other named successor beneficiary

(d)(4)(C) special needs pooled trust provisions provide that the trust is

1. Created with the assets of an individual with disabilities of any age

2. Established by the individual, a parent, a grandparent, a legal guardian, or a court appointment

3. Established and maintained by a nonprofit agency

4. Developed in order to provide for separate accounts maintained for each beneficiary, with the assets of all beneficiaries pooled for investment and management purposes

5. Specified that the trust is not required to repay the state for its Medicaid expenses on behalf of the beneficiary as long as the funds are retained in the trust for the benefit of other beneficiaries in the pool

Each state varies on the trust reimbursement requirements. You should check with your state and your attorney for the requirements you will be responsible for. Although a pooled trust is an option for an individual with disabilities over age 65 who is receiving Medicaid or SSI, those over age 65 who make transfers to the trust will incur a transfer penalty.

There are different pooled trusts throughout the United States that are affiliated with a nonprofit agency that supports individuals with disabilities. For a pooled trust in your state, you may first contact your local chapter of The Arc or AMI. In addition to these resources, there are chapters of the Planned Lifetime Assistance Network (PLAN) in most states that provide pooled trust services for individuals and their families. To find a PLAN chapter or a pooled trust in your state, visit http://www. nationalplanalliance.org.

Funding the Special Needs Trust   Trusts can be funded in various ways, either during your lifetime or upon your death. It is like a bucket that must be filled, and you provide direction to the trustee concerning how the money in this bucket is to be distributed. Without making provisions for assets to funnel into the trust, you would provide only an empty bucket. You can transfer assets during your lifetime to a *living trust* or a *revocable trust* and still maintain access to these funds. A revocable trust can be changed while you are still alive. An *irrevocable trust* does not allow you any access to the funds in the trust.

Because of the complexity and possible ramifications if mistakes are made in funding the special needs trust, either during your lifetime or upon your death, any and all funding strategies should be discussed with your financial, legal, and tax advisors to determine the most appropriate planning strategy to meet your needs. The following are some general guidelines that should be mentioned when speaking to your advisors.

Funding the Special Needs Trust upon Death   There are several reasons why you would only fund a special needs trust upon the death of the parent, grandparent, and/or caregiver. The following are some of the reasons:

- Once a trust is funded, the money can only be used to meet the beneficiary's supplemental needs. This means that the money will be inaccessible for any other needs of the family.

- A separate tax return must be filed for the trust. This will create additional expenses.

- Taxes on any earnings must be paid by the trust. Income earned in the trust is usually taxed at a higher tax rate than an individual rate.

- Once a trust is funded, it becomes irrevocable. This prevents you from making any changes to the terms of the trust.

- Overall, funding a special needs trust while you are alive can reduce flexibility in your plan, because the terms of the trust cannot be changed if needed.

If you and your advisors determine that it would be most beneficial to fund your special needs trust at your death, the following lists the more common ways to fund the trust:

- Provisions of your will can provide direction to your executor to transfer money to the special needs trust.

- You can name the special needs trust as a beneficiary of your life insurance policies, retirement accounts, and annuities.

- Ownership of certain investment accounts may allow **transfer on death** provisions to name the special needs trust.

- Remember, it is important not to make distributions from the trust directly to the beneficiary. All checks should be paid to either the service providers or vendors (see the section on trustee standards and practices later in this chapter for more information on trust administration provisions).

Funding the Special Needs Trust During Your Lifetime Although funding the trust may reduce flexibility, the following are some of the reasons why one may consider funding a special needs trust during the lifetime of the parent, grandparent, and/or caregiver:

- The donor has more than enough money to meet his or her personal needs and transferring assets to the trust will not jeopardize their personal financial security.

- The donor wishes to have the comfort of knowing that there will be a certain amount of money available for the beneficiary.

- Parents who have taxable estates and are implementing strategies to reduce their estate tax liability may wish to make annual or periodic gifts to the special needs trust.

- Grandparents or others may also try to reduce their taxable estate by making annual or periodic gifts to your child. The gifts should be made to a special needs trust to protect the child's eligibility for government benefits.

- Money in the trust can provide some protection from creditors.

- Money directly received by the child, either through an inheritance and/or a legal settlement, which would otherwise disqualify them for benefits, might be directed to a special needs trust with payback provisions.

Special Needs Planning Pointer

A child can be the beneficiary of more than one special needs trust. This is frequently the case when grandparents want to provide for a grandchild without disclosing the specifics of their own personal estate plan to their children. Of course, we always encourage open communications with families regarding the intricacies of planning for their child or grandchild with special needs, but because some families are very private about their financial matters, this may not always be a realistic expectation and may result in more than one special needs trust for the child.

If you and your advisors determine that it would be most beneficial to fund a special needs trust during your lifetime, the following lists the more common ways to do so, although you should discuss these in more detail with your advisors:

- Establish an account in the name of the special needs trust.

- Make gifts of liquid assets out of savings, or regularly fund the special needs trust on a periodic basis. It is, however, important to make sure you stay within the IRS prescribed limits for annual gifts allowed within the provisions of the annual gift tax exclusion ($12,000 in 2007).

- Gift assets that are likely to appreciate to the special needs trust. Generally speaking, this would reduce the estate tax implications at the death of the donor.

- If you do gift investments other than cash, it is important to provide the cost basis of the original purchase price. This will be helpful when or if the assets are sold.

- Own or purchase real estate property in the name of the trust. You need to be mindful of the income tax consequences for both the trust and donor, as well as the potential increase in trustee fees. When real estate is owned in the name of a trust, it is often more difficult to obtain a mortgage on the property.

- Own or purchase life insurance in the name of the trust. You need to be mindful of the impact on the beneficiary's eligibility for government benefits.

- Be mindful of the fiduciary responsibilities of the trustee of the special needs trust. Remember, it is important not to make distributions directly to the beneficiary. All checks should be paid to either the service providers or vendors.

Special Needs Planning Pointer

One planning strategy is to have the special needs trust be both the owner and beneficiary of a life insurance policy—this would be considered an irrevocable life insurance trust with special needs provisions. Although there may be some tax planning advantages to this technique, this may also create problems maintaining eligibility for government benefits to the beneficiary. There may be language that requires a distribution from the trust, known as **"crummy" provisions.** If this is the case, there may be an issue with the beneficiary losing eligibility for government benefits. One strategy to help overcome this potential problem is to include an individual without disabilities as the "crummy" beneficiary. If done properly, this strategy will not jeopardize the government benefits that the special needs provisions protect. In any case, utilizing life insurance can be a complex planning strategy, and many advisors may not be aware of the intricacies. Make certain that your advisors properly address these issues.

Trustee Standards and Practices As with many special needs trusts, an individual such as a family member or friend, rather than a corporate entity, is often named as the trustee. That individual, however, is frequently unprepared to assume the many roles and responsibilities that he or she may have been entrusted with. Generally, the trustee is responsible for investing the money of the trust, making distributions from the trust on behalf of the beneficiary, keeping record of the trust, and reporting any adjustments to the trust. It is important to have a good understanding of trustee laws and government benefit eligibility requirements. In addition to seeking the advice of a qualified attorney, accountant, and financial advisor, the trustee may also want to obtain a copy of the reference book *Special Needs Trust Administration Manual: A Guide for Trustees* (Jackins, Blank, Macy, Shulman, & Onello, 2005). For ordering information, visit the iUniverse, Inc. web site (http://www.disabilitybooks.com).

The following provides some of the important considerations that trustees should keep in mind.

- A trustee is a **fiduciary.** This legal term means the trustee holds a position of the utmost responsibility. A person who is entrusted with someone else's assets is held to the highest standard of integrity.

- Managing property for a beneficiary who has disabilities is different than managing funds for yourself. Record keeping must be flawless, and the beneficiary's money must be zealously guarded. The trustee cannot personally borrow money from the trust, nor can he or she lend money to friends or family.

- A trustee must learn about his or her responsibilities.

In addition to these general fiduciary principles, the Probate Court system in each state will have specific rules and will provide oversight of trustee activities. Unfortunately, the trust document alone will not provide all that a trustee needs to know about his or her fiduciary responsibilities. Trustees should, however, read the entire trust document before accepting the role of trustee. It is recommended that potential trustees seek the opinion of a qualified attorney to help define their responsibilities.

The trustee often assumes a number of responsibilities, the primary ones including collecting the trust property, protecting the trust assets, properly investing the trust assets, and maintaining accurate and complete trust records.

Collecting the Trust Property A trustee must make sure that all trust property is registered in the name of the trust. This is true whether the individual is managing a trust that is going to receive funds for the first time (as **initial trustee**), or whether the individual has taken over the duties from someone else (as **successor trustee**). The specific tasks involved will depend on the kind of property to be transferred.

Trust assets should never be combined with any other person's property. The most common way to identify if assets are owned in the name of the trust is that they are titled properly. The title on an account (i.e., bank accounts, brokerage accounts, stock certificates, real estate deeds) should include the name of the trustee, the name of the trust, and the date the trust was signed. An example of a properly titled account would be "Kyle Miller, Trustee, Alexia Miller Special Needs Trust, Dated 1/1/2007." The tax identification number of the trust should also be used, rather than an individual's Social Security number.

Bank accounts, for example, must be re-titled in the name of the trust. If there is any real estate, a new deed, which names the trust as the owner, must be signed and recorded. Stocks and mutual funds must be re-registered in the name of the trust. Some trusts may have been named as the beneficiary of life insurance policies and retirement accounts. To collect the benefits, trustees must complete the necessary paperwork and provide it to the insurance company or plan administrator. With retirement assets, trustees should consult with an advisor to learn about the different options for electing how to take the distribution of the account. Once the assets have been transferred to the trust, trustees are ready to take control of them.

Protecting the Trust Assets   One of the trustee's primary responsibilities is to protect the assets from loss. If the trust property is lost or mismanaged, there may not be any money remaining to provide for the beneficiary's supplemental needs throughout his or her lifetime.

Properly Investing the Trust Assets   A trustee has a specific duty to make the trust property productive. The trust funds should be properly invested and earn a reasonable rate of return. They should not be left in a checking account that earns no interest. Before embarking on a specific course of investment, however, trustees should consult with a qualified investment advisor and thoroughly review the trust document to determine whether there are any restrictions on the types of eligible investments. Ideally, the investment advisor should be knowledgeable in special needs planning, public benefits, and special needs trust administration to guide trustees.

In most states, trustees are governed by a so-called prudent investor law. (For example, in Massachusetts, the Prudent Investor Act is located in Chapter 203C of the Massachusetts General Laws.) Most prudent investor laws require the trustee to diversify the trust assets. Unless the trust specifies otherwise, trustees should invest the property in a well-diversified portfolio of various asset classes, which would include a mix of cash, stocks, bonds, and other kinds of investments. The specific percentage in each asset class depends on the particular needs of the beneficiary. For example, if the beneficiary is very young and receives most of his or her services through entitlement programs, the immediate cash requirements might be low and the trust could be invested for growth to help meet future long-term requirements. On the contrary, if the beneficiary currently needs a regular subsidy from the trust assets, it may be more prudent to invest the money with an objective of income and **protection of principal.**

Keeping Accurate and Complete Financial Records   It is important for trustees to keep accurate and complete financial records of all trust activities. Even if a trustee is doing a good job managing the trust, his or her actions could be challenged by another trust beneficiary, other family members, the IRS, or state agencies that provide cash payments or services to the beneficiary.

Special Needs Planning Pointer

For any bank and investment accounts, you should keep the monthly statements, cancelled checks, check register, and brokerage statements. The brokerage statements and trade confirmations are especially important, because they will establish the purchase price and date for any investment that was purchased and may be sold later. If there are any notes from meetings or conversations with the investment advisor, these should be retained as well. If a particular investment does not do well, the notes will substantiate that you relied on the investment advisor's advice.

If there are any payments from the trust, trustees should keep receipts, bills, and invoices that support those payments. It is also a good idea to keep any notes of conversations about disbursements from the trust. If there is ever a question about a specific disbursement, trustees can substantiate the logic behind their decisions. Income tax returns and supporting documents (e.g., 1099s, interest, dividend statements) should be kept in a separate tax file. All trust records should be organized and kept in one place.

Trustees should plan to keep any bank records at least until the annual accounts have been approved, if not indefinitely. Keep income tax returns and supporting documents for a minimum of six years. Keep records of all investment purchases, at least until they have been sold and the income tax has been reported and paid. Some trustees keep all these records as long as the trust is in existence. If the records are voluminous and space is limited, storage space could be rented, using the trust funds to pay the rental costs.

Providing an Account to the Beneficiary and Others A trust account is a summary of the trust's financial activities for a specific period of time, usually a year. The purpose of the account is to show the beneficiary, his or her legal representative, and/or any required government agency how the trust funds were managed during the accounting period. Some trusts contain instructions to the trustee to prepare and circulate annual accounts to the beneficiary and other persons who have a legal interest in the trust. Even if the trust does not contain any specific directions to the trustee to provide financial accounts, however, this can be an implied requirement. Financial accounting for the trust property is one of the trustee's fiduciary responsibilities to the beneficiary.

Preparing Income Tax Filings In most cases, a trust is a separate legal entity for tax purposes. This means that the trust should have its own employer identification number (EIN) or taxpayer identification number

(TIN). An EIN can be obtained by contacting the IRS by telephone (1-800-829-4933) or online (http://www.irs.gov). In most cases, the EIN can be assigned on the same day it is applied for. After the EIN is obtained, it should be used on all trust bank accounts and investment accounts. The Social Security number of the beneficiary or the trustee, should never be used. Form 56 (Notice of Fiduciary Relationship) should also be filed with the IRS. This is required for the IRS to recognize the trustee as the legal representative of the trust.

It is important that all trust income taxes are paid when they become due. The taxes are usually paid out of the trust fund account. In some cases, quarterly estimated tax payments must be made to federal, state, and local taxing authorities. Timely payments will prevent any interest and penalties from being imposed on the trust. If the trust fails to pay its income taxes, the trustee might be liable to pay them out of his or her own personal funds.

Successor Trustees   There may come a time when a trustee has to resign. In that case, he or she must take formal steps to end the legal relationship with the trust. To do so, the trustee should sign a formal written resignation (which an attorney can prepare) and provide it to the beneficiary and others who have a legal interest in the trust.

In the event that a trustee resigns, there needs to be a successor trustee to take over. In most cases, the choice of the successor trustee will be named by the trust document. Sometimes a specific person is named as a successor trustee or as a co-trustee. In other cases, the resigning trustee can nominate someone to succeed him or her. In other cases, the choice will be made by a committee that may be composed of the beneficiary's relatives and/or professional advisors. Sometimes the choice is made by the probate court, although this is not always the most desirable action.

Trust Advisor   It is becoming more common to have a sibling serve as the **trust advisor** rather than as the primary or co-trustee of a special needs trust. This removes the fiduciary responsibilities of the sibling, but allows him or her to oversee the actions of the trustee, which can be a paid professional. Instead of having to be the gatekeeper of the money, the sibling can take an active role in simply showing support without having the full fiduciary responsibilities of a trustee. Most likely a family member or friend will be more familiar with the family's values and the needs of the beneficiary than a professional or corporate trustee. Money will not have to get in the way of the relationship between siblings. A professional trustee usually means an attorney, accountant, or other business professional that is not related to the beneficiary. A corporate trustee may be a bank, corporation, or not-for-profit organization.

Removing a Trustee Most trusts contain provisions that describe how a trustee can be fired if they are not doing a good job and must be removed. There are legal standards for removing a trustee who will not resign voluntarily. In some cases, a third party can petition the court to remove the current trustee and appoint a successor trustee. A third party could be the agency or the state department providing services to the beneficiary, a family member, or an interested party of the beneficiary. In other cases, the beneficiary, or his or her legal representative, must apply to the court to have the trustee removed. Court action, however, can be expensive and the result can be uncertain.

• • •   **Special Needs Planning Story**   • • •

I was appointed as a co-trustee of my best friend's son's special needs trust. I was excited about this because I really loved and cared for his son Gerry. However, while working with the co-trustee who was an attorney, I realized that this was a very significant and challenging responsibility. After reviewing the trust account statements, I saw that the other co-trustee was charging what I felt to be an excessive amount of fees. However, because I had no experience in this matter, I truly did not know what a reasonable fee would be. When I questioned the co-trustee, I was told that the fee being charged was comparable to standard legal fees. Initially, I accepted this. But as time went on, I began to worry about my personal fiduciary responsibility as co-trustee.

As a result, I hired an independent attorney. After she reviewed all of the annual accountings and bills, she agreed that the other co-trustee was charging excessive fees for the services provided. She then presented this matter to the court, which made the decision to remove the other co-trustee and have him reimburse the trust for the fees that were determined to be excessive.

• • •   —Gerry's trustee   • • •

Trust Distributions Most special needs trusts give the trustee sole discretion to make distributions from the trust funds. There are specific guidelines to be followed in making distributions. A general rule is that distributions should not be made directly to the beneficiary. Instead, checks should be made payable directly to vendors when goods are purchased, or to providers when services are rendered.

· · ·   **Special Needs Planning Story**   · · ·

As trustee of Sam's special needs trust, I wanted to use the money to provide for his supplemental needs, as was intended by his parents when they set it up. I was finding it difficult to be able to use the money in the trust to provide for what he needed, because the mechanics of getting money to him were difficult. I was afraid that I would jeopardize his benefits in some way.

When his guardian called me to tell me that Sam needed a new television set, I found it difficult to find the time to drive the 1½ hours to take him shopping for one. When I asked the service provider if they could help, they were more than willing. They suggested that their agency pay for the television and send the trust a bill for reimbursement. Since this worked so smoothly to purchase the television set, we now have an agreement that once I approve the expenditures, the agency works with Sam and helps him to select and purchase items as he needs them. Sam takes great pride in being able to buy things that he enjoys. I then pay the bill that the agency sends me. This has made my role as trustee much more manageable.

· · ·   —Sam's trustee   · · ·

Special Needs Planning Pointer

Many brokerage accounts allow provisions to simplify bill paying by the use of a credit or debit card, automatic bill paying services, and/or the basic check writing provisions linked directly to the trust account. The convenience of these services often entail an additional charge, but may well be worth it, especially if they provide additional detail on all transactions.

Trustee Fees   Even if the trust does not contain any specific language about fees, the trustee has a right to be paid. The trustee fee is a tax deduction for the trust and is taxable income to the trustee. The following are some factors to consider in determining an appropriate fee:

- The amount of assets in the trust
- The complexity of the investments
- The beneficiary's needs
- The services being performed

There are two considerations used in determining a fee: the first is the number of hours worked, and the second is the type of service provided. Activities such as paying bills and balancing the checkbook will be charged at one rate. More complicated tasks, such as working on legal, investment, and tax matters, can generally command a higher figure. This is especially important if the trustee has a financial or legal background.

Time and Billing Records The trustee should keep a written record of all the time spent on trust activities. Some trustees maintain a log book in which they write down the date, time spent, and nature of each service. If any personal funds are used for the trust, the trustee should keep receipts for reimbursement from the trust assets. Reimbursements should be made promptly. Plan to keep these records at least until the beneficiaries or the court have approved your account. Table 4 shows a sample trustee log completed for Kyle Miller as the trustee of the Alexia Miller Special Needs Trust.

Trustee's Personal Liability When an individual agrees to be a trustee, he or she accepts some degree of personal risk. If, as a result of his or her actions, the trust suffers a financial loss, the trustee might have to repay that loss out of personal assets. Whether this will occur depends on the kind of action that caused the loss, the laws in each particular state, and any provisions in the trust that govern the trustee's liability.

Table 4. Sample trustee time log for the Alexia Miller Special Needs Trust

Date	Description of activities	Expenses	Hours	Hourly rate
2/13/06	Meeting with attorney to review trust document.	Travel time	1.5	Not applicable
2/15/06	Meeting with financial planner to review goals and cash flow needs for Alexia.	Travel time	1.5	Not applicable
2/15/06	Meeting with guardian and house staff to discuss Alexia's needs and daily routines.	Travel time	1.5	Not applicable
3/1/06	Follow-up meeting with financial planner to discuss and implement plan.	Travel time	2.0	Not applicable
3/5/06	Made arrangements with house staff to have $150 sent to the provider agency each month to pay for Alexia's supplemental needs. The check will be made payable to the agency. Called bank to set up the amount.		.5	Not applicable
4/10/06	Reviewed account online that the bank transferred the money to the account at the agency.		.25	Not applicable

Note: In this example, the trustee, Kyle Miller, is a family member. Although he is currently not charging the trust for the listed activities, it is still important to document the activities to demonstrate that he is fulfilling is trustee responsibilities. In addition, all activities should be carefully documented in the event he does elect to be paid for some of his time or reimbursed for his expenses.

Legal Standards   In general, a trustee is liable for any intentional act on his or her part that causes the trust to lose money. Some trusts contain a so-called **exculpatory clause.** This is a legal term that protects a trustee from personal liability. A common exculpatory clause will exempt a trustee from personal liability if he or she acts in good faith. A trustee would only be personally responsible for a loss if he or she acted in bad faith or was grossly negligent.

Investment Losses   It is not uncommon for one or more of a trust's investments to decline in value in any particular year. Sometimes the trust's entire portfolio will lose money. If that occurs, the trustee in most cases does not have to make up the loss personally. Most states have a prudent investor rule that will insulate the trustee from losses, as long as he or she adheres to that state's requirements.

Most states' prudent investor rules require the trustee to invest and manage the trust property as a prudent investor would. This means that the trustee should not exercise extreme risk or extreme caution. Instead, he or she should consider the size, terms, and purpose of the trust, and use reasonable care, skill, and caution. Also, a typical prudent investor law requires the trustee to reasonably diversify the assets in the portfolio to meet the long-term goals as well as current cash-flow needs of the beneficiary.

How Trustees Can Protect Themselves   To protect themselves from any given potential liability, trustees' best defense is to always act in the best interest of the beneficiary. They should read the trust thoroughly and understand their responsibilities. Trustees need to make sure that all of the trust property that is supposed to be part of the trust is actually registered to the trust. All assets—real estate, automobiles, and investment accounts—should be properly insured. Income taxes must be paid in a timely manner. Trustees should send periodic accounts (annually if not quarterly) to the beneficiary or his or her legal representative. Keeping the beneficiary informed is important. If a trustee has any questions about procedures or requirements, it is recommended that a qualified professional be hired to assist with the specific aspects of the trust and the needs of the beneficiary.

The Surety Bond   A *surety bond* is insurance that protects the beneficiary if the trustee mismanages or misappropriates the trust property. Whether the trustee must post a bond, and if so, what type, is usually stated in the trust instrument. Some special needs trusts excuse a trustee who is a relative of the beneficiary from giving bond, but require a professional or corporate trustee to post a bond.

Estate Tax Considerations

Estate taxes can also play a significant role in determining an appropriate estate plan. A plan that is appropriate for a combined estate of $100,000 is not appropriate for a combined estate of over $3,000,000. Properly addressing your potential estate tax liability could save your family a significant amount in taxes, thus preserving their inheritance. Estate tax planning tools and techniques should be discussed with your financial planner, accountant, and estate planning attorney to explore the most appropriate strategy for your family situation. Table 5 shows the phaseout of the federal estate tax and should serve as a general guideline of how estate tax rates and the exemption amounts are allocated. Estate tax laws will change, as laws do, but Table 5 should give you a rough idea of how much estate taxes will play into your decision making.

RETIREMENT PLANNING TOOLS

Retirement Accounts

The Internal Revenue Code provides dollar limitations on benefits and contributions under qualified retirement plans. Before establishing or contributing to a qualified retirement account, you should consider the maximum annual contribution amounts, any restrictions on withdrawals and loans, as well as the eligibility requirements for each plan option. Your tax advisor should be able to assist you in determining the most appropriate qualified retirement plan for your personal circumstances. Table 6 shows a

Table 5. Phaseout of federal estate tax

Year	Top estate tax rate	Exemption amount
2001	55%	$675,000
2002	50%	$1,000,000
2003	49%	$1,000,000
2004	48%	$1,500,000
2005	47%	$1,500,000
2006	46%	$2,000,000
2007	45%	$2,000,000
2008	45%	$2,000,000
2009	45%	$3,500,000
2010	No estate tax	Not applicable
2011	55%	$1,000,000

Note: The Economic Growth and Tax Relief Reconciliation Act (EGTRRA) of 2001 phases out the federal estate tax through 2009 and repeals it for 2010. EGTRRA expires, however, in 2011, so the estate tax will be restored unless Congress acts. The main elements of the phaseout are a cap on the top estate tax rate and an increase in the exemption amount.

Table 6. Select examples of available retirement plan accounts

	Traditional IRA	Spousal IRA	Nondeductible IRA	Roth IRA
Qualification to make contributions	Individual must have earned income and be under age 70½ at end of year.	Individual must be under age 70½ at end of year. Contributions are based on other spouse's earned income.	Individual or spouse must have earned income.	Individual or spouse must have earned income. May be any age, including over 70½.
Annual contribution limits	2007—$4,000 2008—$5,000 Thereafter, indexed for inflation, in $500 increments Lesser of the above limits or owner's taxable compensation Annual total contribution limit between Roth IRA and traditional IRA is $4,000 (2007). Additional catch-up contributions are available for individuals age 50 and over.	2007—$4,000 2008—$5,000 Thereafter, indexed for inflation, in $500 increments Lesser of the above limits, or total compensation, less your spouse's IRA contribution and less any contributions for the year to a Roth IRA. Additional catch-up contributions are available for individuals age 50 and over.	2007—$4,000 2008—$5,000 Thereafter, indexed for inflation, in $500 increments Lesser of the above limits, or owner's taxable compensation. Additional catch-up contributions are available for individuals age 50 and over.	2007—$4,000 2008—$5,000 Thereafter, indexed for inflation, in $500 increments Lesser of the above limits, or owner's taxable compensation Annual total contribution limit between Roth IRA and traditional IRA is $4,000 (2007). Additional catch-up contributions are available for individuals age 50 and over.
Deductibility of contributions	Above-the-line deduction If active participant in employer retirement plan, phaseout rules apply; phaseout reduction of deduction begins and ends • Single, HOH: $50,000–$60,000 • MFJ: $75,000–$85,000 • MFS: $0–$10,000 Not covered under employer plan and spouse is covered; phase-out begins and ends • MFJ: $150,000–$160,000	Above-the-line deduction Phaseouts apply if the couple's AGI is between $150,000 and $160,000.	Not deductible	Not deductible Phaseouts begin and end • Single, HH: $95,000–$110,000 • MFJ: $150,000–$160,000 • MFS: $0–$10,000
Taxation of distributions	All distributions are taxable	All distributions are taxable	Basis distribution non-taxable; earnings portion is taxable	Qualified distributions are non-taxable, including earnings

(continued)

Table 6. (continued)

	Traditional IRA	Spousal IRA	Nondeductible IRA	Roth IRA
Pre-59½ distributions	Subject to an additional 10% penalty, except in the case of • Death • Disability • Life annuity • "First" home purchase up to $10,000 • Educational expenses • Medical expenses • Health insurance for the unemployed	Same as traditional IRA	Same as traditional IRA	Contributions are withdrawn tax free. Withdrawal of earnings from accounts held 5 years are tax free in the case of • Death • Disability • "First" home purchase up to $10,000 Withdrawal of earnings are subject to tax but no penalty in the case of • Life annuity • Educational expenses • Medical expenses • Health insurance for the unemployed All other withdrawals of earnings are subject to tax plus 10% penalty

	401(k)	403(b) TSA	SEP-Employee	SEP-Self Employed
Qualification to make contributions	Cannot exclude employees who • Are 21 years old • Have completed one year of eligibility service (1,000 hours) • Service eligibility may be 2 years where plan provides for 100% vesting at start of participation.	Employee of a tax-exempt religious, charitable, or educational organization is eligible	Cannot exclude employees who • Are 21 years old • Are employed in 3 of last 5 plan years • Earn at least $450 in current year	Anyone with self-employment income
Annual contribution limits	Employee Elections 2006—$15,000 Thereafter, indexed for inflation in $500 increments Total contributions to the plan cannot exceed 100% of compensation (limited to $220,000, adjusted to inflation) or $44,000, adjusted for inflation.	Employee Elections 2006—$15,000 Thereafter, indexed for inflation in $500 increments Total contributions to the plan cannot exceed 100% of compensation (limited to $220,000, adjusted to inflation) or $44,000, adjusted for inflation.	Employee can contribute up to $4,000 (2007) as an individual IRA contribution to the SEP account in addition to the employer's SEP contribution. Employer may contribute 25% of first $220,000 of compensation up to a maximum of $44,000.	Same as SEP (i.e., 25% of first $220,000 of trade or business income)

	Simple IRA	Defined benefit	Profit sharing	Money purchase
	Additional catch-up contributions are available for individuals age 50 and over.	Additional catch-up contributions are available for individuals age 50 and over.	A Compensation limit of $220,000 adjusted for inflation in $5,000 increments Annual addition limit of $44,000 indexed for inflation in $1,000 increments.	Limited to 20% of net self-employment earnings
Deductibility of contributions	Contributions made pre-tax	Contributions made pre-tax	Employer's contributions are excluded from income. Contributions are independent of employer deducted same as regular IRA; deduction may be reduced because they are covered by employer plan.	Contributions made pre-tax
Taxation of distributions	All distributions are taxable	All distributions are taxable	All distributions are taxable.	All distributions are taxable
Pre-59½ distributions		Subject to an additional 10% penalty, except in the case of • Death • Disability • Life annuity • "First" home purchase up to $10,000 • Educational expenses • Medical expenses • Health insurance for the unemployed	Subject to an additional 10% penalty, except in the case of • Death • Disability • Life annuity • "First" home purchase up to $10,000 • Educational expenses • Medical expenses • Health insurance for the unemployed	Subject to an additional 10% penalty, except in the case of • Death • Disability • Life annuity • "First" home purchase up to $10,000 • Educational expenses • Medical expenses • Health insurance for the unemployed
Qualification to make contributions	Employers with 100 or fewer employees and self-employed, who received $5,000 in compensation in the preceding year Once qualified, can exclude employees who earned less than $5,000 in any two preceding years or expected to receive less than $5,000 in current year	Cannot exclude employees who • Are 21 years old • Have completed one year of eligibility service (1000 hours) Service eligibility may be 2 years where plan provides for 100% vesting at start of participation	Cannot exclude employees who • Are 21 years old • Have completed one year of eligibility service (1000 hours) Service eligibility may be 2 years where plan provides for 100% vesting at start of participation	Cannot exclude employees who • Are 21 years old • Have completed one year of eligibility services (1000 hours) Service eligibility may be 2 years where plan provides for 100% vesting at start of participation.

(continued)

Table 6. *(continued)*

	Simple IRA	Defined benefit	Profit sharing	Money purchase
Annual contribution limits	Employee 2006—$10,000 Thereafter, indexed for inflation in $500 increments Employer Required to make matching contributions of up to 3% of employee wages or 2% of employee contributions with proper notification Additional catch-up contributions are available for individuals age 50 and over.	Lesser of $175,000 (indexed for inflation) or 100% of average compensation during three highest earning years Thereafter, indexed for inflation in $5,000 increments	Contribution limit per employee: 100% of compensation up to $44,000 (adjusted for inflation in in $1,000 increments) Compensation limit: $220,000 (adjusted for inflation in $5,000 increments)	Contribution limit per employee 100% of compensation up to $44,000 (adjusted for inflation in $1,000 increments) Compensation limit: $220,000 (adjusted for inflation in $5,000 increments)
Deductibility of contributions	Contributions are pretax	Employee may be permitted to make nondeductible contributions.	Employee may be permitted to make nondeductible contributions.	Employee may be permitted to make nondeductible contributions.
Taxation of distributions	All distributions are taxable	All distributions are taxable	All distributions are taxable	All distributions are taxable
Pre-59½ distributions	Subject to an additional 10% penalty, except in the case of • Death • Disability • Life annuity • "First" home purchase up to $10,000 • Educational expenses • Medical expenses • Health insurance for the unemployed			

Key: IRA = individual retirement account; HOH = head of household; MFJ = adjust married, filing jointly; MJS = married, filing separately; AGI = adjusted gross income; TSA = tax sheltered annuity; SEP = simplified employee pension.

Note: The Internal Revenue Code provides dollar limitations on benefits and contributions under qualified retirement plans. Consider maximum annual contribution amounts, any restrictions on withdrawals, and loans as well as eligibility requirements before establishing or contributing to a qualified retirement account. Your tax advisor can assist in determining the most appropriate qualified retirement plan for your personal circumstances.

Source: Internal Revenue Code as amended for the Economic Growth and Tax Relief Reconciliation Act of 2001, the Job Creation and Worker Assistance Act of 2002, and the Jobs and Growth Tax Relief Reconciliation Act of 2003.

partial list of select retirement plan accounts and their provisions, which may be available to you.

Traditional Individual Retirement Accounts Traditional IRAs have a number of tax advantages. There are IRS guidelines to determine whether the contributions to these accounts can be used to reduce taxable earnings (i.e., be tax-deductible contributions). Whether the initial contributions were tax deductible or not will determine whether the earnings and/or the total withdrawal may be taxable or not upon withdrawal,

There are two parties involved in an IRA: the owner and the beneficiary. The person who establishes, and most likely funds, an IRA account is the owner. The owner designates a beneficiary (a primary and a contingent beneficiary) who will receive the proceeds of the account upon the death of the owner.

Even though an individual with disabilities is gainfully employed and has earned income to qualify to fund an IRA, an IRA is not always an appropriate planning tool for him or her. Even if the individual does not currently qualify for government benefits, and does not anticipate qualifying for government benefits that require an asset and income eligibility test, there still may not be advantages significant enough to justify establishing such an account. If distributions need to be made prior to the owner's age $59^{1/2}$, the potential tax penalties and consequences will outweigh any advantages that an IRA account provides. Therefore, any decision to fund an IRA should take into account possible changes that might cause an individual to need the funds before retirement age.

Roth Individual Retirement Accounts Another effective retirement planning tool for parents, if they qualify within IRS guidelines, would be a *Roth IRA*. Unlike the traditional IRA, contributions to Roth IRAs are not tax deductible. Earnings also grow tax deferred. The more significant difference is that withdrawals can be tax free (see the Roth IRA web site at http://www.rothira.com).

There are various reasons to fund a Roth IRA rather than a traditional IRA for retirement savings. There are also various reasons to convert a regular IRA to a Roth IRA. Some of the basic reasons to convert are:

- If you are in a low tax bracket, the income taxes due on the converted amount will be moderate

- There are no minimum required distributions at age $70^{1/2}$, giving you more control over the income

- Distributions to beneficiaries are not taxed upon your death

---

Special Needs Planning Pointer

The Tax Increase Prevention and Reconciliation Act (TIPRA) of 2005 (PL 109-222), signed into law on May 17, 2006, eliminated the adjusted gross income test for converting a traditional IRA into a Roth IRA. This change will be effective for tax years after 2009. Taxpayers who convert an IRA in 2010 can elect to recognize the conversion income in 2010 or average it over the next 2 years of 2011 and 2012. While contributions to a Roth IRA are not deductible, the earnings are tax free. Naming the beneficiary of a Roth IRA to your child's special needs trust will provide a tax-free inheritance to the trust under current tax laws. If your adjusted gross income is in excess of $100,000, you should discuss this planning strategy with your tax advisor.

In some cases, it may be appropriate for an individual with disabilities who is gainfully employed, and is not likely to ever qualify for government benefits, to consider funding a Roth IRA for their retirement years. There is a bit more flexibility in withdrawal provisions that may be beneficial for an individual. Before establishing and/or funding a Roth IRA for an individual with disabilities, however, many factors should be considered in addition to tax savings and government benefits eligibility. Participating in one's own financial security can be beneficial to an individual's self-esteem and independence. This is a planning tool that should be considered for individuals who are highly functioning and have no need for government benefits (that would have asset and/or income limitation requirements).

Beneficiary Designations on Retirement Accounts   At the death of the owner of an IRA or company-sponsored retirement plan, the proceeds are distributed according to the beneficiaries that are listed when the application is signed. Generally speaking, if you are married, your spouse is usually listed as the primary beneficiary. At the owner's death, the spouse will be able to transfer the assets into a spousal IRA rollover. This will enable the spouse to defer the taxes until the funds are withdrawn from the account. If you are not married and your intent is for an individual with a disability to receive any portion of the IRA, it is recommended to have those proceeds paid to a trust that has special needs provisions.

If a special needs trust is used as the beneficiary of a retirement plan account, the income earned in the trust will be taxed to the trust, usually at a higher tax bracket than an individual tax bracket. The proceeds from a Roth IRA are distributed tax free upon death of the owner. If an owner has a Roth IRA in addition to other retirement accounts, it may be advantageous to have the special needs trust named as beneficiary of the Roth

IRA and the other children named as beneficiaries of the other IRA and retirement plan assets.

It is not recommended to have an individual with disabilities named individually as the beneficiary of a traditional IRA or a Roth IRA, because an account balance greater than or equal to $2,000 will disqualify him or her for government benefits. Instead, if the owner wants the value of all or a portion of the IRA to be received by a person with disabilities, that person's special needs trust should be named as one of the beneficiaries.

Special Needs Planning Pointer

If you have more than one child and you intend to split your retirement account between all the children, including your child with special needs, you should direct his or her share in the beneficiary designation to the special needs trust. An example would be to have Adam Miller name his wife, Justine, as his primary beneficiary. He would then name two of his children, Kyle and Alyssa, as contingent beneficiaries each to receive 33% of the retirement account; and he would name the special needs trust created for his third child, Alexia, as a third contingent beneficiary to receive the remaining 34% of the retirement account. Adam would list the special needs trust for Alexia on his beneficiary designation form by including the proper registration, "The Alexia Miller Special Needs Trust Dated January 1, 2007."

Pension Plans

Many corporate and government agencies provide a lifetime income stream to the retired employee through *pension plans*. Many years ago, pension plans were very popular in larger corporations. Retirees could often depend upon a steady income stream that was guaranteed for their lifetime, and, if elected, for the surviving spouse or successor beneficiary. At one point, a retiree could feel confident in the pension plan system. Currently, many companies are terminating pension plans for various reasons, primarily due to the high costs of administering and funding such plans. In addition, there are pending situations where companies may be reducing pension plan benefits to retired employees. It was unheard of many years ago for companies even to consider a reduction in income benefits to retirees.

Today, the responsibility to provide retirement income is being transferred to the employee. The establishment of 401(k) and 403(b) plans provides a means by which employees can save for their own retirement with many tax advantages and investment options.

Income Stream versus Lump-Sum Benefit The election of your pension plan income benefit requires careful consideration. Most plans allow the participant (the employee) to elect to receive a reduced lifetime income as well as to provide an income to a surviving beneficiary upon death. The decision on whether to take the reduced income benefit or the lump-sum benefit is based upon a number of factors: the health of the retired employee and his or her spouse, the amount of the reduction required to allow for a spousal benefit upon death, the retired employee's other savings and investments, and other provisions of the retirement plan.

Special Needs Planning Pointer

Although there are exceptions to every planning technique, it is generally not recommended to name a child with a disability as a contingent beneficiary to receive a retirement income stream from a pension plan. Even if the pension plan allows you to name a special needs trust as the beneficiary, the lifetime income will probably be very low, because the income is based upon the life expectancy of all beneficiaries.

In some cases, retired military pension plans allow you to name your eligible child in your survivor benefit plan (SBP). Careful consideration of the effect of this income to your child's eligibly for SSI or related government benefits must be given. The SBP income counts as "unearned income" for SSI purposes. If you are eligible military personnel, you should contact your SBP counselor and state in which you plan to reside to determine whether receipt of an SBP annuity by the child could negatively effect SSI or related government benefits.

If you are married, the usual practice is to name your spouse as the beneficiary of either the income stream or the lump-sum rollover. There may be an occasional exception to this practice, however. Every situation should be carefully analyzed based on the factors mentioned previously as well as consultation with your own personal advisors.

If you are not married, you may consider naming your child with disabilities as the beneficiary. Before you make the decision to name your child with disabilities as the beneficiary of your pension income, you need to first determine whether it will jeopardize eligibility for government benefits either today or in the future. Even if benefits would not be jeopardized, it may still not be beneficial to name them as beneficiary because the income benefit to you will be based on your child's age as well. Naming a younger child as beneficiary will significantly reduce your monthly income during your lifetime. There may be more appropriate options to secure a future income stream for your child.

Determining to elect a lump-sum benefit rather than a monthly pension income can be a complicated decision, requiring professional assistance to at least calculate the present value of what the income stream would provide for you today. It is beyond the scope of this book to provide this calculation, but it is a common financial planning analysis. Because this is an important decision, the following guidelines may be helpful to consider:

1. Income stream election may be preferable:

    If you are healthy and have longevity in your family

    If you are married and your spouse is healthy and has longevity in his or her family

    If you want to have the security of income for life

    If the internal rate of return of the monthly income is very high (a calculation your planner will make for you)

2. Lump-sum election may be preferable:

    If you do not have a long life expectancy, due to health or other factors

    If you are not married

    If lifetime income is not a priority

    If you want to control your investments

Special Needs Planning Pointer

If you have already made the election for your child to be the contingent beneficiary of your pension income, you should check with the retirement plan administrator and/or your former employer to ascertain whether you are able to name the child's special needs trust as the contingent beneficiary, in order to protect eligibility for government benefits.

INSURANCE AS RISK MANAGEMENT

As parents, we instinctively want to protect our family members. We want to somehow manage the risks of: What if I die too soon? What if I live too long? What if I become disabled along the way? How can I protect my family's financial security in the event of my premature death or disability?

Protection planning focuses on managing those risks that we are exposed to by calculating the needs for insurance protection. The principle of risk management is that you self-insure (i.e., by way of a savings cushion) only those financial risks that you can manage. You transfer those financial risks that you cannot personally manage to insurance companies. There are various planning tools that provide for transferring certain risks to insurance companies. The most common types of insurances include health insurance (with or without dental and vision), homeowners insurance, auto insurance, disability insurance (both short- and long-term disability), long-term care insurance, and life insurance.

Health Insurance

Health insurance is critical for the family. Although an individual may be eligible for a government-sponsored insurance program such as Medicaid, it may be prudent to purchase private health insurance for an individual with disabilities. When possible, the dependent child should be included on the parents' health insurance coverage, in addition to Medicaid. Medicaid would then serve as the payer of last resort for medical expenses that are not covered by the private insurance carrier.

Dental health is a pressing problem facing individuals with disabilities in the nation. Many dentists no longer accept Medicaid reimbursements for dental services. Because of this, it is important to maintain *dental insurance* through your employer whenever possible, so that your son or daughter with disabilities can get appropriate dental care.

Some company health insurance policies also allow for *vision health coverage* as an addendum or rider (for an additional cost). Families would need to determine whether this coverage is necessary based on their health history and needs.

· · ·   **Special Needs Planning Story**   · · ·

Shauna is an adult with a medically complex situation. She was awarded a judgment and has a special needs trust that was funded by a medical malpractice insurance settlement. Since the trust has a payback provision, the government has a lien on the assets in the amount of medical payments paid on her behalf. By purchasing a health insurance policy for her using income from the trust to pay for premiums, we had greater flexibility in selecting the doctors and dentist that Shauna was comfortable with. This not only gave Shauna better access to care, but it reduced the reimbursable medical expenses required at her death. Because of this, there was money left in the trust that went to her brother and sister, who were the contingent beneficiaries of her special needs trust upon her death.

· · ·   Shauna's trustee   · · ·

Insuring Property

Obtaining *homeowners insurance* and *automobile insurance* is almost always a requirement before purchasing a home or automobile. It is possible to add additional liability coverage to a homeowner's policy or purchase a separate umbrella policy to provide protection in the event that your children cause harm to others, intended or unintended. This may be advisable if your child with disabilities has behavioral or mental health issues that may affect their social interactions and choices.

It is also possible to insure property against theft or damage if you do not own a home, or if you own specialized equipment or property of value. Renters insurance is sometimes an option for families who are renting a home but wish to have insurance on their furnishings and other belongings. Some homeowner's insurance policies also require special riders for certain types of property with values beyond a certain amount; for example, special art, antiques, or collectables might need to be insured with an additional rider to an existing homeowner's policy.

Insuring for Loss of Income

Disability Insurance   Insurance protection is available for the loss of income due to a short- or long-term disability, illness, or accident. It does not provide for the cost of care. Frequently families overlook disability insurance protection. Statistically, an individual is more likely to become disabled than to die prematurely during pre-retirement years. Because this type of insurance covers your lost income, you are required to have earned income to be eligible to purchase a policy. This can be an issue for families where a primary caregiver is not able to work outside of the home and therefore does not have earned income to insure.

Those with self-employed income, 1099-interest income, or commission income should especially consider purchasing an individual policy. Group coverage does not always cover bonus income or commission income, and the disability payments may be taxable income if paid for by the employer.

Special Needs Planning Pointer

If an individual with special needs is employed and is eligible to purchase additional disability insurance and/or long-term care insurance because the employer offers a guaranteed issued policy, their disability may not prevent them from obtaining such insurance coverage. Many

(continued)

(continued)
high-functioning individuals who are gainfully employed can benefit from such a plan. If so, it may be worth the cost of such coverage as long as it is portable and affordable upon termination of employment. Clearly, any plan provisions should be reviewed with your financial planner.

Long-Term Care Insurance

Long-term care insurance protects your assets in the event of your need for long-term care, either at home or in a long-term care facility. It basically provides you with the money needed to pay for long-term care services and/or nursing home care that you would otherwise have to pay from your own resources. This is an important consideration for a parent. Due to underwriting requirements of insurance companies, you cannot buy long-term care insurance for an individual who currently has disabilities. The planning strategy for an individual with a disability would be to maximize and protect their eligibility for government benefits, which would pay for the cost of their long-term care needs.

· · ·   **Special Needs Planning Story**   · · ·

I purchased long-term care insurance for me and my wife, because if either of us became disabled ourselves and needed to be cared for, we would not be able to help each other and also tend to the needs of our son. Since Cheryl stays at home with our son and does not earn an income, we could not purchase long-term disability insurance for her, but we were able to purchase long-term care insurance for her. Since our assets are not sufficient to pay for the cost of her care in addition to the cost of care for our son, we decided to buy a long-term care insurance policy for Cheryl.
· · ·   —David   · · ·

Life Insurance

Life insurance has many purposes. The primary use of life insurance in the pre-retirement years is to pay for the family's living expenses in the event of a premature death of either parent; basically, the insurance is purchased to protect the family's lifestyle in the event of the death of either or both parents. It is often assumed that the greater need for life insurance applies to the family member that earns the greatest income. In families where there are two parents, however, it is common for spouses to assume varying roles; often one spouse is the primary wage earner, and one spouse is the primary caregiver of the children (who may even work part time). This is often the case with families having a child with disabilities. Insurance on the life of the wage-earner should reflect the income that would be lost if he or she were to die, and insurance on the life of the caregiver should reflect the cost of hiring care for the children as well as advocacy services that the wage earner might not be able to take on. Adequate life insurance should be purchased for both parents.

• • •   **Special Needs Planning Story**   • • •

My husband, Ed, works full time, sometimes 60 to 70 hours per week. He aggressively saves for retirement and for college for our two children without disabilities. He is actively involved in the life and caregiving needs of our son Jonathan, who has disabilities. However, if something were to happen to me, it would not be possible for him to continue with his current work situation. He would also have to hire full-time childcare in our home for the children. Jonathan needs consistency in his life, and the thought of having to rely on hired help is very troubling to me. I want Ed to be able to hire the best of care for my family. We need to purchase life insurance on my life too.

• • •   —Jonathan's mother   • • •

How Much Life Insurance Is Necessary?   In determining the amount of life insurance needed, consider the immediate lump-sum needs for

- Burial expenses
- Estate taxes
- Probate expenses
- Emergency reserve funds (6 months of living expenses)
- Paying off debts
- Mortgages
- School loans
- Automobile loans
- Credit cards

- Personal loans

  Also consider the following lifestyle income needs for

- Living expenses
- Additional child care
- Home care
- Housekeeping as well as maintenance and repair for the home
- Supplemental needs expenses
- Advocacy fees
- Guardianship fees
- Legal fees
- Trustee fees

  In addition, do not forget to include funds for future goals of

- College planning expenses
- Surviving spouse's retirement income needs
- Costs for children's weddings or other milestones
- Costs to purchase a physical residence for your child with disabilities as an adult
- Costs for annual supports to maintain needs of your child with disabilities

Negotiable and Non-negotiable Needs   Table 7 offers some basic guidelines to help you determine the amount of life insurance you should buy. Because there is a cost associated with the purchase of insurance, it may be helpful to make two lists of needs. *Non-negotiable* items are absolutely required, and you will not eliminate them. *Negotiable* items are nice to have, but may not be worth the additional cost in premium needed to provide for them. Because these are personal decisions, we only list typical goals or expenses. It is up to you to decide whether they are negotiable or not.

Types of Life Insurance   There are basically two forms of life insurance, *term* and *permanent*. Term insurance provides protection for a specified period of time. Permanent insurance provides protection for an individual's entire lifetime. There are many opinions regarding the type of

Table 7. Example of classifying needs

Need	Non-negotiable	Negotiable
Income to pay rent, mortgage, or pay off the home loan	X	
Enough money to pay all expenses while children are at home	X	
Money for private colleges		X
Money for state colleges	X	
Money to assist the surviving spouse's retirement needs		X
Money to pay for your child with disabilities		
• Supplemental needs	X	
• Purchase of residence	X	
• Lifetime supports	X	
• Other needs		X

insurance to purchase. It is important to analyze the differences between the policies and determine how to best meet your needs. Because there is a high probability that your child may outlive you, it is suggested that you analyze the insurance options and work with your advisor to design a life insurance plan that provides you coverage throughout the later years of your life. In special needs planning, it is frequently suggested to buy a combination of term insurance and permanent insurance.

Permanent life insurance is designed to provide lifelong financial protection. As long as you pay the necessary premiums, the death benefit—or the amount of life insurance coverage—will be paid. Permanent life insurance policies build cash value. The cash value in the policy can be used to pay the premium in later years, or withdrawn to help pay for other long-term goals.

Term life insurance covers the insured for a certain period of time, known as the "term." A term life insurance policy pays death benefits only if the insured dies during the term, which can be 1, 5, 10, 20, or even 30 years.

Second-to-die life insurance (i.e., survivorship life insurance) is a type of life insurance coverage that insures two people and pays the death benefit at the death of the second insured person. The premiums are significantly less than they would be for two traditional insurance policies, because the policy insures two lives but only pays one death benefit. For older individuals with some health considerations, this may be a viable option for coverage. The policy can be designed using either permanent insurance or term insurance, or a combination of both. Second-to-die insurance is frequently used by families caring for an individual with disabilities, because the major concerns usually develop at the death of the second parent (or caregiver). This is the time when money is often needed the most.

Universal life insurance (i.e., adjustable life insurance) is a type of permanent life insurance that allows you, after your initial payment, to pay premiums at any time, in virtually any amount, subject to certain minimums and maximums. This type of policy can give you flexibility in changing the amount of the death benefit. To increase your death benefit, the insurance company usually requires you to furnish satisfactory evidence of your continued good health.

Whole life insurance (i.e., ordinary life insurance) is one of the oldest forms of permanent life insurance. The premiums and death benefits are guaranteed, remain constant over the life of the policy, and must be paid each year. The policy usually pays dividends. Dividends can be applied towards premium payments, received in cash, or retained in the policy in later years.

FEDERAL AND STATE PROGRAMS

As a rule, federal programs (Social Security and Medicare being the main exceptions) are managed through specific state agencies. For example, states have greater leeway in providing Medicaid services even though the program is part of the Social Security Act. This means you need to first identify the agency in your state responsible for a specific funding or service. States often have different offices for different disabilities. As a rule, there will be an agency department for developmental disabilities, developmental services, human services, cognitive disabilities, or some other related name that will be the best place to begin identifying services available for adults. It is the current trend in many states to avoid the use of specific disability titles for state agencies. There are still, however, many states that have offices labeled with a specific disability. State offices will provide services to individuals with the following conditions:

- Cognitive disabilities

- Cerebral palsy

- Autism spectrum disorders

- Traumatic brain injury prior to age 18 years

- Down syndrome

In some instances, there may be other state offices to cover other disability-related conditions, such as

- Mental illness
- Hearing impairments
- Visual impairments
- Traumatic brain injury after 18 years of age

Some examples of programs or services, which are available in most, if not all, states include

- *Health care:* There are two different public health care programs. Adults over 18 who receive SSI benefits have access to Medicaid. Adults over 18 who receive SSDI have access to Medicare, the same public health care program that provides for seniors. SSDI recipients should try to ensure eligibility to Medicaid, which provides coverage for long-term care in addition to health care. Adults who receive Medicare and Medicaid now must utilize the Medicare Prescription Program to obtain their prescriptions. Medicaid is a state-defined program with national regulations. Individuals under the age of 18 can also have access to Medicaid, if their parents' income and assets allow them to meet the eligibility guidelines for the SSI program. For more information about Medicaid, see http://www.cms.hhs.gov or visit your state's government web site and search for the Medicaid state agency.

- *Early and Periodic Screening, Diagnosis, and Treatment (EPSDT):* For children who are determined eligible for Medicaid, states must provide EPSDT for a child's physical or mental condition if such services are determined to be "medically necessary" until age 21. Some states have established non-Medicaid programs that allow families of middle income and higher to buy into Medicaid services on a sliding scale basis. This then allows access to EPSDT and related services. You have to weigh the cost–benefit by evaluating the benefits received to the amount of premium and co-pays that you will have to pay.

- *Home- and Community-Based Waivers:* States develop waivers to complement their Medicaid State Plan so that they can receive federal funding for part of the costs of the services and can avoid an open-ended service to all Medicaid beneficiaries. It allows the state to focus on a specific population, condition, or type of service or supports for a specific group of individuals, such as those with autism spectrum disorders, cognitive disabilities, mental illness, physical disabilities, developmental disabilities, and so forth. Smith (2006) discussed some common services these waivers include

  - Support coordination
  - Respite

- Home modification
- Assistive technology
- Supplies and equipment
- Health-related services
- Transportation
- Licensed residential services
- Supported living
- In-home supports
- Employment services
- Facility-based day services
- Community day supports

Health care insurance is an important benefit. As an individual reaches adulthood, he or she may be able to continue coverage on a parent's health plan. This is recommended, especially if your son or daughter is gainfully employed and does not have health insurance through his or her employer. Even if they currently have health insurance, you may want to continue to carry them on your policy if you can. In the event that they lose their job, they can maintain health insurance coverage through the parent while they are seeking new employment. Because we often find that individuals with disabilities frequently change jobs, maintaining health insurance on a parent's policy can be a great planning strategy.

State-Funded Health Care

Individuals who have received SSI benefits qualify automatically for state-funded health care. As your child begins to work, he or she can request that the health benefit be retained through special Social Security provisions meant to encourage employment. A good summary guide to employment support for individuals with disabilities receiving SSDI and SSI is the *Social Security Red Book: A Guide to Work Incentives* (see http://www.ssa.gov/redbook to obtain a copy).

In addition, many individuals with disabilities who qualify for Medicare through a parent's Social Security earnings record will also be eligible for Medicaid health insurance. The term that is used for these individuals is **"dual eligibles."**

There are other options for individuals with disabilities who are gainfully employed and do not have health care through SSI. Most states have a buy-in health program, including specific options for individuals with disabilities. This buy-in health program requires payment of premiums that are affordable compared to current private sector health insurance. As with Medicaid health insurance, there will be co-pays for doctors' visits, hospital stays, and prescription drugs.

Long-Term Supports or Care through Medicaid

Children who can qualify through family income for SSI are also eligible for Medicaid health services. The principle of EPSDT was developed to follow the theory that the earlier medical and chronic disability matters are addressed; the more the child will develop and thrive. All children covered under Medicaid are eligible for EPSDT services.

In some states, families who do not meet income eligibility for Medicaid health services can buy into it. This can be beneficial if your son or daughter has complex medical or behavioral needs. The services available include home nursing, home health, and personal assistance services. A special health care option is also available in states through TEFRA (which is also known as the "Katie Beckett" Waiver). This program recognizes that children with disabilities and special health care needs can remain with their families if the right social and medical supports are provided. Eligibility does not count the parents' income or resources. This program has helped many families avoid having to choose pediatric nursing homes, residential schools, and other restrictive options for their children. This program often taps home health agencies for nursing and home health aides. The hours may not be flexible, as the home health service staff may have a large workload and commitments with other families.

Personal Assistance Services

Adults can benefit from personal assistance services that are offered in most states as an optional Medicaid program. Eligibility varies widely, however. In 2002, 22 states were identified to have some type of personal assistance program for individuals with developmental disabilities (Rizzolo, Hemp, Braddock, & Pomeranz-Essley, 2004). This service is not medically based. It is more flexible and thus resembles a "support" (since the individual or family can control the hours of service). The personal assistant provides help to an individual in various activities of daily living, such as dressing, toileting, and preparing meals. The individual or family pay the personal assistant directly and receive reimbursement from the state for the hours that the individual worked. It is a major source of long-term support for people with physical disabilities, even if the rate of reimbursement has not kept up with inflation.

Family Support

Offered in all 50 states, family support services vary widely from state to state. Family support services include respite care or personal assistance, vouchers to purchase special clothing and shoes, and/or access to needed therapies. Each state varies in how the funding or service is provided. The program's goal, however, is the same—to increase the capacity of the entire family. In 2004, 20 states offered cash vouchers (Rizzolo et al., 2004). This number has been increasing over the years.

Social Security Benefits

As mentioned previously, most children and adults with developmental disabilities qualify for Social Security benefits through one of two Social Security income benefit programs: SSDI or SSI. SSDI is a disability income benefit payable to children of parents who have a work history and thus contributed to Social Security. This monthly income benefit is for the children who are disabled at age 18 and who are otherwise eligible due to the death, disability, or retirement of the parent. The specific amount of this benefit is based on either parent's Social Security earnings record.

SSI is an entitlement benefit that is payable to adults or children who are disabled or blind and have limited income and resources. Although this is an entitlement benefit, the value of an individual's resources is one of the factors that determine whether he or she is eligible for SSI benefits. Not all resources are included in making the determination of eligibility for SSI, however. The current limit for countable resources is $2,000 for an individual and $3,000 for a couple (see the web site at http://www.ssa.gov under SSI Resources for a summary of countable and non-countable resources).

The monthly SSI payment received varies, up to the maximum federal benefit rate, which may be supplemented by the state or decreased by countable income and resources. See Table 8 for more information about supplementary services. In addition to the law and regulation, which are both located on the web, you can visit http://www.nichy.org for more information on eligibility according to the federal law and regulations.

Obtaining Services

The best way to identify and obtain services is to go directly to the gateway to those services while gathering information from other families or advocacy agencies involved in that specific service area. A staff person who is handling eligibility or applications may not communicate all the options available. Their role may be more of *gatekeeper* than *gateway*.

Table 8. Some examples of Supplemental Security Income (SSI) sources

SSI Benefits
The maximum Federal benefit changes yearly. Effective January 1, 2006, the Federal benefit rate is $603 for an individual and $904 for a couple.

State Added Supplements
Some States supplement the Federal SSI benefit with additional payments. This makes the total SSI benefit levels higher in those States. SSI benefit amounts and State supplemental payment amounts vary based upon your income, living arrangements, and other factors.

States that Provide No State Supplement
Arkansas, Georgia, Kansas, Mississippi, Northern Mariana Islands, Tennessee, West Virginia

States that Provide Social Security Administered Supplement
California, Delaware, District of Columbia, Hawaii, Iowa*, Massachusetts, Michigan*, Montana, Nevada, New Jersey, New York*, Pennsylvania*, Rhode Island, Utah, Vermont*

States that Provide State Administered Supplement
Alabama, Alaska, Arizona, Colorado, Connecticut, Florida, Idaho, Illinois, Indiana, Kentucky, Louisiana, Maine, Maryland, Minnesota, Missouri, Nebraska, New Hampshire, New Mexico, North Carolina, North Dakota, Ohio, Oklahoma, Oregon, South Carolina, South Dakota, Texas, Virginia, Washington, Wisconsin, Wyoming

Note: * indicates dual administration state. Both Social Security and these states administer some state supplements.
Source: Understanding Supplemental Security Income: 2006 edition. (n.d.). Retrieved October 1, 2006, from http://www.socialsecurity.gov/notices/supplemental-security-income/benefits.htm

In your state, there may be a designated nonprofit agency or agencies that act as the entry point for services. In Maine, for example, there are specific nonprofit groups that determine eligibility for EI services. In other states, you go directly to an EI provider for assessment and services. In California, in-home support regulations are managed at the Department of Social Services, but your actual in-home support comes from a provider agency. California also has a very large regional center system that oversees developmental disabilities services. In Massachusetts, eligibility for personal care services is handled by nonprofit agencies, while eligibility for employment or residential services is determined by state agency officials in regional or area offices (Massachusetts Rehabilitation Commission, Department of Mental Retardation, etc.). Certain states, such as Pennsylvania, may have county staff involved in the process. States vary widely in their handling of services, and the smaller the number of state staff or official bureaucracy, the more likely a provider agency handles the gateway.

Special Needs Planning Pointer

The following are important factors to be considered, and questions to ask, when applying for services:

(continued)

(continued)

1. Are the programs offered by a state office an entitlement or public benefit?
2. How do you obtain the service once eligibility is processed?
3. How long is the application period? An entitlement may be available for your family member, but the state may have six months to process the application once you add up different steps in the process.
4. If the individual is an adult, does the agency look at his or her income alone for prioritization, or do they include the family income? What are the factors that determine his or her priority for services? Ask for a copy of their determination policy.
5. Does the eligibility process complete the application, or is there a second process to determine needs and priority for funding?
6. Are eligibility and needs determinations completed together, or is there another waiting period before we find out about determination of need? How is the priority for funding determined? Is it based on need alone, income, or both?
7. Are there waiting lists if the service is not an entitlement? If so, what is the current waiting time for the specific service or support?
8. If there is a waiting list, can the staff recommend other options that do not require a waiting period? (If there is an urgent need, it is necessary to make this clear to whoever is managing your application.)
9. What do families do to advance the priority of their family member?
10. Are services provided through contracted providers or different state offices?
11. Do we have choice over which provider is involved? If so, ask for a list of potential service providers.
12. If the family member is determined ineligible, is there an appeals process, and how can you obtain a copy of that paperwork?
13. If these services are dependent upon funding, how much funding is available this year? When does that funding get appropriated? How do people assist in advocating for further resources for this service?

When you apply for the service, the gatekeeper staff should give you an overview of the entire process. If he or she does not, be sure to ask. You still may not get all of your questions answered. The process may look intimidating. This is why it is so important to connect with a parent or advocacy group for support. Try to get objective input, even if you have to pay for the information. Even if the group you contact does not provide specific services, the members and/or staff can advise you of the options in your region. Other parents can share what they have done to obtain services. Learning about advocacy activities can ultimately advance service availability.

Special Needs Planning Pointer

Make sure you keep copies of the background material and documents that were requested of you by each state agency you approach and/or Social Security. You may need to contact each agency several times. In addition, develop a list of appointments or steps taken with dates, contact people, and/or agencies and service goals, so you can track the process if you need to appeal at a future date. Always maintain at least one extra copy of such a list in your home, in case you need it for more than one appeal officer. In some states, there may be a single point of entry for applications or eligibility, but this is not the case in most states. Of course, keeping electronic files is best of all, because you may be able to reuse material provided. This information is good to keep attached to your Letter of Intent, as it will be valuable for future caregivers if something were to happen to you.

Bibliography

REFERENCES

Americans with Disabilities Act (ADA) of 1990, PL 101-336, 42 U.S.C. §§ 12101 *et seq.*

Boehner, J., & Castle, M. (February 17, 2005). *Individuals with Disabilities Education Improvement Act (IDEA) of 2004 guide to "frequently asked questions."* Paper presented at the meeting of the Committee on Education and the Workforce, Washington, DC.

Certified Financial Planner Board of Standards, Inc. (2007). *Checklist for interviewing a financial planner.* Retrieved October 1, 2006, from http://www.cfp.net/learn/knowledgebase.asp?id=8

Holburn, S., & Vietze, P. (Eds.). (2002). *Person-centered planning: Research, practice, and future directions.* Baltimore: Paul H. Brookes Publishing Co.

Individuals with Disabilities Education Improvement Act of 2004, PL 108-446, 20 U.S.C. §§ 1400 *et seq.*

Jackins, B.D., Blank, R.S., Macy, P.M., Shulman, K.W., & Onello, H.H. (2005). *Special needs trust administration manual: A guide for trustees.* New York: iUniverse.

Office of Social Security. (n.d.). *Understanding supplemental security income: 2006 edition.* Retrieved October 1, 2006, from http://www.socialsecurity.gov/notices/supplemental-security-income/benefits.htm

Office of Social Security. (2005). *Social Security red book: A guide to work incentives.* Retrieved October 1, 2006, from http://www.ssa.gov/redbook

Omnibus Budget Reconciliation Act (OBRA) of 1993, PL 97-35, 95 Stat. 483.

Rizzolo, M.C., Hemp, R., Braddock, D., & Pomeranz-Essley, A. (2004). *The State of the states in developmental disabilities.* Washington, DC: American Association on Mental Retardation.

Social Security Act Amendments of 1994, PL 103-432, 42 U.S.C. §§ 1305 *et seq.*

Specialized Housing, Inc. (2002). *Passport to independence.* Contact web site for ordering information, http://www.specializedhousing.org

Tax Equity and Fiscal Responsibility Act (TEFRA) of 1982, PL 97-248.

The Tax Increase Prevention and Reconciliation Act (TIPRA) of 2005, PL 109-222, 120 Stat. 345.

WEB SITES TO INVESTIGATE

Academy of Special Needs Planners (http://www.specialneedsanswers.com): A source for families and attorneys to find more information and resources on special needs planning.

American Society for Deaf Children (http://www.deafchildren.org): A national independent nonprofit organization whose purpose is providing support, encouragement, and information to families raising children who are deaf or hard of hearing.

Americans with Disabilities Act (ADA) (http://www.ada.gov): Official web site with information regarding the Americans with Disabilities Act.

Association of University Centers on Disabilities (http://www.aucd.org): Offers different university medical services in each state; some have excellent guides and handbooks.

The Arc of the United States (http://www.thearc.org): Advocates for the rights and full participation of all children and adults with intellectual and developmental disabilities. Identifies state and local chapters and provides links to resources and government affairs.

Autism Society of America (http://www.autism-society.org): Official web site of the Autism Society of America organization.

Centers for Disease Control and Prevention (CDC) (http://www.cdc.gov): An organization globally recognized for conducting research and investigations and for its action oriented approach. CDC responds to health emergencies and applies research and findings to improve the daily lives of individuals. It is 1 of 13 major operating components of the U.S. Department of Health and Human Services.

Certified Financial Planner Board of Standards, Inc. (http://www.cfp.net/): The professional regulatory organization in the United States that fosters professional standards in personal financial planning so that the public has access to and benefits from competent and ethical financial planning.

DB-LINK (http://www.dblink.org): The official web site for the National Consortium on Deaf-Blindness.

DisabilityInfo.gov (http://www.disabilityinfo.gov): The federal government's one-stop web site for information for individuals with disabilities, their families, their employers, human resource and health care professionals, and many others.

Easter Seals (http://www.easter-seals.org): A general service provider for individuals with disabilities.

Financial Planning Association (http://www.fpanet.org): The membership organization for the financial planning community and a good source to help find a financial planner in your area.

IDEA Data (http://www.ideadata.org): This site allows you to compare state statistics on Individuals with Disabilities Education Improvement Act (IDEA) of 2004 services as well as see specific data on your state.

Individuals with Disabilities Education Act (IDEA) (http://idea.ed.gov/): A respository of information from the U.S. Department of Education about the federal laws ensuring services to children with disabilities.

Moving Forward Towards Independence (http://www.moving-forward.org): A nonprofit residential program providing a structured and supported living program for adults with learning and developmental challenges.

National Academy of Elder Law Attorneys, Inc. (http://www.naela.org): A nonprofit association that assists lawyers, bar organizations, and others who work with older clients and their families.

National Alliance on the Mentally Ill (http://www.nami.org): Contains information on mental illness for individuals and their families. Offers connections to local or state chapters.

National Association for Parents of Children with Visual Impairments (NAPVI) (http://www.spedex.com/napvi): A nonprofit organization of, by, and for parents committed to providing support to the parents of children who have visual impairments.

National Association of Councils on Developmental Disabilities (NACDD) (http://www.nacdd.org): Official web site of the NACDD and provides information helpful to locating state chapters.

National Dissemination Center for Children with Disabilities (http://www.nichcy.org): Good starting point to learn more about special education.

National Down Syndrome Congress (NDSC) (http://www.ndsccenter.org): Provides information, advocacy, and support concerning all aspects of life for individuals with Down syndrome.

National Down Syndrome Society (NDSS) (http://www.ndss.org): The mission of the NDSS is to benefit people with Down syndrome and their families through national leadership in education, research, and advocacy.

National Endowment for Financial Education (http://www.nefe.org): Provides a source for general financial information and education.

National Fragile X Foundation (NFXF) (http://www.fragilex.org): Provides support, education, awareness, resources, and research regarding fragile X syndrome.

National Resource Center on ADHD (http://www.help4adhd.org): Repositiory of answers to questions on a broad range of topics including educational rights, treatment options, supports, and services.

No Child Left Behind (NCLB) Act (http://www.ed.gov/policy/speced/guid/nclb/; http://www.ed.gov/parents/academic/involve/nclbguide; http://www.nichey.org/resources/nclb.asp): The NCLB Act is aimed at improving public education and includes considerations for children eligible for special education.

Online Asperger Syndrome Information and Support (OASIS) (http://www.aspergersyndrome.org): An informational web site that focuses on Asperger syndrome, pervasive development disorder, and other high-functioning forms of autism spectrum disorders.

Parents of Galactosemic Children, Inc. (PGC) (http://www.galactosemia.org): A national, nonprofit, volunteer organization whose mission is to provide information, support, and networking opportunities to families affected by galactosemia.

Person-Centered Planning Education (http://www.ilr.cornell.edu/ped/tsal/pcp/index.html): Official web site of the Person-Centered Planning Education Program.

Planned Lifetime Assistance Network (PLAN) (http://www.nationalplanalliance.org): A nonprofit organization dedicated to meeting the planning needs of families with adult children having lifelong disabilities. Many chapters have pooled trusts.

Social Security Administration (http://www.ssa.gov): Social Security information, including benefits, facts, on-line application, and directions.

Special Health Care Needs (http://www.medicalhomeinfo.org/states/index.html): Information about programs for children with special health care needs.

Special Needs Alliance (SNA) (http://www.specialneedsalliance.com): A national network of lawyers dedicated to disability and public benefits law.

Special Needs Contacts (http://www.ed.gov/policy/speced/guid/idea/monitor/state-contact-list.html): Offers connections to state special education offices. You can use these connections to explore your state's specific special education law and regulations.

Special Needs Planning (http://www.specialneedsplanning.com): The web site of the authors' of this book and a resource for families on special needs planning services and information.

Specialized Housing, Inc. (http://www.specializedhousing.org): An organization that promotes independence through home ownership and supportive independent living situations for adults with developmental disabilities, learning disabilities, traumatic brain injuries, physical disabilities, or psychiatric illness.

State Agencies (http://www.nasddds.org/index.shtml): Will help you to identify state agencies that administer programs for developmental disabilities and mental retardation.

Toward Independent Living and Learning, Inc. (TILL) (http://www.tillinc.org): A private nonprofit human services agency, established in 1980, which provides a comprehensive range of services, including creative housing options.

United Cerebral Palsy (http://www.ucp.org): Official web site of the United Cerebral Palsy organization.

U.S. Department of Health and Human Services (HHS) (http://www.hhs.gov): The U.S. government's principal agency for protecting the health of all Americans and providing essential human services, especially for those who are least able to help themselves.

U.S. Department of Housing and Urban Development (HUD) (http://www.hud.gov): Provides information and links on various housing resources.

Glossary

401(K) PLAN A defined contribution plan established under section 401(k) of the Tax Code. A plan in which employees may elect, as an alternative to receiving taxable cash in the form of compensation or a bonus, to contribute pre-tax dollars to a qualified tax-deferred retirement plan.

529 PLAN A college savings plan that provides professionally managed, tax-advantaged investment portfolios designed to help meet tuition and other higher education expenses at any eligible educational institution in the country.

BALANCE SHEET A financial statement that shows the assets, liabilities and owners' equity of an entity on a specific date.

BEQUEST The giving of assets, such as stocks, bonds, mutual funds, real estate, and personal property, to beneficiaries through the provisions of a will.

BORROWING A way of acquiring necessary capital. One form of borrowing is when an individual or a company asks a bank to loan them a certain amount of money, over a certain period of time, and agrees to pay a certain amount of interest.

CAPITAL APPRECIATION One of the investment objectives of mutual funds that purchase securities whose value is expected to rise.

CAPITAL GROWTH The amount that a security's market value increases over the original purchase price, or the amount that a mutual fund increases, as reflected in the price of the shares.

CAPITAL LOSS A decrease in the value of a capital asset, calculated by the difference in price at which an investment was purchased and the price at which it was sold.

CAPITAL NEEDS ANALYSIS The method frequently used by insurance agents and planners to calculate the amount of insurance needed to replace both the future income stream of an individual and the present dollar value of specific future goals.

CASH EQUIVALENTS Short-term, highly liquid investments.

CASH RESERVES The amount of money that should be kept in investments that are easily converted into cash within 5 business days and is available to meet current cash needs and to cover for any unforeseen short-term emergency. Examples are money market funds, treasury bills, saving accounts, and so forth.

CHARITABLE GIFT ANNUITY An arrangement whereby the donor makes a gift to charity and receives a guaranteed lifetime (or joint lifetime) income based on the age(s) of the annuitant(s).

CHARITABLE REMAINDER TRUST Irrevocable trust in which one or more individuals are paid income until the grantor's death, at which time the balance is passed on to a designated charity.

CHARITABLE TRUSTS A form of trust in which the gifter places substantial funds or assets into an irrevocable trust with an independent trustee. The assets go to a designated charity upon the death of the donor, but the donor (or specific beneficiary) receives regular profits from the trust during the donor's lifetime.

CODICIL A legal document that supplements and changes an existing will, generally restricted to minor changes to the original will.

COMMON STOCK One of two types of stock an investor may purchase in a company. Most stock is common stock. Investors who purchase it have voting rights at the company's annual stockholders' meeting. Common stockholders are not guaranteed dividends, but they may receive higher dividends during the company's prosperous periods. If a company fails or liquidates, common stockholders are paid after bondholders and preferred stockholders.

COMPOUNDING The ability of an asset to generate interest that is then added to the previous principal plus interest.

CONSERVATOR A person appointed by the court and given authority to handle the financial affairs of a person who is unable to manage finances on their own. A conservator does not make any personal decisions for the individual.

"CRUMMY" PROVISIONS A trust provision that allows the trust beneficiary to withdraw a limited amount of funds during a limited time period each year. It is used in a life insurance trust to qualify the amount that can be withdrawn as a present interest for the annual exclusion amount.

CURRENT LIABILITIES   Money owed and payable by a company or individual, usually within one year.

CUSTODIANSHIP   Generally, an ownership arrangement in which property management rights are given to a custodian for the benefit of a child beneficiary; a custodian's duties resemble those of a trustee, although the custodian does not take legal title to the property. The custodianship ends when the minor reaches the age of majority as specified by state law.

DEBT OBLIGATIONS   Money an individual owes to a lender. This can be in the form of credit card debt, automobile loans, and mortgages.

DEFAULT RISK   The risk that a company or individual will be unable to pay the principal or contractual interest on its debt obligations.

DEFERRED ANNUITY   An annuity in which the annuitant wishes to allow earnings received into the separate account during the accumulation phase to accrue tax deferred until some future time.

DISABILITY DETERMINATION   Most Social Security claims are processed through a network of Social Security Administration field offices. Social Security field offices review the application and send the paperwork to the federally funded Disability Determination Center. The Determination Center decides if an individual meets the definitions of being disabled.

DISCRETIONARY INCOME   An individual's income that is available to be spent after paying for the essential expenses such as food, clothing, and shelter.

DIVERSIFICATION   The process of accumulating securities in different types of investments, industries, risk categories, and companies in an effort to reduce the potential risk of loss that may be associated with one investment.

DIVERSIFIED COMMON STOCK FUND   A diversified management company that invests substantially all of its assets in a portfolio of common stocks in a wide variety of industries.

DIVIDEND   A cash payment distributed to shareholders. Dividends are financed by profits, and are announced by the company's board of directors before they are paid.

DURABLE POWER OF ATTORNEY (POA)   A legal document that allows one person (the principal) to authorize another person (the attorney-in-fact or agent) to act on his or her behalf with respect to specified types of property and that may remain in effect during a subsequent disability or incompetency of the principal.

DURABLE POWER OF ATTORNEY (POA) FOR HEALTH CARE   A legal document which grants decision-making powers related to health care to an agent; generally provides for removal of a physician, the right to have the incompetent patient discharged against medical advice, the right to medical records, and the right to have the patient moved or to engage other treatment.

EARNED INCOME   Receipt of payments that include wages, commissions, and bonuses for services rendered.

EQUITY   The ownership interest of common and preferred stockholders in a company.

ESTATE   All the assets a person possesses at the time of death, including securities, real estate, interest in business, physical possessions, death benefit of life insurance policies, and cash.

ESTATE TAX   A tax imposed by a state or the federal government on assets left to heirs.

EXECUTOR   The individuals or corporations that are appointed in a will who will have the legal responsibility for carrying out the provisions of the will to the best of their ability, according to the current federal and state laws. The executor may seek the assistance of an attorney to complete the process of settling an estate.

FIDUCIARY   A person, company, or association who is responsible for investing the assets of the beneficiary in a prudent manner (i.e., a trustee).

FIXED ANNUITY   Insurance product that provides for lifetime retirement income in designated (fixed) monthly installments.

FIXED ASSETS   A long-term tangible asset or the real property, plant, and equipment of a business or individual.

FIXED EXPENSES   A cost that remains constant and that the consumer has limited control to change (i.e., mortgage, rent, insurance, taxes).

FIXED-INCOME INVESTMENT   A description of investments in preferred stock, bonds, certificates of deposit, and other debt-based instruments that pay a fixed amount of interest.

FIXED-INCOME SECURITY A security that pays an unchanging rate of interest or dividends. Fixed-income securities include bonds, certificate of deposit, money market instruments, and preferred stock.

FULLY FUNDED MODEL The description of a residential placement that is completely funded by the government.

GRANTOR The person who establishes a trust.

GROSS ESTATE Generally includes the value of all property that the decedent owned, had an interest in, or controlled at the time of death. In addition to property that an individual may own in his or her name, it includes property that avoids probate, such as joint tenancy property, with rights of survivorship and life insurance proceeds paid to a named beneficiary.

GROWTH AND INCOME FUND A mutual fund whose aim is to provide for a degree of both income and long-term growth.

GROWTH OF PRINCIPAL Appreciation on an initial investment.

GROWTH-ORIENTED INVESTMENT Property that was purchased with the intent to appreciate. Any income generated by the property is incidental.

GUARDIAN A person appointed by the probate court to assume some decision-making responsibilities for an individual who is unable to make decisions for him- or herself. The individual for whom one is appointed is called a ward. A guardian is appointed for a ward by the determination of the probate court.

GROWTH STOCKS An ownership interest in a company that is growing earnings and/or revenue faster than its industry or the overall market. Such companies usually pay little or no dividends, preferring to use the income instead to finance further expansion.

HEALTH CARE PROXY A document that contains language that helps an assigned person to make medical decisions if you are unable to do so (also called *power of attorney*).

INFLATION Increases in the general price level of goods and services. Inflation is commonly reported using the Consumer Price Index as a measure and is one of the major risks to investors over the long term.

INFLATION RATE An important economic indicator, this is the rate at which prices for goods and services are rising.

INFLATION RISK Uncertainty over the future value of an investment due to the possibility that the value of assets or income will decrease as inflation shrinks the purchasing power of a currency.

INTEREST   Payments borrowers pay lenders for the use of their money. A corporation pays interest on its bonds to its bondholders.

INTEREST RATE   An important economic indicator, this is the price, calculated as a percentage of the money loaned, that a financial institution charges borrowers for the use of the institution's money.

INTESTACY   When one dies without a valid will, he or she is said to have died intestate and his or her property will be distributed under state succession statutes, generally of the state in which he or she was domiciled at death.

INVESTMENT OBJECTIVE   The documented intent of a particular asset. One example is growth, where the investor wants an investment asset to appreciate. A second example is income, where the investor wants to generate cash flow.

IRREVOCABLE TRUST   A trust that cannot be changed or terminated by the person who created it without the agreement of the beneficiary.

JOINT TENANCY WITH RIGHT OF SURVIVORSHIP   Asset ownership for two or more persons in which each owner holds an equal share and may give away or sell a portion or all that share without the permission of the other owner(s). In the event of death, an owner's share is divided equally among the surviving co-owners.

LETTER OF INTENT   Although not legally binding, this form (see the appendix for a sample and the accompanying CD-ROM for a blank version) communicates your desires and concerns to future caregivers. It covers vital statistics, your child's financial picture, details about what works well or not so well for your child, suggestions about what changes might be needed for the future, a list of the locations of all pertinent documents and records, and individuals that are important in your child's life.

LIABILITIES   See *debt obligations.*

LIFE ANNUITY   Type of settlement option chosen by the annuitant that allows for the payment of retirement income for the entire lifespan of the annuitant. This pay-out option, sometimes referred to as straight life, typically allows for the shortest pay-out period to the annuitant as they are paid over the lifetime of one annuitant. If the annuitant dies, 1 month later payments cease. Since this pay-out will be over the fewest number of years, the annuitant will receive the largest possible check. Because the annuitant is receiving a larger payment, the annuitant is also getting a faster return of the principal amount. This return of principal will allow the annuitant to obtain the largest amount of tax exclusion because the principal amount consists of after-tax dollars that were used to fund the annuity.

LIQUID ASSETS   Those assets that can easily be converted into cash within 5 business days without a penalty.

LIQUID NET WORTH   Liquid net worth includes all assets that can be liquidated within 30 days, exclusive of real estate holdings. This includes, but is not limited to, checking and savings accounts, IRA accounts, all marketable securities, commodity accounts, cash, and money market funds, and precious metals.

LIVING WILLS   A document which allows people to specify in advance of an illness or injury medical treatments to be administered or withheld.

LOCAL EDUCATION AGENCY (LEA)   Another term for a community's school district.

LONG-TERM CARE INSURANCE   Coverage that, under specified conditions, provides skilled nursing care, home health care, or personal or adult day care for individuals with a chronic or disabling condition that needs constant supervision. Long-term care insurance offers more flexibility and options than many public assistance programs.

MARKETABILITY   The ease or difficulty with which securities can be sold in the market.

MATURITY DATE   Date on which the principal amount of a note, draft, acceptance bond, or other debt instrument becomes due and payable.

MEDICAID   Medicaid is a joint federal and state program that helps with medical costs for people with low incomes and limited resources. Medicaid programs vary from state to state, but most health care costs are covered if an individual qualifies for both Medicare and Medicaid. People with Medicaid may get coverage for things like nursing home care and outpatient prescription drugs that are not covered by Medicare.

MEDICARE   The federal health insurance program for people 65 years of age or older and also for certain younger people with disabilities.

MONEY MARKET FUND   A mutual fund that invests in short-term corporate and government debt. Interest payments are passed on to shareholders. The fund aims to keep the net asset value at $1 per share to simplify accounting, but the interest rate does fluctuate.

MUTUAL FUND   An open-ended fund operated by an investment company that raises money from shareholders and invests in a group of assets, in accordance with a stated set of objectives. The market price of the fund's shares fluctuates daily with the market price of the securities in its portfolio.

NONLIQUID ASSETS Investments that cannot be easily converted into cash within 5 business days.

PAYBACK TRUST A section in the Omnibus Budget Reconciliation Act of 1993 governing Medicaid provides that a person can maintain eligibility for government benefits if he or she places excess funds in an eligible trust. This trust is created with the assets of a disabled individual under age 65 and are established by his or her parent, grandparent, or legal guardian, or by a court. They also must provide that, at the beneficiary's death, any remaining trust funds will first be used to reimburse the state for Medicaid paid on the beneficiary's behalf.

PERMANENT LIFE INSURANCE Designed to provide lifelong financial protection; as long as the necessary premiums are paid, the death benefit will be paid. Most permanent policies have a feature known as cash value that increases (tax deferred) over the life of the policy and can be used to help fund financial goals (e.g., retirement, education expenses).

POOLED TRUST Medicaid and federal law also permit trusts that pool the resources of many beneficiaries with disabilities, and those resources are managed by a nonprofit association. Unlike individual disability trusts, which may be created only for those under age 65, pooled trusts may be for beneficiaries of any age, and may be created by the beneficiary. In addition, at the beneficiary's death, the state does not have to be repaid for its Medicaid expenses on the beneficiary's behalf as long as the funds are retained in the trust for the benefit of the other beneficiaries.

POWER OF ATTORNEY (POA) The legal right of an individual named to act on another's behalf during his or her lifetime, in the event that disability or incapacitation renders that person unable to make decisions on his or her own behalf. Decisions may be made concerning assets and property or health care (also called a *health care proxy*).

PRESSURE POINTS The points in time that require a parent or guardian to take specific action to protect eligibility for government benefits, apply for benefits, or work with various government agencies or school systems on behalf of an individual with special needs. This may involve a transition period over time or completing an application on a specific day. In addition to the requirements that pertain to an individual with disabilities, traditional planning points are college, retirement, and death of a parent. The overall goal is to identify these points in advance and implement various strategies to plan for these moments in time.

PROBATE The judicial determination of the validity of a will and the distribution of estate assets under a valid will.

RATES OF RETURN The calculation that measures the gain on an investment over a period of time.

REPRESENTATIVE PAYEE In cases in which an individual is not capable of managing his or her own Social Security benefits and after careful investigation, a person appointed by Social Security, who may be a relative, friend, or another concerned party, to handle that individual's Social Security matters, who is then required to provide detailed records of the distribution of these funds. A person having power of attorney over an individual does not automatically qualify that person to be a representative payee.

REQUIRED MINIMUM DISTRIBUTION A distribution based on the life expectancy of an IRA owner or qualified retirement plan participant designed to satisfy certain minimum requirements imposed by the IRS upon attaining age 70½. Failure to satisfy the distribution requirement may result in a 50% excise tax on the amount not withdrawn.

RETIREMENT ASSETS Money that cannot be accessed by the owner prior to turning age 59½ without paying a penalty.

REVOCABLE LIVING TRUST A trust created during the grantor's lifetime that the grantor may alter, amend, or revoke; the trust may become irrevocable or terminate at the grantor's death.

REVOCABLE TRUST An agreement whereby property is deeded to heirs. This trust may be changed by the grantor or other person.

RISK/RETURN TRADE-OFF A concept that risk is associated to return; the possibility that an investment will not perform as anticipated. In other words, the higher the return, the greater the risk, and vice versa.

ROLLOVER IRA An individual retirement account (IRA) set up by an individual to receive a distribution from a qualified retirement plan. Distributions rolled over into a rollover IRA are not subject to any contribution limits. Additionally, the distribution may be eligible for subsequent rollover back into a qualified retirement plan available through a new employer. To retain this eligibility, the IRA must be composed solely of the original rollover contribution and earnings (i.e., no other contributions or rollovers may be added to or mingled with the IRA), and the new employer's plan must permit the acceptance of rollover contributions. Also known as a *conduit IRA*.

ROTH CONVERSION IRA A Roth individual retirement account (IRA) designated as a conversion IRA. The only permissible contributions to a Roth conversion IRA are amounts converted from a traditional IRA during the same tax year. It is no longer necessary to keep contributory Roth money separate from converted Roth money.

ROTH IRA An individual retirement account (IRA) in which contributions are not tax-deductible, qualified distributions from the account are not taxable, and earnings on the account are taxable only when a withdrawal is not a qualified distribution.

SAFETY OF PRINCIPAL Preserving the value of an investment.

SECTION 8 HOUSING ASSISTANCE The Section 8 Housing Choice Voucher Program is the federal government's major program for assisting very low income families, the elderly, and individuals with disabilities to rent decent, safe, and sanitary housing in the private market. Since the housing assistance is provided on behalf of the family or individual, participants are able to find and rent privately owned housing, including single-family homes, townhouses, and apartments. The participant is free to choose any housing that meets the requirements of the program and is not limited to units located in subsidized housing projects.

SECURED DEBT Borrowed funds that are backed by a specific asset. For example, a home mortgage is backed by the value of the residence. If the borrower does not abide by the terms of the agreement, the lender has a legal right to the residence.

SEMI-LIQUID ASSETS Money that is intended for long-term savings that may be subject to early withdrawal fees or fluctuations in price or value.

SINGLE PREMIUM DEFERRED ANNUITY Method of purchasing any annuity in which the annuitant deposits one lump sum of money into the account. The money will then remain in the account and accrue as tax deferred until the annuitant elects to begin the pay-out phase. At pay-out, the annuitant will pay ordinary income tax on all earnings in the account that are in excess of the cost basis.

SOCIAL SECURITY DISABILITY INSURANCE (SSDI) A program financed with Social Security taxes paid by workers, employers, and self-employed persons. In order to be eligible for a SSDI benefit, the worker must earn sufficient credits based on taxable work. Disability benefits are payable to workers with disabilities, disabled widows or widowers, or adults disabled since childhood who are otherwise eligible. Auxiliary benefits may be payable to a worker's dependents as well. The monthly disability benefit payment is based on the SSDI earnings record of the insured worker on whose Social Security number the disability claim is filed.

STOCK   An instrument that signifies an ownership position in a corporation.

SUCCESSOR TRUSTEE   The person that is named as a back-up to the original individual appointed trustee.

SUPPLEMENTAL SECURITY INCOME (SSI)   The SSI program provides monthly income to people who are age 65 or older, or are blind or disabled and have limited income and financial resources. Effective January 2006, the SSI payment for an eligible individual was $603 per month and, for an eligible couple, $904 per month. If only one person of a married couple is eligible, a portion of the spouse's income may be counted. In addition, the individual's financial resources (savings and assets owned) cannot exceed $2,000 ($3,000 if married). Individuals can be eligible for SSI even if they have never worked in employment covered under Social Security.

SURETY BOND   Secures the performance on fiduciaries duties and compliance with court order.

SURVIVOR BENEFIT PENSION PLAN (SBP)   Established by Congress effective September 21, 1972, (PL 92-425) to provide a monthly income to survivors of retired military personnel upon the member's death when retired pay stops. Survivors of members who die while on active duty, and survivors of members recalled to active duty from retirement that die while on active duty, may also be protected by the SBP.

SURVIVORSHIP LIFE INSURANCE   This type of life insurance covers two individuals and pays the death benefit at the death of the second insured. The premiums are significantly less than two traditional insurance policies because the policy insures two lives for one benefit. For older individuals with some health considerations, this may be a viable option for coverage. The policy can be designed using either whole-life insurance, term insurance, universal life insurance, or a combination of these. This product is frequently used in the disability market because the major concerns usually develop at the death of the second parent (or caregiver), a time when money is often needed the most.

TEMPORARY GUARDIAN OR CONSERVATOR When a guardian or conservator is required on a temporary basis, or pending the general guardianship appointment. A temporary guardianship may be granted until a problem is settled or a permanent arrangement can be made. Such a court appointment can either be responsible for the person, the estate, or both.

TENANTS IN COMMON A form of ownership held by at least two persons. Each owner has a specific percentage interest in the account and, upon death of one of the owners, those shares become part of the deceased owner's estate.

TERM LIFE INSURANCE This type of life insurance covers the insured for a certain period of time, or term. The policy pays death benefits only if the insured dies during the term, which can be 1, 5, 10, or even 20 years.

TESTAMENTARY TRUST A trust that is funded at death.

TIME VALUE OF MONEY The concept that money available today is worth more than that same amount in the future.

TOTAL RETURN A measure of investment performance that starts with price changes, then adds in the results of reinvesting all earnings, such as interest or dividends, generated by the investment during the period being measured.

TRANSFER ON DEATH ACCOUNT An account registration used to help avoid probate, transferring assets to a pre-assigned beneficiary upon the death of the account owner.

TREASURIES Debt obligations of the U.S. government. They are secured by the full faith and credit of the U.S. federal government. The interest on treasuries is exempt from state and local taxes but is subject to federal income tax. There are three types of treasuries: treasury bills, with maturities of 1 year or less; treasury notes, with maturities ranging from 1 to 10 years; and treasury bonds, long-term instruments with maturities of 10 years or more.

TRUST A legal arrangement under which an individual (grantor) gives fiduciary control of property to a person or institution (trustee) for the benefit of a beneficiary.

TRUST ADMINISTRATION The act of implementing and following the terms of the trust.

TRUST ADVISOR An individual, often a family member or friend, who will provide input on behalf of the beneficiary to the trustee that can be a professional trustee. This role removes the fiduciary responsibility of the individual but allows them to be involved in the activity of the trust.

TRUSTEE The individual or individuals who manage the trust. There is a fiduciary responsibility for seeing that trust funds are properly invested and disbursed according to the wishes of the individual who created the trust.

UNEARNED INCOME Income derived from sources other than wages, consisting of interest, dividends, rental income, and capital gains.

UNIVERSAL LIFE INSURANCE A type of permanent life insurance that allows you, after your initial payment, to pay premiums at any time, in virtually any amount, subject to certain minimums and maximums. This policy also permits you to reduce or increase the death benefit more easily than a traditional whole life policy. To increase your death benefit, the insurance company usually requires you to furnish satisfactory evidence of your continued good health.

UNSECURED DEBT A debt or money owed that is not backed by assets or collateral; such as credit card debt.

USE ASSETS Property that is owned by an individual that cannot be used to generate an income (e.g., a personal residence).

VARIABLE EXPENSES Expenses that will change over time and items that an individual may have control over. They generally consist of necessary expenses that may vary, such as utilities.

WARD The legal term for a person under guardianship or conservatorship.

WILL A legal document that defines how a person wishes his or her estate or property to be dispersed after his or her death. The document must be signed by the testator in the presence of two witnesses, who must also sign. An executor or executors are appointed by the testator to ensure that his or her wishes are carried out.

WILL CONTEST The challenge of a will's validity by heirs in probate court.

WHOLE LIFE INSURANCE The most common type of permanent life insurance. With this type of policy, premiums generally remain constant over the life of the policy and must be paid periodically in the amount specified in the policy.

YIELD The calculation used to determine income as a percentage of the investor's capital investment.

Appendix

LETTER OF INTENT

Prepared for: Joseph Richard Brown

Prepared by: Patricia and Richard Brown (Richard's parents)

Date: November 15, 2006

Copies given to: Andrew Brown (Richard's brother) and Judith Lambert (Patricia's sister)

[Current photograph of Joseph]

Contents

Introduction

The most important asset your child has is YOU.

Think for a moment about the specific instructions or guidelines you give to your child or his or her caregiver when you leave for just an evening out or a weekend away. Imagine if you never came back. Certainly, you have an idea of what you would like your child's life to look like after your death. Your child's next caregiver, however, may not have the same ideas and insights as you. Your child's future trustees may not have the same values of money that you have. A Letter of Intent will guide your child's future caregivers in making the most appropriate life decisions for your child and will provide direction to your child's trustee in fulfilling his or her fiduciary responsibilities.

When we first began providing special needs planning for families in the early 1990s, the field of future planning for individuals with disabilities was virtually nonexistent. Our research in this area told us that parents should make a list of things for future caregivers to know about, which has developed into a Letter of Intent. Providing a long list of ideas to include in the Letter of Intent, however, did not motivate families to create their own Letter of Intents. When our initial Letter of Intent was created in 1995, it was designed to provide a user friendly format for parents to be able to simply fill in the blanks rather than try to follow a list of things to include in creating their own Letter of Intent. Over the years, we have made modifications based upon the input that we have received from families using our Letter of Intent to make it more comprehensive.

Many families need a catalyst to encourage them to begin the planning process. A Letter of Intent simplifies the planning process by initially asking basic biographic information and progresses to more thoughtful and provoking questions. Since developing the Five Factors of comprehensive special needs planning, we have reorganized the content based upon these key elements in planning for your child's future. By completing a Letter of Intent for your family member, you will begin to develop goals and objectives to assist you in the overall planning process. Ultimately, it will provide the details required for future caregivers to fulfill their expected roles based upon your desires and concerns.

No matter who you have entrusted to care for your child when you are gone—sibling, friend, relative, trustee, guardian, or organization—you can help guide that person by providing them the knowledge that only you, as a parent, possess. This is not a legally binding document, but it is still perhaps one of the most important documents you can prepare for the future well being of your child. This is an opportunity to leave a legacy of all that you have accomplished with your child.

You need to periodically review and revise this Letter of Intent, perhaps on your child's birthday, making certain to provide your child's future caregiver with an updated copy. As every child is unique, so should this document be unique. Feel free to expand where needed and omit areas that are not applicable. Be flexible, be clear, and feel free to make it as personal as you wish.

Best of Luck!

John W. Nadworny
and
Cynthia R. Haddad

Emotional Factors

The Emotional Factors section allows you to provide your personal vision that you have for your child's future. Taking time to express this vision will accomplish three goals: 1) it helps you to set personal goals for you to achieve for your child's future, 2) it helps future caregivers to better understand your child and your wishes, and 3) it will help future caregivers understand your expectations of their roles in your child's life.

When faced with the responsibility and the reality of their role in your child's life, the future caregiver(s) may feel similar emotions as you did when you first learned about your child's diagnosis. Depending upon your child's age and the familiarity that the future caregiver has with your child and his or her routines, you may want to expand in some areas of this section more than in others. It is important to put yourself in the future caregiver's place and look at it from the perspective that you first had—wanting to know as much as possible, as soon as possible.

Some parents' may wish to provide every detail of his or her child's being in this section—what makes their child the person that he or she is, what makes the child happy, sad, or mad. They want to pass along their nurturing instincts so that the future caregiver not only sees their child from the outside but understands the child's heart.

Another set of parents' may be more analytical or factual about their child's future in this section. They may emphasize the accomplishments their child has made and set periodic milestones for both the family and the child to achieve.

Only you can decide what type of information you wish to provide. Whatever you decide, please remember that it is helpful for you to work together with your child's future caregiver in developing this Letter of Intent for your child.

CREATE THE VISION

What is the vision that you have of your child's life with you?
We want Joseph to enjoy life to his fullest potential. He brings such joy to all those he meets with his enchanting smile, beautiful blue eyes, and chubby little arms that give great big hugs!

We often forget that Joseph has Down syndrome. And we hope that others will, too. We want him to grow and develop as any other child. We want to make sure that Joseph receives whatever supports are required for him to do so.

What is the vision that you have of your child's life without you?
We are worried about Joseph's future and his well-being, especially when we are not here for him. At this point, Joseph is developing very similar to Patrick's development at age 1. We really do not know what to expect from him. We just want him to be happy and to be safe.

We hope that the information here will serve as something of a blueprint for others to know who Joseph is and what our wishes are for his future. We can only share what we know and how we feel about things today. We will update this document as often as possible.

What is your vision of the role of your child's guardian? What do you expect him or her to do for your child?
We hope that you will care for Joseph and guide him as you would your own child. Please include him as an equal member of your family. Instill the family values that we share with him.

What is your vision for the role of your child's trustee? How should he or she make financial decisions?
We want to make sure that Joseph is never a financial burden to anyone. Meet with his guardian regularly to know what his needs are and what his needs could potentially be. Although we tried to provide adequate money for Patrick and Joseph's long-term needs, we realize that needs and expenses change. Overall, we divided our estate equally between Patrick and Joseph. We currently expect their expenses to be somewhat similar during their years as children. There may, however, be a need to hire advocates for Joseph, which would contribute to a greater expense. We would consider this situation to be very good use of trust assets. We see this to be an issue for the trustee when Joseph reaches adulthood: We need you to properly budget Joseph's money to make sure there will be adequate resources available to provide for assistance in Joseph reaching his fullest potential.

What is your vision for the role of your child's trust advisor? How should he or she best help the trustee?
You need to make sure that the trustee will always provide for the expenses and materials that will help to support Joseph's independence. This includes spending money to hire private therapists and providers to help Joseph.

What is your vision for the potential relationship with all of your children?
Joseph and Patrick truly love each other. Patrick does not realize that Joseph is any different than other babies. We hope that they will always share the special closeness that they have with each other.

What are the family traditions you wish to always be continued?
Celebrating Joseph's birthday with his family and friends each year is so important to us!

We want Joseph to also be a part of Patrick's birthday parties. Christmas should be a magical time with our extended family.

What personal thoughts would you care to share with future caregivers?
Right now we cannot imagine what Joseph's full life will be like. He is doing well in his early intervention programs.

BIOGRAPHICAL AND PERSONAL INFORMATION

Child's information

Joseph Richard Brown	November 15, 2005
Full name	*Date of birth*
24 Shady Lane	123-45-6789
Home address	*Social security number*
Hometown, New Jersey 12345	732-123-4567
City, state, zip code	*Home telephone*
Catholic	
Religious preference	
St. James Church	Father David Anzley
Place of worship	*Contact person*
564 Main Street	732-122-3456
Address	*Telephone*
Hometown, New Jersey 12345	Weekly Mass on Sundays
City, state, zip code	*Services attended or involvement*
We would like Joseph to learn the basic beliefs of our faith.	
Why this is important	

MEDICAL INFORMATION

Overview of Current Medical Information and Concerns

General diagnosis (medical, developmental, psychiatric, physical)
Joseph was born with Down syndrome. We were not aware of this from any prenatal screening. Otherwise, he is a healthy baby boy.

Most recent hospitalizations (reason, date, follow up care, location)
Joseph was taken to the Newark Beth Israel Medical Center emergency room to check for pneumonia on November 3, 2006. He did not have pneumonia, just a bad cough.

Current health concerns
Joseph is a very healthy baby. He had an echocardiogram to test for any heart conditions. The test went well. There are no indications of any heart problems at this time.

Current health treatments
Early intervention services are provided to Joseph each week for speech, physical, and occupational therapies.

Current health precautions and recommendations
Joseph has received all the recommended immunizations since birth. At this point, Joseph is developing very similarly to his older brother Patrick. Although Joseph has had a recent heart test, we will continue to monitor his heart. We have been told that it is very common for children with Down syndrome to have a heart condition. Please watch this carefully.

Insurance, Physicians, and Specialists

Insurance information

Blue Cross/Blue Shield #123456	Not applicable
Health insurance company and policy number	*Other health insurance information (e.g., Medicaid)*
Richard	Not applicable
Subscriber	*Subscriber*
Not applicable	Not applicable
Dental insurance information and policy number	*Prescription drug coverage information*
Through Richard via his employer. Note: In the event that Richard and I both die prematurely, this health insurance will stop. Their Human Resources Department told me that coverage could continue under COBRA or Medicare Survivor benefits for the boys.	
Insurance coverage through parent/child/guardian/other	

Physician information

Dr. Roberta Joyce	732-765-4321
Name of primary care physician	*Telephone*
Arlington Pediatrics—2 Water Street	Arlington, New Jersey 02731
Address	*City, state, zip code*
Joseph goes every 3 months for routine well-baby visits to monitor his head size, growth, height, and weight.	
Approximate frequency of visits	
All normally scheduled immunizations so far. Please continue.	
Note any tests, immunizations and frequency (e.g., flu shots, thyroid testing)	
Joseph loves Dr. Joyce's nurse, Christine.	
Additional information	

Not applicable	Not applicable
Name of dentist	*Telephone*
Not applicable	Not applicable
Address	*City, state, zip code*
Not applicable	Not applicable
Specialty or affiliated hospital	*Approximate frequency of visits*

Not applicable

Note any tests and their frequency

Not at this time. We plan to use Dr. Paul Horgan who is our family dentist in Hometown Center.

Additional information

Dr. Alan Hookset	732-723-2222
Name of specialist	*Telephone*
New Jersey Children's Down Syndrome Clinic	Newark, New Jersey 12345
Address	*City, state, zip code*
Developmental Pediatric Specialist	Every 6 months until he is 3 years old
Specialty or affiliated hospital	*Approximate frequency of visits*

Muscle tone, verbal, visual, and other common tests for children with Down syndrome.

Note any tests and their frequency

We really enjoy our visits to Dr. Hookset—He is the best! We hope to continue with annual visits after Joseph is 3 years old.

Additional information

Susan Love	732-765-4326
Name of specialist	*Telephone*
Not applicable	Not applicable
Address	*City, state, zip code*
Physical Therapy Early Intervention	Weekly
Specialty or affiliated hospital	*Approximate frequency of visits*

Works on mobility and sitting up.

Note any tests and their frequency

Joseph loves her!

Additional information

Elijah Morris	732-765-3233
Name of specialist	*Telephone*
Not applicable	Not applicable
Address	*City, state, zip code*
Speech Therapy—Early Intervention	Weekly
Specialty or affiliated hospital	*Approximate frequency of visits*
Not applicable	
Note any tests and their frequency	
This is coming along slowly with some verbal sounds.	
Additional information	

Pharmacy

Note: No medications at this time.

Shore Drug in Hometown Center	732-847-9876
Name of pharmacy	*Telephone*
16 Ash Lane	Hometown, New Jersey 12345
Address	*City, state, zip code*

Preferred Hospital for Emergency Treatment

Newark Beth Israel Medical Center	732-123-5656
Name of hospital	*Telephone*
Mt. Auburn Street	Newark, New Jersey 12345
Address	*City, state, zip code*

Medications, Health, and Related Information

Allergies (such as medical or environmental) and required treatments
None known.

Medical facilities (include medical record numbers if necessary)
Joseph was born at Mt. Auburn Hospital.

Medications—prescription drugs
None.

Medications—nonprescription drugs (including vitamin supplements)
None.

The best ways to give your child medications are...
Orally with a liquid dropper.

Other important medical information
Check with Dr. Joyce or Dr. Hookset's office before giving Joseph any medicine. This includes over the counter cold or flu-type medicine.

PERSONALITY TRAITS AND PREFERENCES

Describe what living with your child is like.
A lot of fun! Very exhausting sometimes!

Basic characteristics and personality
Joseph is generally a happy baby and always smiling!

Abilities and skills in reading and writing
None yet!

Abilities and skills in financial matters (money skills)
None yet!

Abilities and skills in household chores
He likes to drop his toys a lot!

Abilities and skills in other areas
He is working with his therapists from early intervention on different things. This helps us too.

Sleeping habits
Joseph loves his naps. And generally loves to sleep.

Safety issues
At this time, only typical safety issues for a 1-year-old child.

Explain any issues your child has in being able to identify an unsafe situation or individual.
Not applicable.

Sensory issues
None known.

Provide suggestions to address any sensory issues or challenges.
Not applicable.

Behavior issues
No real behavior issues at this time.

Provide suggestions to address any behavioral challenges.
Not applicable.

If you have to contact one or two people to help you on the above, who would they be?
Not applicable.

What is most important to your child about his or her personality?
Not yet developed.

What is most important to you about your child's personality?
His good nature!

Preferences

Preferred setting and/or environment (rural or city, large or small house)
Not yet developed.

Favorite places to visit
His Grandmother Lambert's house.

Hobbies and interests
Listening to music.

Favorite entertainment
Music! Joseph loves Raffi songs and the Wiggles.

Recreation
Our stroller walks.

Favorite type or brand of clothes
We prefer Joseph wear cotton—flame resistant.

Favorite colors and patterns
Not yet developed.

What is most important to your child about his or her preferences?
Not yet developed.

What is most important to you about your child's preferences?
Not applicable.

Clothing and Shoe Sizes

Article of clothing	Size
Pants/shorts	12 months
Shirt/blouse	12 months
Skirt/dress	
Shoes	2–3 (infant)
Coat	12 months
Hat	12 months
Gloves	12 months
Underwear	12 months
Other	

PERSONAL CARE INFORMATION

Physical Abilities

Communication skills
Joseph knows what he wants but is not able to express it. This is frustrating to him, and he will cry until he gets his point across.

Physical mobility
We are working with his physical therapist so Joseph can sit up.

Hearing ability
Seems normal.

Eyesight
Seems normal.

Special equipment
None.

What is most important to your child about his or her physical abilities?
Joseph gets tired easily after his therapy sessions.

What is most important to you about your child's physical abilities?
It is very important to continue and help Joseph achieve each milestone at his own pace.

HABITS AND HYGIENE

Specific grooming routines and nature of assistance required.

Shaving
Not at this time.

Bathing
Joseph loves his bath time. He does not like his hair to be washed very often.

Dental care
Joseph has almost a full set of teeth in his mouth!

Dressing
Standard care for 1-year-old.

Toileting
We hope that Joseph will be able to be toilet trained at a typical age of 4 or 5 years old.

Personal care
Standard care for 1-year-old.

Male or female personal hygiene care
Standard care for 1-year-old.

Is your child aware of his or her own issues of sexuality? Are there issues or concerns to be aware of?
Not yet developed.

What is most important to your child about his or her habits and hygiene?
Joseph does not like to have sticky fingers.

What is most important to you about your child's habits and hygiene?
We want Joseph to have good personal hygiene habits.

MEALS AND DIETARY REQUIREMENTS

Food allergies (with suggested treatments if required)
None that we know of. We have not introduced Joseph to peanuts or strawberries yet.

Food preferences (likes and dislikes)
Joseph loves his milk. He still enjoys baby foods and sometimes Cheerios—with help.

Assistance needed in meal preparation
Not applicable.

Assistance needed in feeding self
We feed Joseph in his high chair with lots of assistance in feeding him.

Eating habits
Eating time is fun time for Joseph.

Mealtime issues or behavior concerns
Joseph likes to drop his food on the floor—messy for me, but fun for him!

Cleanliness and neatness
Keep the wipes close by. Joseph is a messy eater even with our help. He will scream when his hands are too dirty.

What is most important to your child about his or her mealtimes and dietary needs?
Fun! Fun! Fun!

What is most important to you about your child's mealtimes and dietary needs?
We think family mealtimes are important time together. We try to provide a healthy and balanced diet to our children. I encourage healthy snacks, too.

IMPORTANT DAILY ROUTINES

Include Times and Preferences

Wake-up time
Around 6:30 A.M. is a typical wake up time. Joseph is a very happy baby when he wakes up. He still does not like to have his diaper changed. He loves his bottle and to play!

Morning
After breakfast, we usually play more. Then we have a snack and a bottle. Then it is usually naptime around 10:00 A.M. until around 11:30 A.M. or so.

Noon
After naptime is lunchtime. Then we have more playtime.

Afternoon
I usually do some errands and pick up Patrick at preschool. Snacktime when we get home and then nap time around 3:00 P.M.

Evening
Dinnertime is when Richard comes home. Joseph loves to see his Daddy!

Bedtime
Joseph loves to listen to his music before bed, snuggling with his bottle. His lullaby music player always puts him to sleep. He will cry if it is not playing at bedtime. He is almost starting to sleep through the night.

What is most important to your child about his or her daily routines?
Playtime and snacktime!

What is most important to you about your child's daily routine?
Joseph's schedule should be the same each day. He does not do well when he misses his naps or bedtime.

Family and Support Factors

The Family and Support Factors section allows you to identify all the important people in your child's life, which will help you create a directory of resources for future caregivers so that they will know who else plays an important role in your child's life and how those individuals can be contacted.

There are a number of different individuals and agencies that will be in contact with your child. Some will be paid employees of government agencies and have specific responsibilities to meet the needs of your child in his or her capacity. You should identify the agency that each employee works for so that the future caregiver will know who to contact and what to expect from their services or supports. There is often a high turnover of support staff in human services provider agencies throughout the country, so it is very important to be in regular contact with the agencies and keep the contact information current. It is also a good idea to introduce future caregivers to these individuals early on.

Some individuals are fortunate enough to have family, friends, and extended family members who help and support them without monetary payment. If this is the case in your situation, it is important that you include enough resources in your financial planning to allow these individuals to continue to be a part in your child's life regardless of their own personal financial abilities.

You should try also to make it financially possible to continue any special traditions that are important to your child's life for holidays, birthdays, vacations, or special occasions.

FAMILY INFORMATION

Mother's information

Patricia Brown	August 26, 1978
Full name	*Date of birth*
24 Shady Lane	012-60-6789
Home address	*Social security number*
Hometown, New Jersey 12345	732-123-4567
City, state, zip code	*Home telephone*
Not applicable	Lambert
Place of work	*Maiden name*
Not applicable	Not applicable
Work telephone	*Cellular telephone*

Father's information

Richard Brown	October 1, 1977
Full name	*Date of birth*
24 Shady Lane	012-60-6000
Home address	*Social security number*
Hometown, New Jersey 12345	732-123-4567
City, state, zip code	*Home telephone*
Hines Engineering Company	
Place of work	
732-423-6894	732-718-1848
Work telephone	*Cellular telephone*

Sibling information

Patrick Brown	August 6, 2003
Full name	*Date of birth*
24 Shady Lane	123-45-5891
Home address	*Social security number*
Hometown, New Jersey 12345	732-123-4567
City, state, zip code	*Home telephone*
Joseph's older brother. They are very close.	
Current status of relationship	
We hope they remain close for their whole lives.	
Future status of relationship	

List any health concerns and or medical conditions of parents, guardians or siblings.

All family members enjoy good health.

List any medical family history or concerns

Richard's mother died at age 55 of pancreatic cancer. Richard's father died at age 66 of lung cancer. Patricia's father died at age 68 from a heart attack. Patricia's mother, at age 68, is very healthy.

Guardian information

Judith Lambert	April 10, 1979
Full name	*Date of birth*
14 Pennybrook Road	321-54-9865
Home address	*Social security number*
Hometown, New Jersey 12345	732-123-6464
City, state, zip code	*Home telephone*

From home.	jlambert@aol.com
Place of work	*E-mail address*
732-123-5656	732-141-1269
Work telephone	*Cellular telephone*

Successor guardian information

Nancy Rooter	March 1, 1977
Full name	*Date of birth*
12 Meadow Glenn Road	213-69-7412
Home address	*Social security number*
Wheatlock, New Jersey 02463	732-421-6407
City, state, zip code	*Home telephone*
Smithtown Middle School	nrooter@yahoo.com
Place of work	*E-mail address*
732-432-6492	732-421-1243
Work telephone	*Cellular telephone*

PROFESSIONAL SUPPORT INFORMATION

Professional service providers (e.g., residential, employment, respite, personal care attendant, transportation, education)

The Family Network	Sally Jackins
Primary state agency	*Director*
123 Adam Street	Cathy Waters (social worker)
Address	*Contact person*
Hometown, New Jersey 12345	732-123-9876 extension 131
City, state, zip code	
Early intervention services. Cathy helps coordinate all services.	
Services provided	

The Outreach Center	
Family support agency	*Director*
333 High Street	Mark Hyman
Home address	*Contact person*
Hometown, New Jersey 12345	732-141-9888
City, state, zip code	*Telephone number*
Family support and respite.	
Services provided	

SOCIAL AND RECREATION SUPPORT INFORMATION

Social and recreation activities and interests (e.g., social clubs, hobbies, sports, arts, recreation)

Not applicable
_____

Organization name   *Director*
_____

Address   *Contact person*
_____

City, state, zip code
_____

Why important

FRIENDS AND EXTENDED FAMILY SUPPORT INFORMATION

Additional important individuals in your child's life (e.g., friends, neighbors, relatives)

Rose Ludwood   732-431-1234
_____

Name   *Telephone number*

123 Hurd Street   Haverhill, New Jersey 12356
_____

Home address   *City, state, zip code*

Patricia's close friend for years. Patrick calls her "Auntie."
_____

Relationship

Richard and Maureen Cleveland   732-412-1444
_____

Name   *Telephone number*

1 Apple Street   Haverhill, New Jersey 12356
_____

Home address   *City, state, zip code*

Richard's college friends. They have children similar ages as Patrick and Joseph.
_____

Relationship

Sandra Bruin   732-431-1919
_____

Name   *Telephone number*

5 Lake Street   Wellesly Hills, New Jersey 12345
_____

Home address   *City, state, zip code*

We met in the hospital when Patrick was born; she also has a 1 year old.
_____

Relationship

Emily Larch	732-412-9991
Name	*Telephone number*
Not applicable	Not applicable
Home address	*City, state, zip code*
We met at early intervention, she has a 2-year-old daughter with Down Syndrome.	
Relationship	

OTHER FAMILY AND SUPPORT CONTACTS

Individuals who may be in contact with your child but share different philosophies or may jeopardize your child's well-being and safety. None at this time.

Financial Factors

The Financial Factors section is where you should provide financial information that you feel is important to future trustees, estate executors, and those individuals that will handle your financial matters when you are no longer able to in the event of your disability or death. You should include all individuals that you have a professional relationship with as well as those who assist you in making important financial decisions. A solid team of advisors is the key in assisting future caregivers to follow through with your plans for you and your family. Do these advisors know each other and the role that they play in your overall financial plan? You may want them to have a copy of this Letter of Intent as a means of communications and/or perhaps introduction.

You should also include the assets and income sources to be anticipated to assist in the future care needs of your child. This assumes that you have taken the necessary steps so that these assets will be properly directed into your child's special needs trust when appropriate.

Take some time to help guide those that you have entrusted with your financial resources to understand the values that you have about money. This should help them to make important decisions on spending and perhaps investing your assets to meet your overall goals. This will help them to maintain the lifestyle that you have achieved for your family and for your child.

Personal and financial situations often change. As your children grow their personal and financial needs will develop and change. These changes will affect how you divide your assets among your children. As you work with your advisors to modify your plan to adapt to these changes, so too should you modify the information of your Letter of Intent. It is important to review this information with your advisors and make any appropriate changes.

LIST OF ADVISORS

Financial Planner

John Stevens	Financial Planning, LLC
Name	*Firm name*
5 New Street	john.stevens@fpllc.com
Work address	*E-mail address*
Pleasant, New Jersey 12345	781-893-0909 extension 242
City, state, zip code	*Telephone number*

In addition to investing and insurances, John helps coordinate our financial matters and connects us with other families and professionals.

Relationship

Attorney

Sally Brown	Brown and Wallace
Name	*Firm name*
41 Nisson Road	brown@lawfirm.com
Work address	*E-mail address*
Garden City, New Jersey 01237	732-423-6791
City, state, zip code	*Telephone number*

Sally has become a friend; she has a son with Down syndrome.

Relationship

Accountant or Tax Preparer

Charles MacAvoy	MacAvoy, Murphy, and McCarthy
Name	*Firm name*
94 Newcomb Road	macavoy@cpa.com
Work address	*E-mail address*
Flower City, New Jersey 01237	732-987-6543
City, state, zip code	*Telephone number*

Charles does tax preparation, one time per year.

Relationship

Trustee of parents' trusts

Richard Davis	SBR Associates
Name	*Firm name*
1 Timberman Lane	davis@art.com
Work address	*E-mail address*
Concorde, New Jersey 01236	732-921-7777
City, state, zip code	*Telephone number*
Close personal friend.	
Relationship	

FINANCIAL INFORMATION ABOUT PARENTS

Summary of Net Worth as of January 2007

Note: Indicates amount allocated to your child's needs. This column estimates the approximate amount that would be distributed to the child's special needs trust if parents were to die as of the date of the current market values.

Assets	Current estimated market value	Amount allocated to your child's needs
Liquid assets (cash, checking, money markets)	$25,000	$12,500
Semi-liquid assets (stocks, bonds, mutual funds)	$60,000	$30,000
Retirement plan assets (401[k], IRA, 403[b])	$225,000	$112,500
Other assets (annuities, other)	$0	$0
Real estate (residence, rental property, other)	$457,000	$228,500
Business assets	$0	$0
Personal property (autos, antiques, artwork)	$45,000	$22,500
Total assets	**$812,000**	**$406,000**

Liabilities	Current estimated market value	Amount allocated to your child's needs
Liabilities (mortgage, credit cards, loans)	$195,000	$0
Other liabilities	$20,000	$0
Total liabilities	**$215,000**	**$0**

Net worth (assets less liabilities)	Current estimated market value	Amount allocated to your child's needs
Total net worth	**$597,000**	**$298,500**

LIFE INSURANCE, POTENTIAL GIFTS, AND INHERITANCES

Life insurance on father

Insurance company	Policy number	Type of policy	Death benefit	Owner of policy	Primary beneficiary	Contingent beneficiary
Metropolitan	24901	Group	$50,000	Richard	Patricia	Children's trust
John Hancock	4239981	Universal	$250,000	Richard	Patricia	Children's trust
Pacific Life	1237249	20-year term	$500,000	Richard	Patricia	Children's trust

Life insurance on mother

Insurance company	Policy number	Type of policy	Death benefit	Owner of policy	Primary beneficiary	Contingent beneficiary
Mass Mutual	426948	20-year term	$500,000	Patricia	Richard	Children's trust
Prudential	9276532	Universal	$200,000	Patricia	Richard	Children's trust

Life insurance on guardian
None at this time.

Life insurance on child
None at this time.

Are you aware of any potential gifts or inheritances that your child will receive? If so, please provide details including the source (e.g., person, estate, trust), the anticipated amount, and estimated date(s) of gifts or inheritances.
At this point we are not anticipating any large inheritances.

Beneficiary Designations of Assets

Father's retirement plan assets

Investments	Account number	Type of plan	Current market value	Potential income benefit	Primary beneficiary	Contingent beneficiary
Company plan	123456	401(k)	$16,000		Patricia	Children's trust

Mother's retirement plan assets

Investments	Account number	Type of plan	Current market value	Potential income benefit	Primary beneficiary	Contingent beneficiary
IRA rollover	654321	IRA	$65,000		Richard	Children's trust

FINANCIAL INFORMATION FOR CHILD

Current income sources of child
No income currently.

Potential income sources from parent

Type	Financial amount	Payable
SSDI	Yes, unknown	Upon death or disability?
Pension-survivor benefits	$0	Upon death or disability?
Other sources	None	Upon death or disability?

YOUR FINANCIAL VALUES

General thoughts on your values about money in making financial decisions.
We want to make sure that money will provide for an independent life for Joseph and for Patrick. We make a point to save money with each paycheck and to live within our means. If we want to buy something, we try to budget for it and not buy it on our credit card. We do not like to have any debt other than our mortgage. Teaching these values to our children is also important to us.

What is important about money to your child?
Nothing right now.

What does money mean to your child?
Nothing right now.

What is important about money to you and to your family?
Feeling that our family is financially secure is very important to us.

If there is more than one child, provide an overview of how the trustee should evaluate financial priorities.
We do not want Patrick to feel that he is not as important to us as Joseph. We hope that there will be enough money for both of our sons to be as independent as possible. College tuition for Patrick is just as important as Joseph's needs. We would also like to help Patrick with any wedding plans or a down payment on a home some day. It is important that the trustee evaluate the needs of both children at all times. Currently, it is too difficult to project how much money is required to provide for Joseph. We have been told that early intervention is a great program and as Joseph moves to the school system, it may become more difficult for him to get the supports and services he needs. We feel that it would be a good use of money to hire an advocate or other professionals to help secure resources for Joseph. As you plan ahead, it is important to know that after Joseph leaves the school system there may be less public resources available for him. Because of this, it is suggested that you plan ahead in budgeting his resources to try to make sure there will be adequate funds available to supplement any of Joseph's needs.

Legal Factors

The Legal Factors section is where you should provide information about the legal and estate planning documents that you have prepared that will assist others in the event of your disability or death. You should also have a checklist of important documents and their location. If your important papers are in your safe deposit box, make certain that the executor of your estate or your power of attorney has proper authorization to access it and its contents. If you have a safe in your home, these individuals should also know where to find the code so that they may access its contents.

Not only is it important to identify those individuals that you hope will execute your wishes, they should also have a copy of this Letter of Intent to use as a guideline in making important financial decisions. In fact, as you are completing your Letter of Intent, it may be helpful to share some of your thoughts with your child's future trustee because they will have the fiduciary responsibility involved in spending the money that will help to fulfill your vision for your child's future. The more clear your vision and the details of your child, the easier it will be for them to fulfill their expected role.

When you work with your attorney to create your legal documents, you are creating the vision that you have for the ultimate distribution of your estate. During this process, you should be clear in expressing to future trustees, guardians, powers of attorneys, and health care proxies how you want your financial and legal matters tended to. The role of the attorney is to place those wishes in writing by utilizing the proper documents. Coordinating your financial resources with these legal documents is critical.

OVERVIEW OF ESTATE DISTRIBUTION

Patricia	April 30, 2006
Executor of father's estate	*Date father's will signed*
Richard	April 30, 2006
Executor of mother's estate	*Date mother's will signed*
The Joseph Brown Special Needs Trust	April 30, 2006
Name of trust	*Date of trust*
Andrew Brown	5 Thomas Avenue, Milton, New Jersey 45673
Trustee name	*Address*
732-222-4589	732-232-6060
Home telephone	*Work telephone*
Richard's brother	Yes
Trustee's relationship to child	*Is trustee aware of role?*
Each other	April 30, 2006
Power of attorney for parents	*Date of most recent filing*
Each other	April 30, 2006
Health care proxy for parents	*Date of most recent filing*

LOCATION OF IMPORTANT DOCUMENTS FOR PARENTS

Wills
Originals with our attorney.

Trusts
Originals with our attorney.

Special needs trusts
Originals with our attorney.

Life insurance policies
In safe in basement. Judith Lambert (the guardian) and Andrew Brown (the trustee) have the combination to the safe.

Guardianship papers
In safe in basement.

Power of attorney papers
In safe in basement.

Health care proxy papers
In safe in basement.

Mortgage papers
In safe in basement.

Investment paperwork
On file in filing cabinet.

Retirement plans
On file in filing cabinet.

Real estate deeds
On file in filing cabinet.

Property titles
In safe in basement.

Birth certificates
In safe in basement.

Marriage certificates
In safe in basement.

Social Security cards and passports
In safe in basement.

Safe deposit boxes/access information
Andrew has this information.

Bank records and tax returns
On file in filing cabinet.

Funeral instructions and related documents
Keefe Funeral Home. No specific plans filed.

FINAL ARRANGEMENTS FOR CHILD

Details of prepaid arrangements (if any)
Not applicable.

Describe your desires for final arrangements you wish for your child in the event that you are not available to make these plans.
Keefe Funeral Home. Our family has always used them. See Father Anzley at St. James Church. Keep it simple and make sure there is music for Joseph.

LOCATION OF LEGAL DOCUMENTS
SPECIFIC TO CHILD

Birth certificate
In safe in basement.

Burial instructions
In safe in basement.

Special needs trust paperwork
With our attorney.

Names of those with copies of this Letter of Intent
Andrew Brown and Judith Lambert.

Government Benefit Factors

The Government Benefit Factors section is where you should include any and all government benefits that your child is currently receiving. You should also include how they are used for your child's needs. It is also helpful to provide a directory of state agencies and resources to contact that may be utilized for future needs. Government benefits and eligibility are predetermined. Planning to maximize and protect your child's eligibility is paramount to your child's future security and independence.

Many families, however, chose not to utilize government benefits for a number of reasons. If this is the case in your family, you should make certain to express it.

CURRENT GOVERNMENT BENEFITS

Joseph has no current government benefits. Richard does pay into Social Security, and Patricia did contribute when she was working.

POTENTIAL GOVERNMENT BENEFITS

We still need to look into this.

Index

Page references followed by *t*, *f*, or *b* indicate tables, figures, or boxes, respectively.